W9-BCF-417

the
depths
of
the
soul

mental
health
series

6

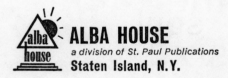

ALBA HOUSE
a division of St. Paul Publications
Staten Island, N.Y.

A CHRISTIAN APPROACH
TO PSYCHOANALYSIS
BY IGNACE LEPP

the
depths
of
the
soul

This book was originally published by Aubier, Editions Montaigne, Paris under the title, *Clartés et Ténebrès de l'âme.*

Nihil Obstat:
Austin B. Vaughan, S.T.D.
Censor Librorum

Imprimatur:
Terence J. Cooke, D.D., V.G.

New York, N.Y., December 27, 1965

Library of Congress Catalog Card Number: 66-16470

Designed, printed and bound in the U.S.A. by the Pauline Fathers and Brothers of the Society of St. Paul at Staten Island, New York as part of their communications apostolate.

contents

preface

This book is not new treatise on psychoanalysis. There are too many good books on the subject already, and there is no point in repeating what has already been said. Our objectives are at once both more modest and somewhat more lofty.

Psychoanalysis is interested only in the unconscious, that is, the *dark side* of the soul. Classic psychology, as it has always been taught in the schools, is interested only in the *light* in the soul, that is, the conscious part of the psyche. It seems to be acquainted only with the rational soul. As for the experimental and natural sciences, they generally act as if there were no soul, tending to see psychology merely as a subdivision of biology. But, thanks to the specialized studies of today and in particular thanks to the popularizations which have been appearing, almost everyone is more or less familiar with some of the broader theses of psychoanalysis, in which the soul appears as fundamentally irrational.

Under such conditions, there is much confusion on the part of those who are pursuing the study of medicine, natural science, or psychology, and even in the boader field of literature and general culture. Many times I have heard people ask: "What is the soul? What can a man actually know about it today?" These are the questions which we hope to answer in this volume.

Our intention is to pry as deeply as possible into both the

light and the darkness of the soul. The different human sciences and various methods of psychology, far from contradicting each other as a general rule, are really complementary. It might perhaps have been necessary, at a preliminary stage, for each discipline to present its teaching with a certain degree of exclusivity. But now that work relative to the manifold activities of the soul, the conscious and unconscious faculties of the psyche, is both widely spread and well investigated, we have the right — and perhaps even the duty — to go one step beyond these contradictions and work out a psychosynthesis.

The interest of such an undertaking is not merely theoretical. There must obviously be answers to some pointed questions: "What is the soul? What is man?" Still, like every other science, psychology has other applications in the domain of "praxis." Its role is a fundamental one in the education of children and adolescents. More and more people are turning to psychology as a factor in deciding on the choice of a school or profession. Teachers, social workers, businessmen, journalists, politicians, in a word everyone who has any social responsibility towards other people, all need to have some grounding in psychology. Many have this by natural intuition, but inuition itself, at least in our civilization, cannot function properly without some solid scientific training as well.

Modern medicine, in its turn, is more and more aware of the fact that many diseases affect not only the body, but also the mind and soul. The therapy, as a result, cannot be applied merely to the sick organ, but to the totality of the person: it is psychosomatic. Then too, specifically psychic diseases, neuroses, are growing more and more frequent as our civilization grows more refined and specifically differentiated. Diseases such as these, obviously, are within the domain of psychology, not medicine as it has always been understood.

The soul is not something divided into airtight little compartments. Whether we are speaking about education and teaching, about therapy, or any other branch of the application of psychology, it is always the totality of the soul towards which psychology must be directed. The promotion of the personality, as well as mere knowledge of personality, demands attention on both the conscious and on the unconscious mind. Analysis is obviously necessary but analysis has real meaning and effect only when it is a conscious preparation for the synthesis to follow.

* * * *

There is little point in underscoring our immense debt to those who have gone before us in this work. I frequently find myself in the most fundamental disagreement with certain theses of both philosophical psychology and Freudian psychoanalysis. But my argument against them is never meant to be dogmatic; it is always dialectic. Psychosynthesis is conceivable only insofar as both psychoanalysis and rational psychology have reached a high degree of perfection.

Even if we wished it otherwise, it would be impossible to present psychoanalysis without constant reference to Freud and the other masters of depth psychology. Our debt is particularly great with regard to the psychology of Jung, which seems more open to the understanding of the true depths of psychic reality. Our psychosynthesis is not, however, properly speaking, the work of Jung. Some of his speculations will always remain completely foreign to our perspectives and, on the other hand, our work embraces problems in which Jung was not ever interested.

* * * *

I am well aware of the imperfections of this work. Who, in so immense a domain as that of psychic life, would dare to claim that he had exhausted his subject? We were forced to limit our work to only those aspects of psychoanalysis which appeared particularly important for understanding and advancing the development of human personality, or those which we had occasion to explore in somewhat greater depth. The reader must bear in mind that this is not a definitive work, but only a modest essay.

On the other hand, it is not the learned specialist we are addressing here. We are attempting to answer the questions and anxieties of all educated people who have neither the time nor the necessary background to undertake the study of more advanced and specialized works on the subject.

The modern world is in a state of turmoil. One gets the frightening impression that the immensity of the Cosmos is weighing down upon us. How could it be otherwise, since our materialistic science has almost completely destroyed the sense of human dignity? This dignity cannot obviously reside in the body. If it exists at all, its source can only be in the soul, that soul which is still so imperfectly known at a time when the physical sciences have made such gigantic progress. A better understanding of the soul is, moreover, an indispensable prerequisite for the advancement of humanity. Psychosynthesis has a definite contribution to make to this advancement.

1 new paths in psychology

In stating that our psychological studies are hardly out of their infancy, that they are thus far behind the development of the physical and mathematical sciences, I will probably surprise a good many people.

I. *Science of the Soul*

Socrates and Plato frequently talked about the human soul. The neo-Platonists and the Christian thinkers of the first centuries who were influenced by them were almost exclusively taken up with the subject. Many of their insights have an extraordinary depth: they stand up well under comparison with the analyses of the best Hindu masters and the most penetrating work of modern psychology. But as far back as in Plato's day the orientation of the scientific spirit of the Mediterranean world had already been set. It is no longer possible for us to discover today whether it was due to the congenital structure of the Mediterranean mind or to mere chance that our first thinkers turned their attention to the outside world. Ever since, for many, many centuries, the study of man, to be taken seriously, had to be set up along the model of the nature sciences.

In reading their works, we frequently have the impression that

Plato, Plotinus, St. Augustine . . . , used concepts drawn from the world of physics only in an effort to make themselves understood by a world that did not yet know how to think in other terms, a concession to the spirit of the age. The Aristotelians, on the other hand, were naturalists by conviction. Following their lead, almost every thinker who takes up the subject of psychology from the thirteenth century on seems to speak quite naturally about the soul as if it belonged to the same order of realities as the phenomena accessible to the study of physics.

The obvious consequence of following such a method was that psychology could only know the soul insofar as it had some common grounds or resemblance with the world of nature. St. Thomas Aquinas and the other Christian thinkers had to have a very acute feeling for the profound originality of spiritual reality. In order to cast some light on what makes the human soul different from the body and the physical world, they made lavish use of the analogical method. This is not the place to question the merits of analogical reasoning. Taking into account the general direction taken by intellectual research, this method was obviously the only way to escape the monism of materialism or naturalism. But still, its positive results are relatively poor. If Christian theodicy offers an infinitely richer and much less anthropomorphic image of God than that of Aristotle's "First Mover," this is not owing to the fact that it made better use of analogy. It is rather because it was drawing on the sources of biblical revelation and the experience of the mystics.

In order to know the human soul, we neither can nor ought to count on any revelation. Since the soul is our own deepest reality, we must try to penetrate its nature only through the unaided faculties of our mind.

We know that the development of Oriental thinking, particularly Hindu, followed a much different path than our Western speculation. As a result, the Indian masters are in possession of a complex of knowledge of the soul that is extremely profound and developed. In this area they have at their disposal techniques whose rigorously scientific character can hardly be called into question, provided scientific methodology is not defined in too narrow a sense. On the other hand, the Orient is very far behind the West in the knowledge and mastery of the external world.

Is it possible to conjecture what the modern picture of the world would be if Western reflexive thinking had started out by addressing itself to the intimate depths of its own personality? If it had built up its sciences of nature only after it had elaborated as complete as possible a science of the soul? Henri Bergson, among others, likes to ask this question. In his opinion, the scourges from which humanity now suffers would not have ever existed; instead of being overwhelmed by the world of matter, man would have become its lord and master. The famous philosopher is probably not too wrong.

Another result would be that Western man, becoming attentive to the real depths of his own personal existence, would have lost nothing of his taste for life and activity. The Hindu civilization, notwithstanding its extensive psychological knowledge, is far from being completely satisfactory. Who could say whether it was not their respective civilizations that have made the Oriental an introvert and the Occidental an extrovert? Isn't it just as probable that our science is directed towards the outside world precisely because we are, taken as a whole, congenitally extroverts, and *vice versa* as regards the Hindu?

One thing is certainly true: if our psychology were not so beholden to the sciences of nature, no intelligent man would have ever dared to refuse to believe in the reality of the soul "unless he could find evidence of it under the surgeon's scalpel." The soul can and should be scientifically known, but in a different way than the body.

The Greek word *psyche* is almost synonymous with our word *soul*: and thus psychology is — or ought to be — a *science of the soul*. Some modern psychologists are opposed to this definition, for fear that they are being forced to concede, *a priori*, the existence of a substantial soul. With Segond, they prefer to call psychology the "knowledge of the interior life, in which the spiritual values of a man rise and come to light." By spiritual values, they understand sentiment, thought, *etc.*

II. *The First Awakening of the New Psychology*

Until a century and a half ago, the official psychology, the only one which enjoyed any rights at the Universities, was rigorously rational. It was built up on the model of metaphysics rather than physics or biology. In an effort to keep faith with Aristotle and Descartes, psychologists studied the substance of the soul, its faculties, and its functions. The far too famous dispute between rival schools as to whether or not the soul and its faculties were "really distinct" was not based on an observation of scientific facts, but only on a reasoning process which proceeded from commonly admitted metaphysical principles. What is more, this psychology is far from being completely dead. I can recall a professor of scholastic philosophy who was scandalized at my ignorance of the fact that such problems could still be posed in psychology, in the twentieth century.

In the writings of a St. Augustine or a Pascal, in the numerous works of the many mystics and spiritual writers we can trace the rough outlines of another kind of psychology, based on an experimental knowledge of the soul. But it remained something purely empirical, and thus it was considered non-scientific.

In the beginning of the nineteenth century, as a consequence of the criticism of Hume and Kant, metaphysicis fell into great discredit. As a repercussion of this, rational psychology could not help suffer in its turn. It was at this time that, with Jouffroy and primarily with Maine de Biran, the first tentative steps were taken towards the construction of a psychology that was scientific in the modern sense of the word.

Aware of the existence of "inner realities" which human consciousness touches upon without an intermediary, Maine de

Biran claimed that he could study them with the same scientific objectivity that is applied to the study of phenomena within the range of our external senses. The Scotch psychologists carried this approach still further; they were the first to establish a psychology that was basically a phenomenlogy. It was content with a description of the inner realities and categorically refused to pronounce on the essence of the soul. But if, for lack of appropriate techniques, these psychologists were unable to lay the foundations of scientific psychology in the proper sense of the term, they still managed to open the paths along which the science of the soul was to make its further progress.

The English disciples of David Hume and Stuart-Mill carried the work one step further. They considered the mere description of inner realities as insufficient for the foundation of a scientific psychology, and attempted to explain these realities, to explore the bonds that connected them in a system. The law of association of ideas was destined to play the same role in the science of psychology as the law of universal gravitation played in physics.

* * * *

The weakness of the associationists, like that of the psychologists of the Scotch school in the nineteenth century, was due to their fascination for the materialism of their age. They believed they could rely only on realities whose materiality was beyond question, or which could at least be deduced on the basis of causes which were accessible to the senses. Since it was understood that only matter could claim the title of reality, the originality of the mind and spirit was necessarily denied, if not even ridiculed. Without realizing it, they took an active role in the construction of that intellectual monstrosity — a methaphysics of matter. Mind and spirit, when it was necessary to mention them at all, were treated as simple "epiphenomena" of matter. The extremists of the school (or rather the *sect*) went so far as to claim that thought was a mere secretion of the brain. That was the triumph of psychology without soul.

Despite their claims, the psychologists of the nineteenth century did not succeed in building a really objective science of psychic realities. Just as in the past, psychology remained dependent upon philosophy; and there were as many psychologies as there were philosophical systems. In my own opinion, it could hardly have been otherwise. The most lucid physicists and biologists of our own day all turn their backs on the scientific faith of the nineteenth century. They realize that wherever science goes beyond the simple stage of exploration and undertakes the construction of a system, it implicitly leans on a philosophy. But, in the preceding century, philosophy was a word which was widely looked down on. In order to be taken seriously, psychologists thought they had to prove they had no connections with any philosophy. But the worst philosophy is precisely the one philosophy that is unconscious of its own existence.

The psychophysics of Charles Henry and Lasareff, the form theory of Ehrenfels, the behaviorism of Watson — all seem satisfactory enough to many psychologists today. Still, they are all impregnated with the scientific prejudices of the nineteenth century and, for that reason, they can touch only the outside of the soul. They do, however, have all the authentically scientific techniques at their disposal and thus they can arrive at extremely valuable material for the real psychologists to work on.

The considerable underdevelopment of psychology with respect to the natural sciences, seems to be at least partially owing to an error in methodology. Heirs to Aristotle and Descartes, our thinkers all remained generally convinced that there was only one really scientific method, and that it could be applied to every aspect of reality. How many physicists still deny the scientific value of our conclusions at which the biologists have arrived by methods other than those proper to material physics. The biologists themselves are hardly more tolerant with respect to the psychologists. There are not yet very many thinkers who can consistently recognize the fundamental differences between these various orders of reality. As far as physical facts are concerned, they are simply irreducible not only to the category of physico-chemistry, but even less so to the category of biology.

Every science, in order to succeed, has to develop its own proper methods, in keeping with the specific demands of its proper object of investigation. In order to penetrate deeper into the essence of psychology, says Jung,[1] in order to treat it as a science and not condemn it to a miserable existence within the limits imposed by the methodologies of the natural sciences, we must first of all recognize the fact that the experimental method has never been able, and never will be able, to do full justice to the human soul, nor even outline a moderately faithful picture of its complicated phenomena.

Traditional philosophical psychology, and also the scientific psychology of the nineteenth century, both set out from the postulate that the soul is an exclusively rational reality. Poets and mystics had been denying this fact for centuries, but their insights were regarded as unscientific. Today, when we know that the vast majority of psychic facts are not rational but emotional in origin, we can understand the very fundamental reasons behind the essential failure of the psychology taught by the schools. Whatever was not reducible to rationality completely escaped them. No wonder that the neuro-physiologists could so easily deny the existence of a soul which the psychologists had already divested of its most specific elements.

Humanity has a right to look to psychology for something more than mere speculative knowledge. If physics, chemistry, or biology offered only theoretical knowledge, they could have never played the role they did in the formation of modern civilization. And if this civilization is, as Bergson says it is, one big body without a soul, this is largely due to the fact that psychology has not accomplished its mission in the field of practice.

---

1. *Psychological Types*, p. 420 (French edition)

Psychology can and must become the most useful of the sciences, since it is taken up, not with the world around us, but with man himself. It must instruct us on the nature of man, but also on the scope of human potential. A better acquaintance with human conduct, a better understanding of self and others, will necessarily make a big contribution along this direction. How many miseries, social and individual as well, are the direct result of psychic disorder. Instead of being a personal satisfaction of the narcissistic intellect, psychology must set out to correct this disorder. In this sense, it is a therapy as well as a science.

It is also, and even more so, a pedagogy. The individual and collective disorders from which human beings have to suffer can be in large measure avoided, thanks to a better knowledge of the soul and the perfection of techniques which put psychology in a position to work effectively.

III. Depth Psychology

It does not take a Freudian to recognize that the modern human sciences in general and psychology in particular owe their rapid progress to Dr. Sigmund Freud (1856-1939). Freud obviously did not create this science *ex nihilo*. He owes a lot to the psychologists we have mentioned above and even more to such philosophers as Leibnitz and Schopenhauer, and to psychiatrists such as his teacher P. Janet, Charcot, Bernheim and his fellow Viennese Breuer. But it is true that he was the one who set psychology along the path it was destined to follow. We might agree with hardly a single one of the particular theses advanced by Freud, and we would still have to recognize our debt to him.

Freud was not content to study the external manifestations of the psyche, as most of the psychologists of the nineteenth and early twentieth centuries were doing. He had very little interest in them. What counted particularly, if not solely, for him was the depth life of the soul, a life which he held to be so hidden that the subject himself was unaware of it most of the time. In order to find a way into this mysterious universe of the unconscious, Freud, on the basis of his clinical experience, elaborated his famous analytic psychology which we shall have frequent occasion to discuss throughout this book. Whereas, before Freud, the attention of the psychologist was directed primarily to the cognitive and rational functions of the soul, Freudian psychoanalysis effected a complete reverse of perspective which the future might well consider as important as the Copernican and Newtonian revolutions in the world of physical realities. The emotional psychic activities become much more important than the rational.

* * * *

Unfortunately, Freud was not a philosopher. In fact, he was not well enough grounded in philosophy to be able to understand the real nature of his own discoveries. A typical nineteenth century man, he was caught up in a network of prejudices and postulates that were rigidly confined to the limits of the natural sciences. Looking upon psychology as a rigorously natural science, the founder of psychoanalysis believed that he had to postulate, as a basic principle, the biological origin of the psyche. He was much too clever an observer not to recognize the specific character of psychic activity. But in the name of science, he tried to "prove" that all psychic functions, even the most spiritual, are reducible, in the last analysis, to instincts which are basically biological in origin. Psychology could be no more than one of the branches of biology.

Freudian psychogy was thus hampered, at the outset, by being unable to grasp the real nature of ego. Thus it is in no position to grasp the freedom exercised, in varying degrees, by the higher functions of the soul. Psychological determinism is not only a matter of methodology for Freud (in the way that many modern speculators speak of physical and biological determinism), but a matter of rigorous dogma. As frequently happens with men who have a contempt for philosophy, Freud gives evidence of a particularly rigid philosophic dogmatism.

Since there is no morality either in physics or in biology, Freud affects a sovereign contempt for moral values which, according to him, are an undue incumbrance on psychic life. As a result, to quote the American psychologist Karen Horney, the Freudian vision of man and humanity is necessarily a pessimistic one. The social phenomena are only an amalgamation of psychic phenomena for him, and these in turn can be reduced to biological phenomena. This tendency, she says, has induced Freudian thinkers to believe, for example, that wars come from the death instinct, that our economic system of today is basically rooted in analerotic impulses, that the reason for the industrial revolution's not having begun some two thousand years earlier was the narcissism of Antiquity.[2] And, since there is little that can be done to control instinct, there is very little hope for any real human progress. The most that can be hoped for is that psychoanalysis will succeed in "sublimating" the more dangerously antisocial instincts.

As is typical of so many Jewish thinkers (and this was the case with Karl Marx as well), Freud had a strong inclination to generalize and systematize. Refusing to recognize that psychic disease is not the normal condition of a man's mind, but rather a disintegration, he based his observations, frequently the insights of a real genius, on conditions which he claimed to be valid for every man as such. In a word, despite his horror of metaphysics, Freud was unable to escape the worst elements of most metaphysics, a tendency to generalize beyond the evidence afforded by the case.

* * * *

---

2. *The Neurotic Personality of Our Time*, p. 186 (French edition)

As far as the history of psycholgy is concerned, Dr. Freud's worst misfortune was due to the excessive zeal of some of his disciples. Once the hostility and mistrust which pyschology based on psychoanalysis had to face were completely overcome, the number of men who followed Freudian thinking grew in leaps and bounds. Unfortunately, many of those who claimed to be the most orthodox of his disciples, understood only that the one imperative obligation of the true disciple is to surpass his master, to correct whatever was necessarily incomplete or imprecise owing to the limitations inherent in the personality of the master or the historical and social "atmosphere" in which he lived and worked.

The disciples of Freud locked themselves up within a narrow and highly sectarian dogmatism. What had frequently been nothing more than an imprecise wording or provisory hypothesis in their master's teaching they soon hardened into rigid dogma. Thus Freudian thinking turned into *psychologism*.

Freudianism claims to explain everything "psychologically." And psychology remains for it, at least theoretically, a rigorously positivistic science. It recognizes, in the psyche, only the rigid laws of determinism. It seems to ignore the fact that many of our modern physicists now realize that they have to abandon a like determinism, even in the area of the natural world.

If Freud's followers were the only representatives of psychology in this mid-twentieth century, we would have to conclude that this science had miserably shipwrecked, after offering such great promise. The ingenious insights of Dr. Freud would have remained forever undeveloped and our knowledge of the human soul would be no further advanced than it was in the days of David Hume or Auguste Comte.

* * * *

Paradoxical as it might seem, the authentic continuators of Freud's work are the disciples who disagreed with him. They retained the master's teaching only on uncontrovertible points. But they broke with the simplifications and dogmatism, and were not afraid to set out along paths whose very existence Freud himself had not even suspected. As a result, though Freud remains the undisputed founder of the new psychology, it has long since ceased to be really "Freudian."

Among Freud's first disciples, Alfred Adler was no doubt the most famous, but also one of the first to grasp the inadequacies of Freud's thinking. Freud's pansexualism, in particular, seemed indefensible to him; he felt it threatened to lead psychology to a final impasse. But Adler's mind was just as systematic as his master's. He replaced Freud's sexual monism with another monism of his own, the "will to power." As a result, Adler's thinking is in no better position than Freud's when it comes to a question of understanding the whole complexity of psychic life. This is probably why Adler can count only a few faithful followers, and why his positive contribution to the new psychology was so minimal.

The Swiss doctor Carl Jung is a much different case. With a boldness that is both characteristic and praiseworthy, he advanced psychological investigation to unexpected depths. The theories and theses that Jung claimed to draw from these investigations do not all possess an equal value. More than once, his poetic genius seems to have overruled the rigor of his scientific methodology. Still, he did open prodigious horizons for the future study of the human sciences, and we can now hope that the underdevelopment of these sciences can quickly be remedied. Only ignorance can excuse the persistence of certain psychologists and other thinkers in the illusion that the human soul is a mechanism which can be taken apart and put back together again.

Freudians and some other positivists criticize Jung for not having respected the taboos of scientism. They accuse him of having played with philosophy, or even metaphysics. But even a superficial familiarity with his work is enough to prove that his scientific rigor is at least equal to that of his detractors. His long medical experience with the subject of psychotherapy combines with his immense grasp of history, ethnography, literature, and philosophy to set a broad foundation for his writings. He studies firsthand, and without any prejudices, the mythologies and religions of many peoples, ancient and modern, primitive and civilized. There was no sectarianism, no narrowness of mind, to vitiate the objectivity of his observations and his vision. It is small censure to say that, in the speculative part of his work, he sometimes went beyond the strictly empirical domain. In my opinion, there is no real science that does not tend to transcend itself. Emmanual Mounier, without specific reference to Jung, remarks that no psychology can succeed without a metaphysics to point out its horizons, its limits and its proper object.[3]

* * * *

It is not possible here to mention all the names which, for the last fifty years, have contributed to the construction of the new psychology. Still there must be some mention of a man like Charles Baudouin, whose famous psychology is particularly geared for exploring the spiritual reality of the soul. Karen Horney, on her part, has stressed the social conditioning of the psyche, calling very opportune attention to the fact that man is only an individual, that the dramas and conflicts of which his soul is frequently the stage, cannot be laid solely to his own neurosis but that there is an intimate interaction between the individual and the collectivity of his environment. The "psycho-politics" of Rene Laforgue is another door opened in the science of psychology.

As far as the Marxist school is concerned, Marxist theory is extremely reticent and mistrustful on the subject of depth psychology and psychoanalysis. Actually if we maintain, with the orthodox Marxist position, that man is causally determined by the forces of economic production, that his psychic activities are nothing but epiphenomena of these economic forces, what value could there possibly be in the method and theories of Freud or

3. *Traité du caractère*, p. 47

Jung? In Russia, up until very recently, all real psychological research was forbidden. The old associationism and mechanistic theories, more or less corrected along the lines of Pavlov's thinking were *de rigeur* in all official instruction. Psychology was nothing more than a branch of biology. The Marxist Robert Desoille did, however, manage to amalgamate Pavlov's theories with some methodological procedures that were psychoanalytic in inspiration. It is still too soon to predict how much of his thinking will be retained and continued by scientific circles in the Soviet Union.

The Christian attitude towards psychoanalysis was at first just as openly suspicious as that of the Marxists. Theology is opposed, on principle, to the irrational. The positivism and irreligion of the famous founder of psychoanalysis, as well as his pansexual bent, were not likely to reassure the Christian mind. Little by little this mistrust began to yield to a more positive attitude. At present, there are many priests and many Catholic doctors and teachers who profess and practice analytic psychology. The works of Professor Dalbiez, the publications of the *Études Carmelitaines*, the quarterly *Psyche*, directed by Maryse Choisy, — all have played an important role in this change of attitude. It is surprising that most Catholic psychologists profess a somewhat corrected Freudianism, whereas the psychology of Jung would appear to be infinitely more attractive: the reason probably lies in their basically dogmatic intellectual habits.

* * * *

There is one principle that is admitted by almost all contemporary psychologists: psychology as such has nothing to say about God, the nature or origin of the soul, immortality, nor the question of instincts, emotions, or ideas, *in themselves*. Psychology can be concerned only with the psychological function of these concepts. Only on this condition can psychology claim the title of scientific discipline. But neither does psychology have the right to cast doubt or deny the transphenomenal reality of concepts which accomplish one or another psychological function. Philosophers and theologians and artists can use these concepts as they see fit. And on occasion, the psychologist himself might play the role of philosopher or theologian or artist. There is only one basic demand that can be made of the psychologist in such a situation: he must not ever falsify the data of science for the purposes of whatever non-scientific use he proposes to make of them.

2 soul or psyche ?

Poets, philosophers, theologians, psychologists, the man on the street — all speak of the soul as something familiar to everyone, a substance whose precise meaning does not need further definition. Spiritualists and materialists, believers and unbelievers, all seem to know that the soul exists and what it is. Even those thinkers who theoretically deny the body-soul dichotomy still use the words in their everyday conversation. But when we come to a formal definition of the soul, we soon see that there is much less agreement and that, for that matter, hardly anyone is in a position to define it.

I. *Philosophical Approaches*

Aristotelian philosophy has always defined the soul as the "substantial form of the body." But, in order to accept this definition, there has to be an acceptance of the Aristotelian and Thomistic system of hylomorphism, and few moderns are inclined to accept this system. The psychologist in particular, whose proper object is the science of the soul, categorically rejects a definition that is so foreign to the scientific spirit. In his eyes, there is much more to be said for the more or less metaphorical and symbolic descriptions that come from the mystics, the poets, the masters of Christian spirituality. They are certainly not scientific in the modern sense of the word, but they can surely be viewed as more or less successful attempts to describe the knowledge of experience.

The psychologist cannot obviously be content with Christian experience alone. Christian thinking, after all, could have been more or less seriously influenced by doctrines and dogmas that are not the fruit of empirical observation. It is thus important to compare Christian experience with our knowledge of the experiences of the same order realized by other peoples who are foreign to our civilization and our intellectual concepts. The moral and religious literature of China and India is particularly precious in this respect, because the Orientals have a much finer adaptation to this type of experience than the Western world.

Carl Jung devoted long months to the on location study of the soul among the primitive tribes of Africa. He managed to familiarize himself with the concrete nature of the soul with better success than he experienced among civilized peoples. The soul appeared there not as a vague entity or a handy word to describe the complex of psychic functions, but as a solid reality expressing itself in psychic functions.

Christian theologians speak of the soul as a substance: a point of view which can only violently shock the sensibilities of educated persons in our modern world. In the minds of modern people, the word substance conjures up an image of something static, whereas the soul must necessarily be fundamentally a dynamic entity. It makes little difference that, in the philosophy of Thomas Aquinas and his disciples, substance is not a static concept. Post-Cartesian philosophy has changed these concepts. Our contemporaries are inclined to conceive of the soul more as a pure dynamism, thus approaching, to some degree, the experience of the mystics, both Christian and Hindu.

Perhaps we could come to at least a provisory agreement by accepting the definition of the famous psychologist Wilhelm Steckel, who defines the soul as an *existential act*.

* * * *

Most people have learned to speak almost indiscriminately about soul and spirit as if the two were synonymous. Even the materialists think they can use terms like "spiritual values," "spiritual faculties," etc., in reference simply to the higher values of civilization. But if the word spirit has any meaning at all, it can only mean something that is radically different from matter. And it must mean this both as a principle of activity and as an *essence*. With his usual penetrating insight, the philosopher Louis Lavelle says that soul must not be confused with spirit. But the human soul is a participation of the spirit. . . . The soul is a "spirit engaged in the world."[1]

To keep from falling into the confusion of pantheism, the radical transcendence of the spirit must always be vigorously maintained. On the other hand, the soul is inconceivable without essential reference to the world of matter. Christian theology, which is generally little interested in the reality of body and material, still cannot conceive of the soul's eternal happiness as taking place before the resurrection of the body. What is more, a biologist such as Paul Chauchard believes that he is in perfect accord with St. Thomas when he categorically rejects the theory of the dualism of body and soul. We can all agree with Louis Lavelle when he says that the problem here is to understand how the soul and body can be separated, not how they can be united.[2] Later on, we shall have occasion to examine which important psychological truths have thus been intuitively experienced by a philosopher who was also a sage. Together with its spiritualization, the soul also affects the progressive spiritualization of the whole universe.

---

1. *De l'ame humaine,* pp. 17-18
2. *Op. cit.,* p. 104

It is extremely important to insist on the little known fact that the radical dualism between soul and body is not Christian in origin, but Cartesian. The theologians of these last centuries, unfortunately, have been caught up with the phrase, seeing it as the expression of a Christian truth when it is really the denial of Christian teaching. It is largely because of this unnatural barrier erected between the two that the soul has appeared as a superfluous luxury which can be denied without any great damage to man as he actually exists. Angelism, as Pascal so well described it, is closer to gross materialism than is generally realized. Depth psychology, in denouncing this dualism, does a service not only to science, but also to religion.

II. *Soul, Object of Psychology*

What we have just said about the soul is a matter of philosophy, or even theology. Psychology is not in a position to speak about the substantiality, essentiality, spirituality, or immortality of the soul, and it is wrong to criticize psychology on these grounds. It can, moreover, even establish the fact that these metaphysical claims are not contradicted by its own findings. As the occasion warrants, these claims might even be taken as working hypotheses, and psychology will frequently admit that they are fertile hypotheses. But there is nothing to keep other psychologists from constructing their own hypotheses on the denial of these same metaphysical notions. Acually, as we said in the preceding chapter, psychology as we understand it today is not in a position to speculate on the *per se* reality of the soul and its faculties: it studies only the various psychic functions and activities.

It might perhaps be desirable for psychologists not to use the word soul when they are making a serious claim not to pass beyond the limits of phenomenology. The term is so bound up with a metaphysical (or metapsychological) coefficient that confusion is inevitable in the mind of the average layman, especially when Freud or Freudian psychologists use the word.

It would be better to use the term psyche for that complex of psychic facts which can be scientifically observed, and the word soul should be reserved for theology, philosophy, and naturally also for metapsychology. Etymologically speaking, of course, psyche is almost synonymous with soul, but in the minds of men of our time and civilization, the first term is much less familiar and would thus give rise to much less confusion. Soul includes psyche, but it is more than psyche. Thus we have good reason to say that Freudian psychology is without soul, and still no one would deny that it has made great contributions to the understanding of the psyche. Indirectly, too, our knowledge of the soul has also profited.

III. Body and Soul

As a result of the discredit into which metaphysics had fallen, the psychologists of the nineteenth and early twentieth centuries believed they had grounds for denying the existence of the soul. There were only a few functions that were called psychic, and the word soul was only a metaphor. These psychologists had lost all their faith in the independent existences of the object of their own science. Only an object that could be studied and observed by the instruments in common use by physicists could possibly have any scientific bearing. The soul, according to all evidence, eludes the realm of physical investigation. It took a lot of time for biology, first of all, and then psychology to re-establish their autonomy.

Is it possible, scientifically, rigorously possible, to deny that there exists within man some "inner life," not reducible to the activities of the body? Intellectual activity is something more than the secretion of even the best developed brain, no matter how much more complicated than that of the animal. Human affections — love, sense of beauty, feeling of honor — can these be considered as products of one of our bodily organs, or one of our external senses? Is moral conscience only the result of a long social development? The answers to these questions, which are all very solid ones, are extremely important, not only for the psychologist, but for every man. If we have to answer no to these questions, then we could speak only metaphorically of the soul. The specificity of the psychic functions once being denied, the soul, which is presumed to be their subject, has no further reason to exist.

On the philosophical plane, the work of Bergson and his disciples, guided by the most rigorous scientific methods of observation, has concluded to the specificity and irreducibility of numerous psychic functions. For them, this is not a more or less plausible hypothesis, but a pure and simple scientific certitude.

Obviously there is no question of the autonomy of the psyche, in the Cartesian sense. The bonds of interdependence, and reciprocal conditioning that exists between the psychic and the psysiological are one of the truths on which both the Thomistic disciples of Aristotle and the immense majority of modern thinkers are in perfect accord. Conditioning does not always mean that the first principle proceeds from the second the way an effect proceeds from its cause, and dependence is not the same thing as subordination.

The work of psychologists and psychosomatic doctors has established the fact that neither dependence nor conditioning are unilateral. It is true that brain damage has direct repercussions on the most "spiritual" psychic activities. But it is equally true that bodily ills, such as tuberculosis and stomach ulcers, and probably also cancer, are often symtoms of psychic disorder.

IV. *The Nature of the Soul*

The soul appears to the psychologist as the psychic totality, in somewhat the same way as the body can be considered to be the biological totality of man. Its faculties and functions are manifold; there are probably many functions of whose existence we are not even aware. But this does not seem to be a denial of its basic unity and permanence. It is because the soul is one that I am more than a simple aggregate of feelings and sensations. It is because the soul is endowed with permanence that, notwithstanding the incessant transformation of the cells which make up my body, I can legitimately refer to what I was, what I am, and what I will be as *ME*.

Still, nothing authorizes us to consider the spirituality, unity, and permanence of the soul as the privilege of man alone. Quite the contrary, and as Father Teilhard de Chardin has so magnificently demonstrated, what is present in man in a state of some perfection is already preexisting, in germ, in animal life and even in the lower spheres of being.

Even in the case of man, the soul does not possess its definitive perfection from the outset. It is not the simple sum of a man's psychic functions, and yet it is nothing without these functions. Philosophically, we are surely right in saying that the soul exists before our psychic activities are awakened. For the psychologist, the soul is something that gradually and slowly *becomes*, as these functions begin to develop within man. The opposition between essence and existence is without foundation in reality. There is never any existence without essence, nor any essence without existence.

V. *Structures of the Soul*

Ancient psychology (it is still generally taught in the schools) believed that the soul could be known only through the medium of its conscious functions. Some Christian writers, in particular, had well grasped the fact that conscious activity was far from exhausting all the riches of the soul, and that within the real depths of the soul there were a number of processes which only rarely bobbed up to the light of consciousness. But the unconscious, by definition, seemed inaccessible, and thus it was felt that it had no information to offer about the soul. As for the post-Cartesian positivist, the very idea of unconscious and irrational seemed intolerable. This rationalistic prejudice was so deeply anchored in the minds of men of scientific pursuits that even today a psychologist as well known as Robert Desoille still refuses to speak of the unconscious.

The unconscious will be the object of more profound investigation in the chapters which follow. Psychoanalysis has unveiled the extent, depth, and importance of our unconscious psychic life, and many psychologists who are in sympathy with the methodology of psychoanalysis have a tendency to counterbalance the rationalist prejudice by identifying the soul with the unconscious. For them, it is the conscious mind that is a more or less accidental epiphenomenon.

* * * *

As we have just said, psychological observation and philosophical reflection make us consider the soul as a psychic totality. It thus embraces equally and simultaneously both the conscious and the unconscious.

The conscious part of the soul is called the ego. With the appearance of the ego, man becomes capable of assuming his own destiny. In step with his growing autonomy, the ego becomes more individualized, asserts its feeling of distinct entity with respect to the milieu to which it belongs, and begins to exercise control over nature. Ego must not be confused with consciousness: it is the ego that has the consciousness, that supports the identity of the person.

The ego has its sense of shyness, and it has its "complexes." Only rarely does it show its true face, not only to other people but even to itself. Many men never are aware that they are wearing a mask. Let us take a very simple example. The children of a famous professor have formed an image of their father as a silent, timid, and overly self-effacing man. That is how they see him at home, where their mother is the undisputed master of the house. Then one day the children happen to stop by the university and listen to a class. They can hardly recognize their father in the man who is delivering the lecture there. Sure of himself, authoritarian, brilliant, caustic: the very image of a great professor. Because society has formed a certain idea of what a good professor ought to be, this man instinctively assumes the role. But can we be sure that his real ego shows up any more truly at home, in the company of his wife and children? There is good reason to believe that he is still wearing a mask, a different one. As Jung so well phrases it, identification with one's profession or with one's title has something fascinating about it. Many men are really nothing more than the social dignity that society has conferred on them. It would be a waste of time to look for any real personality under this facade.[3] Jung refers to the original Latin meaning of the word, and calls this mask *personal*. Such a person is no longer a *person* really, but a *personage*, as we might put it in English.

In the case of superior people, the personage does not completely take the place of the ego. It hides and sometimes even protects it. In certain circumstances, in the presence of persons who can understand, the ego will drop its mask and show what it really is.

The ego asserts itself, grows, by winning territory from the unconscious, the "primitive," the "id" of Freudian psychology. But there must be no illusions here: no matter how strong an individual ego is presumed to be, it will never manage to integrate

---

3. *Beziehungen zwischen dem Ich und dem Unbewussten*, p. 42

the whole of the unconscious. Nor must it destroy the bridge between itself and the id. Maintaining a contact and a living communication between the two parts of the psyche is of the utmost importance for our destiny. The ego separated from the unconscious necessarily dissolves into a mask, whereas a communion between the two gives rise to the "self," the subject of psychic totality.

Experience shows that only a very few humans actually arrive at this stage of self, that is, the adult age of their psyche. Most of them never get far beyond the stage of ego, always wearing a mask, and always playing a variety of different roles in life.

For the self to come into being and consolidate, people must not live solely, nor even primarily, in tune with the outside world; they must make as great an effort as possible to see their own inner harmony. Now it seems that our modern world of today, with its frantic rhythm of life and its constantly increasing robotization is less in a position to promte this self-realization. Losing sight of self, that is, a too radical division between the ego and the treasures accumulated in the unconscious is in the eyes of the psychologist who is open to social realities, the principal cause for the disorder and disequilibrium, both individual and collective, that are becoming more and more widespread. The unconscious abandoned to itself, in its turn, can only live in utter anarchy.

Still, even under the most propitious conditions, perfect self-realization remains an ideal which cannot be realized existentially. In order to realize it, the ego has to be in a position to communicate with the totality of the unconscious, and this seems beyond our powers. Christian and Hindu mystics, through recourse to certain ascetical practices, are unquestionably as close as men can come to such an ideal, but not even they ever really managed to attain it. At the very most we might suppose that they were really themselve during those brief and privileged moments of ecstasy. As for the claim of some Freudian psychoanalysts that they can arrive at the fullness of personality by means of their own proper technique, we must consider this no more than a childish boast. All the more so, in that these philosophical presuppositions of their system do not even afford a proper conception of the real nature of the human self.

Each individual thus has a moral obligation to tend towards maximum self-development. Perfection necessarily varies according to the depth and individual potential of each soul. The moral obligation spoken of here does not arise from any external imperative; it is based on the fact that it is the only condition in which a man can acquire a certain degree of perfection which is in keeping with his specific nature. The mystics, in claiming that God is to be discovered in the self, are well aware of what they are saying. It is by neglecting self that so many men have become really incapable of finding God.

VI. *Kindred Souls*

The ego's function of individuation makes each soul rigorously distinct from every other soul. The more the ego is asserted, the stronger this individuality. The "primitives," whose ego has hardly begun to bud, give the impression of being barely distinct from the social group in which they live. As for the over-civilized society in which the personage has replaced the ego, there is nothing particularly "personal" about them: their uncompromising individuality is still only a mask to hide the emptiness within.

Still, the kinship of all souls, whatever their race or degree of evolution, is just as incontestable a fact as their individuality. The source of this fundamental resemblance is to be found in the unconscious. It is there that we find the accumulation of the fruits of experiences realized by individual men over thousands of years of human existence. It is here too that we must obviously look for that by which the Creator wanted to make all men resemble a certain image. Rather than through the intermediary of the community of culture and education, it is owing to this common fund (Jung calls it the "collective unconscious") that men of all times and places are, despite individual differences, still capable of understanding each other and communicating in an existential way.

VII. *Affective Nature of the Soul*

We have already said that psychology was, until very recent times, always oriented towards the intellectual, cognitive functions of the soul. St. Thomas himself maintained that beatitude was the perfection of knowledge. Obviously he was no less aware than the professional psychologist of today that the soul is also the seat of the functions of feeling and loving. But these functions appear too much bound up with the obscure and mysterious part of the soul to which the conscious ego has no access. This overemphasis on the rational activities of the soul is probably responsible for very much of the inhuman rigidity of our civilization.

One of the most precious benefits of depth psychology seems to be the discovery of the primacy of the effective element. This is obviously not to depreciate the rational. As Bergson has so well demonstrated, in the domain of pragmatic activity, reason renders inestimable service to man. On the plane of the ego, intelligence must always occupy first place. But, in the light of the scientific observations of depth psychology, the depths of the soul, the unconscious, is affective or emotional in nature.

The soul is thus a burning furnace of love, if it is true that love is the supreme expression of affectivity. This could hardly surprise the Christian, no matter how little acquainted he is with the Gospel of St. John. God being love and man being made in the image of God, what could be more normal than for love to occupy first place in man as well? Such, moreover, has ever been the deep-seated conviction of the saints and mystics even when, as children of their times, they theoretically professed the primacy of reason.

3 the unconscious and its "darkness"

The importance of the studies and discoveries realized by depth psychology in matters relating to the unconscious can be compared, without undue exaggeration, to the importance, in physics for example, of the law of universal gravitation or Einstein's theories of relativity. Even supposing that all the other theses of his psychology turned out to be erroneous, the debt humanity owes to Sigmund Freud would still be an immense one, for having discovered the primordial role of the unconscious in the life of the psyche.

I. *From Preconscious to Unconscious*

Freud did not invent the unconscious. Long before his time, philosposhers and psychologists had spoken of it. How could they miss the fact that psychic reality is not the same thing as conscious reality? There are some facts that any intelligent man must necessarily observe. A friend's address, a name that is on the tip of my tongue: despite my efforts, I cannot recall them now. What has happened to them? It is impossible to suppose that they have been destroyed or lost, because I know from experience that the least hint might bring them back to the field of consciousness.

Elementary reflection is enough to convince us that only a

very small fraction of what we have learned and experienced is actuated by our conscious mind. In order to avoid the chaos that would make it impossible for us to carry on any organized activity, the conscious mind is forced to reject whatever is not needed for its current occupation. Still it does not destroy the images and ideas that are, for the moment, superfluous; most of them can be useful again later on. It has to keep them in reserve.

Moreover, everyone knows that, especially in moments in which the activity of consciousness is reduced or suspended (for example in sleep or when we are daydreaming), images and ideas rise up of their own accord, coming from some mysterious abyss to invade our conscious mind. It is this deposit of psychic elements which the conscious mind does not need at a given moment that we currently call either unconscious or subconscious, with no appreciable difference in terms. Traditional psychology, although it was aware of its existence, did not believe it could be put to any profit.

* * * *

It is obvious that the unconscious, such as we have described it, is equally familar to the psychoanalysts. Their works, however, are not directed primarily towards this unconscious which is still so close to the conscious mind that Freud calls it the *preconscious*.

Beyond and below this *preconscious*, their therapeutic experience with mentally ill patients has led psychoanalysts to discover an *unconscious* that is much more radically separated from consciousness. The conscious mind can do very little to draw voluntarily upon the content of this unconscious properly so called. It is only independently of our volition that, as a general rule, the images and emotions of the unconscious irrupt into the field of consciousness. There they almost always throw things into confusion. Neurosis and mental abnormality are no longer such mysterious things, thanks to the new psychology. The behavior of the neurotic or the "madman" is only apparently incoherent: such people are obeying a different logic, the logic of the unconscious.

* * * *

Freud very early observed that the unconscious is not content with spawning the specifically pathological symptoms of psychic activity. In our everyday life, how many apparently incoherent words and acts we are guilty of: slips of tongue, mistakes in reading, the loss of a gift we were not particularly happy to receive, and many other little slip-ups — are these always due to chance alone? Freud was convinced they are not. For example, if I read "John died," instead of "John did," this might be due to some unconscious feeling of animosity I have for John, or because whatever he "did" was not agreeable to me. My unconscious mind would prefer him dead. If my fingers prove to be clumsy, dropping and breaking some gift I did not particularly like, that is because my unconsious mind is not satisfied with the gift.

We must obviously not push this Freudian theory to the absurd. Some of his over-zealous disciples claimed that every mistake in speech or act could be explained on the basis of unconscious motivation, thereby completely abolishing chance and freedom. Actually, there has to be a good deal of investigation before we dare maintain that a certain automobile accident, for example, was due to the unconscious suicidal tendencies of the driver or simply to some chance error in his judgment or lack of skill, or, again, to some mechanical failure in the car itself. In very many cases, Freudian interpretation is perfectly justified.

Later we shall devote an entire chapter to the study of one of the most important manifestations of the unconscious activity, dreams. Here it is enough to merely mention their existence.

* * * *

To sum up: the *preconscious* is the home of all the psychic facts, both cognitive and affective in nature, which have, for the moment, lost their energetic value, but can always recover it under a variety of external or internal stimuli. As for the *unconscious* properly so called, the Freudians consider that its content is made up of all the experiences accumulated over the whole course of existence, by all the memories, by all the residues of events we have been witness to, by all the feelings we have ever had on the occasion of these events, by all the desires that have never been satisfield.

These experiences, traces, feelings, and desires have been rejected by the conscious mind, either because they have now played their role in the individual's life and have thereby lost all their usefulness; or because they are incompatible with the social conventions of our living and "social censorship" has kept them from ever rising to the conscious mind. They might easily expose the individual, who would give them a role to play in his conscious life, to the pressures and punishments which society reserves for those who do not conform to its precepts and customs.

The philosopher Schopenhauer was certainly one of the precursors of the Freudian theory of the unconscious. In a most dramatic way, he experienced the fact that "man is unaware of the motives behind his actions." But there is also the influence of C. G. Carus, one of the first to consider the dream as an irruption of the unconscious into the conscious. There is the influence of E. von Hartmann, who saw the unconscious as the source of all conscious life, particularly the source of genius. On the rigorously experimental plane, the founder of psychoanalysis has a debt to acknowledge to Charcot, Bernheim, Janet.

The psychologists who followed Freud added many nuances and some modifications to the master's theses. As we shall discover, they saw the unconscious as the resting place of many things which have never been conscious and never will have a chance to be conscious. In all its essential elements, however, the insights and discoveries of Freud will remain of inestimable value for the whole future progress of psychology.

II. The Primitive

In speaking of the unconscious, it is important to avoid all use of image, all static comparison. The unconscious, as it is conceived in modern psychology, is not a vast "storehouse" which holds all of our psychic experience that consciousness, for one reason or another, either does not want to recall or cannot. Even Pavlov, whose inspiration is far removed from that of psychoanalysis, insists on the essentially dynamic character of the psychic depths: the unconscious gets its energy from instincts and impulses. However, the arguments of those who claim to see instinct and impulse as the whole source of psychic activity do not convince us at all. The specific character of psychic life seems to be beyond question, on the basis of experimental investigation, and instinct and impulse are only a biological substructure. But that much they surely are, and that is enough to condemn Cartesian dualism out of hand.

What is more, when we as psychologists speak of instincts, we understand the word to mean something very much more complex than what the biologist refers to under the same term. In order to avoid confusion, many writers prefer to use a more supple expression, one which is less flavored with biologism: "instinctual impulses."

These instinctual impulses, by their very nature, escape the control of the conscious mind. The conscious mind, being the principle of individuation, is concerned primarily with the welfare of the individual. The instincts, on the other hand, the most specifically psychological as well as the most fundamentally biological, all tend towards the good of the species, even to the possible detriment of the individual. But it frequently happens that they aim at these goals under the form of a more or less personalized disguise. Thus the instinct might say, "I want . . ." even when it is possible that the ego has no desire whatsoever.

Among primitives, the motivation of instinct is almost the

only operative force. In civilized man, the extension and consolidation of the conscious psyche results in a more or less large scale emancipation from the control of instinctual impulse. Instinct can even undergo a certain transformation. Beyond the physiological ends of the organism, beyond the survival and wellbeing of the species, instinct is engaged in the service of higher human goals. Instinctual impulse is at work in the life of artist and thinker and even in the mystic ecstasy. Not only the sex instinct (this is the one that had held the almost exclusive attention of the Freudians), but also the instincts of security, power, *etc.*, can all be "sublimated."

But there must be no illusions here. No matter how great we imagine the power of sublimation to be, the unconscious, in itself, will always remain "primitive"; it will never become "civilized." Instinct holds sway there, absolutely, in the doctor of physics as well as in the pygmy of central Africa. In fact, instinct is even more dangerous in the case of the doctor, if he ever tries to subdue the instinctual forces in order to live "in accordance with the laws of reason alone." The bizarre behavior, the "stupidity" of so many men of obviously superior intelligence can be explained in this way.

The education of children and self-formation must, therefore, never aim at suppressing the life of instinct, nor even reducing it to slavery and bondage. From the numerous revolutions known to history we must retain the lesson that nothing is more cruel or senseless than the sudden violence of the slave whose bonds are broken. Only consenting to a "peaceful coexistence" can give rise to a certain mastery over instinct life by the conscious and voluntary within us. The evil of instinct, according to Emmanuel Mounier, is inertia and regression.[1] An instinctual impulse that has been forced into silence will some day have its revenge. Then it might very well break into areas in which it normally has no

---

1. *Traité du caractère*, p. 135

rights at all. There is truth in the Freudian theory of repression, even if we reject the dogmatism with which he advanced it.

III. *Unconscious Depths*

The extent and depth of the unconscious cannot ever be measured. The most ingenious processes of psychoanalysis can never make more than an infinitesimal part of it come to light. The unconscious, according to Freud, is like a big circle which encloses the conscious mind like a smaller circle. There cannot ever be any conscious fact without an unconscious preparation, whereas the unconscious can do without the conscious stage and still have a psychic value and a meaning of its own. The unconscious is the psychic element itself and in its essential reality.[2]

The discovery of the uncharted abysses of the unconscious has given way, in many psychologists who base their thinking on Freud, to a serious underestimation of the conscious psyche. Frieud, however, while professing that the conscious has no dynamism of its own, that it owes its whole life to the unconscious, still did not underestimate the primordial value of conscious facts in the study of psychology. We do not mean to say, he writes, that the quality of the conscious has lost its value in our eyes. It remains the only light we have to guide us through the darkness of psychic life.[3] No matter how rich we suppose it to be, the unconscious is never immediately accessible to us. Its structures and all its secrets are yielded up only in the proportion that our conscious mind succeeds in projecting some of its own light upon them. The conscious mind alone is able to assimilate and interpret the facts experienced by the unconscious.

In practice, a given psychic activity must never be attributed to the unconscious, unless detailed investigation has made it

---

2. *Science of Dreams*, p. 599 (French edition.)
3. *Abrégé de la psychanalyse*, p. 20

certain that the activity cannot be explained on the basis of the conscious mind. Moreover, though it is obviously true that the unconscious contains immense treasures, it is still far from being as omniscient as some thinkers like to believe it is, and it is not all-powerful. Our consciousness, according to Jung, is only the vanguard of our psychic life. This is obvious. But the role is not a negligible one. Jung goes on to say that there are basically only a very few moments in which man is really conscious, in which consciousness attains a certain level and intensity.[4] Education and psychological therapy still demand that we promote the activity of the conscious mind as much as possible.

* * * *

Freud and his disciples are interested only in the most superficial strata of the real unconscious. Certain psychic facts have become unconscious only after being conscious first. Others have never been able to enter into the field of consciousness, repression having been operative upon them from the very outset. But we must not conclude that the unconscious is nothing more than a depository for the discarded psychic phenomena of the conscious mind. Quite the contrary; Freudian theory teaches that it is rather the poverty of our conscious mind and its fundamental incapacity to open to the profound riches of the unconscious, that has given rise to this repression.

Jung's view of the matter is a more rewarding one. The master of Zurich was able to observe, very early in his career, in dreams and other expressions of the unconscious mind, that there are numerous elements which, on all evidence, have never been conscious and certainly could never even want to be. This not a denial of the existence of unconscious repression, in the sense that the words are understood in Freudian psychology. But, in addition to the unconscious of Freud, there is another, earlier unconscious which precedes the emergence of consciousness.

---

4. *L'homme à la découverte de son âme,* p. 74

IV. *Collective Unconscious*

This unconscious depth which we might rightly consider the essence of the soul is not personal. In studying the legends, the mythologies, and the poetry of peoples far removed from each other in space and time, where there could be no possible question of mutual influence or borrowings, the psychologist observed that certain themes and certain figures appear in every culture. On the other hand, the dream analysis of many different people, belonging to different races, cultures, and religions, all uncovered the same themes and figures. Just as the little chick comes out of his shell in the same way all over the world, writes Jung, in the same way there are certain psychic modes of functioning, that is, certain manners of thinking, feeling, imagining whose existence can be demonstrated in every place and at every time, independently of any tradition or continuity.[5] With more or less significant variations, every mythology shows some signs of the evil dragon, the crafty serpent, the wise old man. The sacred character is recognizable in almost every religion by a certain number, or a certain gesture.

Jung called these figures and symbols that are common to all souls "archetypes." By this he meant to say that they are not the result of the repression of personal experiences, but rather part of a heritage in which every member of the human race has a share. The archetype, he writes, is a symbolic form which functions particularly wherever there is not yet any conscious concrete concept, or when external or internal reasons make it impossible. The content of the collective unconscious is represented in the conscious mind under the form of inclinations or characterized conceptions.[6]

The collective unconscious transmits by way of heredity, under the form of archetypes, not the representations as such, but

5. *Guérison,* . . . p. 24
6. Jung: *Types,* p. 387

rather the faculty of producing or evoking them. Thus, Jung is not advocating a restoration of the age-old philosophical concept of innate ideas. More simply, the human soul is everywhere identical, everywhere possesses the same faculties and functions. The work of ethnographers and prehistorians shows that certain fundamental patterns are to be found in every human person. These are the archetypes on the psychological plane.

In drawing up this theory, Jung was not pursuing any objectives of the metaphysical order. The usage that some theologians might make of such a theory, to assert the essential unity of the human race, is thus all the more valuable.

* * * *

Proceeding everywhere in the same psychic function, the same archetype does not always present an absolutely identical form. Each particular civilization leaves its own stamp on the archetype. The Western soul, for example, has been molded by twenty centuries of Christianity; it would be surprising indeed not to find some trace of this in our collective unconscious. Actually, the deep and obscure powers of the psyche are manifest within us in the symbols that are used in Christianity, even if personally we do not adhere to that religion. Thus the archetype of the wise old man frequently takes on the form, in our dreams, of a particularly popular saint, or a picture of God the Father. The cross, the Blessed Virgin, or the ceremony of baptism also frequently accomplish the same archetypal function. Naturally enough, for the Hindu, the Buddhist, the Mohammedan, the archetypes make use of symbols proper to each of these religions. It takes a deep and thorough analysis to establish their underlying identity.

Only in virtue of this fundamental identity of the depths of the unconscious among all human beings are we, the Westerners of the twentieth century, in a position to understand something of the poetry or sculpture or painting produced by civilizations that have disappeared thousands of years ago. Once again, owing to this identity of the unconscious, once we learn Chinese or a Chinese learns English, we are able to communicate our thinking and feeling, no matter how different the conscious structures of our respective psyches. And all this is even more true on the affective plane than on the level of rational intelligence.

As the very essence of the psyche, the collective unconscious is the privileged source of metaphysical speculation and mystic insights bearing on the nature and activities of the soul. It is not a dead sea, but rather a volcano in a constant state of eruption. From time to time, it breaks through into the smaller world of the conscious, and it is then that we can verify its existence.

The collective unconscious implies several strata of unequal depth. There is the family collective unconscious and the national, the unconscious that is common to a given civilization, and finally the unconscious which is common to all men everywhere. The farther removed it is from the individual himself, the more difficult of access it is. It seems probable that the deepest strata are permanently closed to our investigation.

At first sight, the theory of a collective unconscious appears to involve us in full psychological determinism. Emerging from the ocean of the unconscious whose sources are as ancient as humanity itself, what can the conscious ego ever possess and call its own? And yet it is really the Freudian psychology, notwithstanding its ignorance of the collective unconscious, which actually professes determinism, whereas the psychology of Jung remains perfectly open to a philosophy of human freedom. In recognizing the immutable character of psychic functions, it makes it possible to concentrate better on the conditions of personal freedom.

Obviously, such freedom is never total. It is proportioned to each individual's degree of individuation. The more the ego has succeeded in assimilating the treasures of the unconscious, the more it escapes from this determinism. But just as it is inconceivable for the whole of the unconscious psyche to ever be conscious, human freedom will not ever be perfect, at least not in the temporal stage of human existence.

V. *The Unconscious as a Destructive Element*

We have already said that Dr. Freud was led to explore the unconscious by the demands of his medical practice in dealing with psychic maladies. How could he help notice the maleficent activity of the unconscious? Equilibrium and the values recognized by the ego appeared to be of the most extraordinary fragility. At any moment, they are threatened by the destructive irruption of instinct. Primitive man, living only under the sway of instinct, looks like a sort of monster. But this monster is still living within every man; only very imperfectly have the trappings of civilization and social custom managed to keep him hidden within the civilized man.

Here once again we run afoul of Freud's famous penchant for unwarranted generalization. He seems never to have suspected the illegitimacy of the applications he made on the basis of his investigations into the diseased psyche. What is more, he let himself be too easily influenced by his own characteristic pessimism. We shall see later on how small a chance, within the perspective of Freudian sublimation, the soul actually has of being saved, that is, escaping the clutches of the demoniac unconscious. Still it is important to note that, in speaking of the unconscious as a monster, Freud is simply using a common manner of speaking, without, in his own eye, meaning to imply anything like a value judgment.

We cannot share Freud's pessimism any more than we were able to agree with his exaggeration of the role of the unconscious. A more serene attitude appears to be that of Jung, who says that the unconscious is not a demoniacal monster; it is a natural organism, morally ambivalent, esthetic and intellectual, which can become really dangerous only when our conscious attitude towards it is desperately false. The deeper we try to repress it within ourselves, the greater are the dangers which actually threaten us from that source.[7]

The unconscious becomes unfavorable and dangerous, he goes on to say, only when we are in discord with it, when we are in opposition to the major tendencies that operate within our psyche.... As a result, a lack of contact and formal bonds with the unconscious is synonymous with the uprooting and instability of our instinct. But if we succeed in reestablishing this function, the disunion with self will cease and the subject will be able to benefit from the favorable influences of the unconscious.[8]

In the primitive and in the child, the domination of the unconscious is almost total. Neither the one nor the other is a monster, however; quite the contrary, most often they are endowed with a remarkable degree of psychic health. The civilized adult can share this same psychic health, provided only that the assimilation of the unconscious by the ego takes place harmoniously, and the contact between the two is never broken.

What is more, the conscious can be just as serious a source of danger to the psyche as can the unconscious. This is particularly true whenever its behavior tends to be too exclusively individualistic or totally oriented towards the external world. Cut off from the compensating function of the unconscious, the ego runs the risk of losing all its consistency, being only a mask, the superficial personage described above. Only after really proving the fact, should psychic disorder, neurosis, be attributed to the unconscious: it can just as easily be the work of the conscious mind. Or rather, it is the conscious that can be *responsible*, if it is the conscious that has broken the vital contact with the unconscious.

---

7. Jung: *Psychologie de l'inconscient*, p. 221
8. Jung: *L'homme à la découverte* ..., p. 301

It is thus absolutely imperative to never lose sight of the
fundamental unity of the psyche. In the psychic totality, the
unconscious serves as the "organ" for what the mystics call the
"interior life," without probably realizing how far their insights
correspond with the scientific truth of the matter. The ego is not
capable of realizing itself unless it maintains a state of communication with the unconscious. Thus it can utilize the psychic energy
for which the unconscious is the vast reservoir. If there are
dangers to the ego, they do not come from the unconscious, but
from the attempt to act as if there were no unconscious, as if we
directed our behavior solely according to the light of reason. A
source of energy as potent as the unconscious can never be stifled:
the volcano will almost always erupt with more than savage
velocity.

VI. *Synthetic View of the Psyche*

Having examined almost all we need to understand, in psychology, about the unconscious — and, correlatively with this,
the conscious — we are now in the position to complete what we
have said about the structures of the soul in the preceding chapter.

The Freudians distinguish three strata in the soul. There is
first of all the *unconscious*, the home of instincts and repressed
emotions. They call it the *"id"* or *"it"* in the sense of: *"It* is
stronger than I am, I have to act this way." The *ego* makes up the
second stratum, the area of conscious psyche. It is almost necessarily at constant grips with the *id*. Finally, there is the *superego*,
the artificial and monstrous product of social constraints which
chafes at both the *ego* and the *id*. Like true heirs of their master's
somewhat magically inclined mentality, many of Freud's disciples
speak of the *id*, the *ego* and the *superego* as if they were autonomous little people living within us. The fundamental unity of the
psyche is thus practically denied.

Richer, more elaborate, and thus more apt to take into account all the fundamental unity and immense complexity of the soul is the Jungian schema. I have adopted its broader outlines here, with the one important distinction that, in my view, the ego is not an entity distinct from both the conscious and the unconscious, in which it simultaneously has a share, but rather the *subject* of the conscious psyche. It remains true, however, that whenever this conscious ego ceases to communicate in a vital way with the unconscious mind, the ego is exhausted. In this sense, there is no real ego in my outline either, excepting in virtue of the energy that is constantly drawn from the unconscious.

The principal functions of the conscious mind are thought, intuition, sensation, and feeling.

Thought is oriented towards the objective outside world. Its proper function is the comprehension of the universe, and through that knowledge it makes it possible for man to adapt to the world. We are thus, with Jung, very close to Bergson's idea of intelligence. Intellectual cognition is the specific act of thought: knowing. But we must be on guard against depreciating the role that thought plays in our existence. The soul could not ever realize itself without drawing upon the outside intelligible universe.

Feeling is also a rational function. However, it differs greatly from that of thought, insofar as it does not take in the outside world in its objectivity, but rather takes a subjective grasp of reality. This means that it accepts what is agreeable to the ego and rejects what is disagreeable.

Sensation and *intuition* Jung calls irrational. They are independent of the judgment of reason, content with registering perceptions which they neither evaluate nor interpret. *Sensation* grasps things in themselves, such as they are in their real objectivity; it is thus somewhat related to rational thinking. Intuition, however, grasps the possibilities inherent in things, by an inner perception. Like sensation, it establishes a certain mediation between the conscious ego and the unconscious psyche.

Obviously we are not so bold as to claim that we have encompassed the whole reality within our little schema. Reality goes far beyond it on every side, and reality always has more nuances to explore. Jung himself considers the case of *empirical* thinking, and a second type of thought which might be called *intuitive*, while a third class ought to be called *speculative*. In like manner, there is *sensory feeling* and also *intuitive feeling*. One thing must be avoided at all costs: there are no closed compartments in the psyche, no little persons who are more or less autonomous and concurrent. Such a vision of the psyche is doomed to failure from the very outset.

4 libido, psychic energy

When the average layman hears the word psychoanalysis, he thinks primarily in terms of the famous "libido." He generally has a rather confused idea of it. What is more, the last-ditch opponents of the new psychology have continued to offer the most vehement criticism against the theory of the libido. We must admit that they are not completely wrong, for a number of so-called Freudians have said so many foolish things about the libido, that, in the eyes of serious thinkers, it looks more like a slogan geared for publicity than a really scientific notion. As for Freud himself, he never managed to present a really unequivocal definition of the term.

I. *Affective Energy*

It is wise to insist once more on the fundamental truth of the new psychology (of all the schools) that the psyche is basically *dynamic* in nature, a constant wellspring of energy. It can suffer momentary interruption and limitations, but only because the psyche is intimately bound up with matter, with the body of the individual, and also the outside world. On this subject, we are only repeating one of the fundamental theses of the old metaphysical psychology, which also conceived of the soul as a principle of life and activity.

The originality of the psychology which serves as the basis for psychoanalysis is somewhat greater when it establishes the fact, on the basis of innumerable experiences and investigation, that psychic energy is affective in nature. Freud chose the term *libido* to refer to that energy: it is a Latin word and means *"passion, desire, envy, caprice,"* and, in the more recent authors, *sexual desire.* Was it a happy choice of terms? We might well ask such a question in view of the fact that the word has contributed much to making psychoanalysis suspect or even ridiculous. In English and in many other languages, the words derived from libido have a decidedly bad connotation: libidinous, libidinosity, etc. At any rate, and notwithstanding the efforts of some psychoanalysts, it is difficult, if not absolutely impossible, to speak of the libido without bringing up the thought of sex. We might well protest against the depreciation of sex on the part of a civilization that has retained only a few taboos from its Christian origins, even though it is not by provoking the problem, as did Freud, that we might hope to remedy the situation.

Affective energy has been officially christened *libido,* and the conclusion that both the admirers and the adversaries of Dr. Freud have more or less consciously drawn from this fact is that, for psychoanalysis, sex is the source and center of all psychic life. How can we profess such a theory without appearing to be ridiculously pedantic?

II. *Freudian Pansexualism*

The exegetes and commentators have some grounds for dispute when they set about establishing the exact thinking of the founder of psychoanalysis on the subject of the libido. His writings on this subject yield expressions and ideas which appear to be as contradictory as possible. Arguing against criticism and accusations which were often treacherous, Freud frequently had to defend himself by claiming that his opponents had not properly interpreted his teaching: at other times his aggressiveness gets out of hand and then he himself packs the libido with a full charge of dynamite. Then again, he sometimes tries to reconcile all these different points of view.

In perfect keeping with the intellectual bent of the nineteenth century, Dr. Freud was constantly trying to correlate psychic activities with biological instincts. The libido, he writes, is the force with which the instinct behind the assimilation of nourishment is manifested.[1] Still the sex instinct, no matter how biological it is, takes on a particular dignity in the whole complex of Freudian teaching. Libido, as he understands the term, is the source of all psychic activity. No wonder, under such conditions, that he was accused of having professed pansexualism.

Present day Freudian thinking is resigned to this charge, and even professes to teach pansexualism with a certain pride. But Freud himself could not help being aware of the harm such a charge could do to the success of his whole system. In order to escape it, he tried to establish a fine distinction between *sexual* and *genital*. Only the first really deserves the name of libido. It embraces the second, but never identifies with it. Freud claims that all the impulses of the libido, in themselves, always necessarily tend towards genital satisfaction. If they do not always actually arrive at this satisfaction, that is the work of inhibition and repression, unless there is also some element of organic deficiency. Sexual is not thus equivalent to genital, but the relationship between the two is such a close one that I cannot see how it can possibly dissolve the stigma of pansexualism.

* * * *

Today, and in large part owing to the work of Freud, hardly anyone, among the educated classes, claims to identify sexual and

---

1. *Introduction à la psychanalyse,* p. 336

genital. But this is far from saying that this distinction obliges us to consider sex as the only principle of human affectivity, to say nothing of psychic activity in general. That sex does actually occupy a primary place in the psychic life of the neurotic is beyond question. Since it was from the observation of such people that Freud first developed his theories, the excesses are easy to understand, but this does not justify the conclusions that are drawn with respect to mankind as a whole. We shall have occasion to treat this subject of Freudian sexology again, in the next chapter, in greater detail.

The Catholic followers of Freud like to refer to the following passage, in which Freud speaks of the libido in terms acceptable to all: Libido is a term borrowed from the theory of affectivity. We use it to mean the energy (considered as a quantitative magnitude, but not yet measurable) of tendencies which are related to what we sum up under the word love, and naturally made up of what is commonly known as love as it is sung by the poets, that is, sexual union. But we do not separate any of the other varieties of love, such as self-love, the love we have for parents or children, friendship, human love in general, any more than we exclude an attachment to concrete objects or abstact ideas. To justify the extension we thus make of the term love, we can cite the results of psychoanalytic research, namely, that all the varieties of love are equally expressions of one and the same complex of tendencies, which, in certain cases, lead to sexual union, while in other cases they turn us away from this objective or hinder its achievement, all the while preserving those characteristic traits which make their underlying identity unmistakable.[2]

It would be really very hard to find, in all of Freud's writings, a text which offers a clearer and more developed summary of what he understands by libido. But how can this definition be used to refute the charge of pansexualism? In an earlier phase,

---

2. Quoted by Maryse Choisy, *Psychanalyse et catholicisme*, p. 40

Freud seems to come very close to the traditional Christian doctrine of the primacy of love. He even refers explicitly to St. Paul, in the passage from Corinthians, where he asserts the primacy of love over all other moral values, natural and supernatural alike. But there is some confusion. For Paul, and for the whole history of Christian thought, the charity he exalts does not have the same origin as sexual love, even if sexual love were not directly ordered towards the genital.

If Freud had been content to enumerate the "varieties" of love, we might perhaps agree with him. But how can we fail to notice, in the text quoted above, the absolute primacy he accords to strictly sexual love, that is, genital love? It is obvious that, in his eyes, the libido tends towards other goals only because it is prevented from arriving at its primary end, sexual intercourse.

In a fine little book, *Three Essays on the Theory of Sexuality*, Freud himself condensed his teaching on the libido in a series of lapidary formulae which leave no room for doubt about its pansexualistic character. All pleasure, even the pleasure of the newborn child in sucking the nipple on his mother's breast, can be reduced, in the last analysis, to the sex instinct. The growing curiosity of the child is exclusively centered on the genital organs, *etc.* Not that the other impulses and biological tendencies are only an illusion, but according to Freud, they all relate back to the "libido stock."

Pansexualism seems to be an unwarranted deduction on the basis of scientifically observed facts, and thus we cannot adopt Freud's theory of the libido in our system of psychology.

III. *Libido as Psychic Energy*

We have no preference, *a priori*, for the psychology of Jung over that of Freud. But it does seem that Jung's psychology has left a better description and definition of the true nature of the psychic dynamism.

Perhaps it would have been wiser for Jung to give up the term libido, since the word can hardly be understood any longer in a sense that is radically different from the meaning Freud gives it. But, if Jung has kept the word, he has given it new connotations and enriched its meaning to the point where we no longer find ourselves involved in pansexualism, or sexualism at all, for that matter.

Even though we are devoting the whole of Chapter V to the subject, it is still necessary to insist, right here and now, on the fact that we are not minimizing the extremely important role of sex in the life of the psyche, any more than Jung does. It is our intention simply to allow it to have the place it really deserves and thus put an end to myth and confusion. Some of Jung's disciples, it is true, who were possessed of neither their master's general culture nor his vigorous thinking, show a tendency to speak of the libido as if in Jung's writing, it were primarily sexual and its extension to other domains were to be understood only on the basis of analogy. But such is not the thinking of Jung: and this is not the way it looks to us.

Since, despite my own personal regrets, the word libido seems to have definitively established its citizenship in the field of psychology, it is pointless to keep questioning the legitimacy of its use. With Jung, we understand libido as the totality of psychic energy, affective in nature, the whole complex of forces and tendencies which animate and connect all the activities and functions of the soul. In art and scientific research, in religion and morality, in love and friendship, the libido is everywhere at work. For the libido to be absent in a given activity or way of behavior, a man would have to remain completely uninvolved. This might be the case in some extremely mechanized industrial work, where a man is little more than a cog in the machinery.

Psychic energy, the libido, obviously also lends its force to man's sexual activity, precisely to the extent that this activity is human. But — in order to clearly demonstrate the fundamental difference between Freudian theory and our own (closely related to Jung)— it is at least theoretically conceivable that there can be sexual relations that are so exclusively bio-chemical that the libido is totally absent. In any case, the sexual libido does not enjoy any priority over the other forms of affective energy.

There is absolutely nothing "metaphysical" in this conception of the libido as the Freudian orthodox like to claim, in an effort to discredit it. It might be premature to speak of scientific evidence in this respect, but at very least we have a working hypothesis that has proved to be extraordinarily fertile.

We might say, writes Jung, that in the psychological domain the concept of libido has the same general meaning that energy has in the domain of physical sciences since the time of Robert Mayer.[3] Thus we have every right to speak of it as *psychic energy*. Nor do we expect to put our finger on the libido, any more than the physicist expects to find material energy under his microscope. Its reality is expressed through the permanent activity of the psyche, and we might well consider that the theoretical postulate finds its practical confirmation every day of human existence. Just as the formation and disintegration of cell life maintain equilibrium in the physical economy of the organism, psychic energy — to use Jacobi's rather elementary comparison — determines the relationship among the various psychic elements: all the disturbances which are evident in its proper functioning give way to pathological symptoms.[4]

IV. *Differentiation in the Libido*

Psychic energy has its source in the collective unconscious. Consequently it is the hereditary property of every member of the human race. But it does not exist in the same quantity and same quality in every person. In speaking of men of strong libido

---

3. *Metamorphoses de l'âme et ses symbolses*, p. 237
4. Jolan Jacobi *La psychologie de C. G. Jung*, p. 64

or weak libido, we mean to describe something real; it is not a mere metaphor.

The reasons for this unequal division of a fundamental "family inheritance" can be of the individual or the social order, just like the reasons for physical inequality. The existential possibilities of individuals who have strong libido are obviously superior to those individuals who have weaker libidos. Still, no matter how powerful we suppose the libido of a given individual to be, it can never produce any good effects automatically. The role of human freedom is never restricted in our psychology.

* * * *

The so-called normal man uses his libido in an "equally balanced" way among the various functions of the psyche. One part is at work in sex, another in his professional activity, a third in his leisure occupations, a fourth in his religious and moral life, *etc.* Actually, such perfect balance is rarely encountered in practice, and those who approach this ideal generally do not belong to the rank and file of humanity.

In the vast majority or cases, we can observe an over-accumulation of psychic energy towards one particular function. That is why we can notice a predominance of the will to power in one person, and a predominance of sex in another, whereas a third might be consumed with artistic passion or mysticism, or simply love and hate. This intensive expenditure of libido in only one of its many functions inevitably involves a more or less noticeable atrophy in the others.

In itself, the libido is thus perfectly undifferentiated, neutral. We can make whatever use we wish of it. In saying this, I am obviously not thinking of a positive will on our part, acting according to the imperatives of free and deliberate choice. Most of the time, the orientation of the libido is pretty well determined by the various structures of the personality. If a person is not endowed with musical talent, no amount of will or desire is going to orient his libido towards the creation or study of music. Of itself, the libido neither creates nor destroys anything. Genius and personal aptitude are not the offspring of libido. But if the energy of the libido is not directed towards them, neither genius nor the most extraordinary individual aptitude could ever pass over into exercise.

What has just been said of the libido in general is equally true of the sexual libido. In most people, the energy consumption of the sex function is so considerable that Freud and the Freudian school might well be excused for having confused libido with the sex instinct pure and simple. But this energy consumption is markedly different in degree, according to individual differences and civilizations, and probably also in keeping with the degree of psychic maturity. There is nothing surprising in the fact, for instance, that in the neurotic, sexual conflict is generally to be found at the heart of psychic activity. This is generally the case, not because their sexual function has undergone any exceptional constraint or inhibition, but because the other important areas of their psychic activity are not normally developed and the energy that is thus at their disposal has no other outlet than sex. It is not by encouraging such a patient to sexual indulgence and dissipation that his neurosis will be cured, but rather by orienting the libido towards one of its "higher" psychic functions.

V. *Good and the Bad Use of the Libido*

The "equal and proper" division of the libido's energies among all the functions of the psyche, as we have observed above, is an ideal that can hardly be achieved in reality. Some kind of "abuse" is practically inevitable and perhaps even necessary. It is certainly a real shame that geniuses and highly endowed men in general are always so excessive, so unbalanced; but genius will come at no other price.

In many cases the psychic imbalance in the cases described above manifests itself in the area of sex. Sexual abandon, perversion, and similar sexual disorders, really do seem to be much more frequent in the more highly endowed man than in the common man. But this must not lead us to the hasty conclusion that these men have a stronger sexuality — this would be in contradiction to our way of looking at the libido. Sexual disorders, as any perceptive psychologist will admit, result not from too much, but from too little sexual libido. This deficiency is, in the cases mentioned above, the inevitable result of using too much of the energy in the specific activities to which the "superior person" likes to devote himself.

Everyone knows that most religions consider renunciation of sexual activity as an indispensable condition for anyone who wants to approach the mystic life. That is because they feel, more or less confusedly (and experience can only confirm the opinion), that the mystic function of the psyche demands a particularly concentrated use of libido. Where will it come from? Obviously from the one area in which its natural consumption is greater than anywhere else, that is, from the sex function.

The limited quantity of libido in each human being and its undifferentiated character explain why all human superiority is necessarily relative. No genius is ever universal; quite the contrary, the greatest artists and thinkers are frequently very "backwards" in any field apart from their particular specialty.

* * * *

Depth psychology made a mistake in taking the medical field as its primary field of activity. This erroneous concentration can be explained by the fact that the founders of this psychology were psychiatric doctors; but still it is primarily on the pedagogical plane that the activity of the psychologist is more necessary and appears to be more fruitful.

Only the intelligent usage of the libido can help a man to lead a beautiful and socially useful existence. Now, whether it is owing to the existence of external or internal obstacles, experience proves that in many cases the libido does not develop normally. It even seems that deviations or inhibitions have become more frequent than ever before, in our modern civilization. It is the province of the psychologist to fight against these obstacles, to help people control their problems and properly direct their affective energies.

Jung observes that, both in mythologies and in dreams, the libido is frequently symbolized by the sun or personified by heroes who have solar qualities. Thus the libido can hardly be a force that is maleficent by nature. It can become so only accidentally, when it is prevented from distributing its warmth and light. To the degree that his libido operates freely, a man will experience happiness.

Once again we must insist: this is not a question solely, or even primarily, of sexual libido. Still it does seem that, with the exception of the genuine mystics and certain geniuses in whom "sublimation" is perfect, the sexual usage of energy is always necessary for the maturity and health of the psyche. More than the atrophy of any of the other psychic functions, sexual atrophy leaves the libido partially unemployed. It remains blocked in the unconscious, and threatens to break loose in anarchical irruptions, to the serious mental harm of the individual. Still, in certain periods of particularly intense intellectual, spiritual, or artistic activity, the "ordinary" man himself can turn the libido away from the sexual function not only without any danger, but to his own real profit.

In these serious cases, the irruptions of the repressed libido give rise to neuroses; this is not the time to discuss them fully. In less serious cases, the false virgin (that is, the person in whom chastity is not associated with any higher psychic activity) easily turns into a miser, a sickly hypochondriac, a vain and childish weakling. Psychoanalysts are not wrong in considering these deviations of the libido as auto-erotic manifestations. In the saint, perfect chastity not only is not harmful to psychic equilibrium, but it is actually a condition for this equilibrium. It must furnish the necessary "fuel" for an intense spiritual activity. The same is not true of those who, voluntarily or otherwise, repress their sexuality, without however mobilizing all their affective energies in the service of some absolute. The weird behavior of the old spinster or bachelor is not the invention of the cartoonist. Obviously, not everyone can really be a saint, just by wanting to. Still, the Catholic Church demands perfect chastity from all her monks and priests and sisters. This is not the place to question whether or not she has good reason for doing this. The psychologist is never in a position to impose his own theories, particularly when dealing with institutions such as the Church, whose ultimate goals are far above the psychological order. The psychologist must behave existentially, that is, he must do what he can to help human beings to self-realization in the conditions in which they actually exist and as they want them to be.

The libido must be kept from leading souls who are consecrated to the service of God back to the infantile auto-erotic stage of sexuality. Can there be any authentic spiritual progress, any real purification, in the case of those who are chaste only because they have become miserly or gluttonous or vain and childish? Such unfortunate results can easily enough be avoided provided those who are in charge of the formation of young religious are equipped with a solid psychological training. Such a foundation, obviously will not guarantee that all their young charges will turn into staints. But it can stimulate intellectual activity, or other interests. The libido unemployed in sexual functions would then have a chance to burn itself up in some positive direction and would no longer pose such a threat.

In no case must there be any voluntary and deliberate repression or slavery of the libido. Even supposing that we could manage to produce such an effective repression that no treacherous outburst is any longer to be feared, the result would be such a radical impoverishment of human existence that life would lose its taste and interest. Ascesis must not ever be an end in itself. Richness and variety of psychic life are the prerequisite of all true religious living.

VI. *Anarchy in the Collective Libido*

The seat, or rather the source, of the libido is to be found in the unconscious. It is essential to recall now that this unconscious is not only individual, but also (and primarily) collective. The former is "refueled" in the latter. Let us suppose that, as a result of repression and inhibition, the psychic energy remains unused. Not only the individual unconscious, but the collective unconscious as well, will be fatally upset in its normal functioning. The crises and revolutions that darken the history of mankind all have their psychological explanation in this fact: they are, for the collective unconscious, what neurosis and the other mental disorders are for the individual unconscious.[5]

An American disciple of Jung, Esther Harding, in a work which must be considered as the best synthesis of Jung's psychology, applies his ideas to Hitler's madness: "In the depths of the German soul," she writes, "the Nazi cause conjured up the forces which, instead of being repressed or held in check by the archetypes of Christian religion, had regressed towards the pagan forms of the cult of Wotan. The energy that was capable of transforming a beaten and disorganized Germany, in the ten years from 1930 to 1940, into a superorganized, optimistic nation, with a demoniac power must have issued from some very deep source; it could never have been produced by a conscious effort or by the application of rational planning in the fields of administration or national economy."[6] The responsibility of the authors of the Treaty of Versailles and the Franco-English politicians who prevented the energies of the German people from focusing upon a positive and authentically constructive objective, contributed enormously to the crimes of Nazism. It is at least equal to that of those millions of Germans who followed Hitler with enthusiasm

---

5. We do not mean to imply that the psychological explanation of these historical phenomena is sufficient for the whole understanding of history: but it does deserve a most important place.

6. *Réalité de l'âme*, p. 13 (French edition)

and even fanaticism, all the while protesting their innocence. They are sincere when they claim that they cannot begin to understand the intoxication and madness that turned a nation of poets and thinkers (*Volk der Dichter und der Denker*, as the Germans like to describe themselves) into the butchers of Poland and the torture-masters of Buchenwald. It is less a question of having acted themselves than having been acted upon by the repressions of a collective libido.

It would not be difficult to show the same influences at work in other countries and in other human horrors. There is, for instance, the sacrilegious fury of the Spaniards, burning churches and massacring priests and nuns. Closer to our own time, there is the McCarthyism of America, a very characteristic symptom of the unconscious phobias of a people who have no roots. Dr. Rene Laforgue's ambition, to create a "psychopolitics," does not seem to be a particularly far-fetched project, and far from useless. The exact knowledge of the deep and shadowy forces which act on peoples as well as individuals could make a great contribution towards alleviating the apocalyptic threats which menace the future of humanity.

VII. *Loss of Libido*

The libido which, under the influence of a variety of causes, is directed towards one of the "normal" functions of the psyche, can always be directed towards another equally normal function. We can observe, for example, a considerable diminution (if not a complete cessation) in sexual urgency during a period of intense intellectual or artistic activity. The conscious ego is well aware of this fact, and, frequently, it is the ego itself which, in such relatively simple cases as these, acts as a sort of regulator over the libido.

Frequently, though, it happens that the libido withdraws from one function on which it was expended, without the ego being aware of the reasons for this withdrawal and without being able to redistribute the psychic energy.

Annette, nineteen, applied herself to her studies with a surprising energy for one of her years, and was rewarded with brilliant scholastic success. Then, much to her chagrin, for several weeks she had not really been able to concentrate on any subject at all, she no longer understood what the professors were lecturing about, she no longer knew what she was reading. Instead of a model student she turned into a scatterbrain and daydreamer; her teachers were already beginning to reprimand her for her flightiness.

The psychoanalysts refer to this not uncommon phenomenon as loss of libido. The expression is not entirely exact. Just as the physicist refuses to recognize any loss of material energy, but only its transformation, in the world of material physics, even so the psychologist knows that libido cannot ever be really lost. It goes somewhere else; it is transformed.

It is not impossible that, even without the regulatory interventions of the ego, the libido which withdraws from one psychic function will spontaneously reorient towards another equally normal function. It can happen that a young lady like Annette in the case above, unable to apply herself to any formal studies, will suddenly experience a particularly intense craving for love and tender affection. Parents and educators frequently act, in such cases, as if the only reasons behind such a loss of interest in one's studies were flightiness or inattention; particularly when they see the young girl begin to take a more active interest in attracting the young gentlemen she meets. The truth is that she has become more "inattentive and flighty" because she has lost her interest in studies. And her energies have to find another outlet.

Marie, a fervent and virtuous Christian, followed her heart's desire and entered the convent. Six months later she left, because of a fundamental character difference with the novice mistress — as she put it. Before that time — she was 25 — not only had she been absolutely chaste, but her chastity had never appeared as a source of constraint or anxiety, or offered the least difficulty. From the day she left the convent, she began to experience such imperious sexual desires that she was no longer able to resist. She went from one affair to another, without ever being satisfied. To say that her religious fervor had only been a "sublimation" — in the Freudian sense — of her repressed sexuality is an ungrounded assertion which explains nothing and is an unjustifiable simplification. I had an opportunity to observe Marie's case firsthand, and I believe that in keeping with the observable facts of the case, her strong libido had found sufficient object for its energies in her religious life, without the least need for repression. But as a resut of her disillusionment at the convent this psychic energy was left without an object and burst violently into the area of sex. The fact that she was not instead oriented towards some transcendent activity — social, political, or artistic — probably is owing to her natural predispositions, or the chance circumstances of her education.

The loss of libido can be followed by a great anxiety, apparently without cause, by gastric disorders or pulmonary disease, verbal disturbance or a state of nervous excitement. The psychologist's duty is to "unblock" the psychic energy that is thus dangerously immobilized and direct it towards a positive psychic function.

5 sex-psychological instinct

The general study of instincts belongs rather to biology than psychology. Still, even the most "material" of the instincts — for example, nourishment — have their repercussions or their projections in the psyche: it must always be remembered that the distinction between biological and psychological does not ever imply a series of neat little compartments, tightly shut off from each other.

Among all the instincts, sex is unquestionably the one with which the psychologist most frequently needs to deal. Freud elevated sex to the dignity of *life instinct*. Like all instincts, sex also operates according to the "pleasure principle": it tends to resolve the state of tension which is the source of the instinct.

I. *Love and Sex*

The similarities between animal and human sexuality are so obvious that there is no point in describing them in any detail. It is more important for us to examine what it is that distinguishes sex in the human person and thus escapes the only methods of investigation open to the biologist.

Freudians and other materialists, in whose eyes there are only biological elements in any instinct, deny as a consequence all essential difference between animal and human sexuality. It is the animal sexuality that is, in their opinion, really "normal and healthy." What we call love can thus be nothing more than a simple disguise of the instinct, without doing anything to modify the instinct in itself. A certain naturalism, pseudo-psychonalytic in origin, has gone so far as to advise a "return to the primitive simplicity of animal sex life."

In the first years of the Soviet regime, this was a concept much discussed in Russia, and without any particular reference to Freud. A certain psychoanalyst whom I know severely reprimanded one of his clients who was exposed to strong sexual desires for having refused the advances of a man because, though the man did arouse a great deal of physical attraction in her, she did not experience any feeling of love for him. "Did you ever see animals stop to worry about love when their natural urgencies took hold of them?" the doctor asked her.

To conclude from similarities to identity is another example of the "original sin" of the modern mind which has to be scientific everywhere. It thinks it can and must explain the higher by the lower, as if the process of evolution had nothing creative about it.

The original impulse in the sex instinct is unquestionably a biological one, in the same way, for example, as the instinct of nourishment. But can we be just as certain that, even in the case of human nourishment for that matter, there are not some elements that have no real relation at all to the demands and ends of mere biology? At all events, in the case of sex, such a transformation — which is more than a simple "sublimation — seems to be supported by quite clear evidence.

Even among the primitives, and among the most frustrated members of our civilized societies, the attentive observer will note that sex life is not uniquely, nor even predominantly, a simple search for physical pleasure, ordered by "nature" towards the procreation of the human species. It is not because the reproductive power possessed by sexual union seemed mysterious to them that primitive societies enveloped it in rites and religious ceremonial and surrounded it with numerous taboos. It is rather because the very soul of man seems to be bound up in the sexual. More or less confusedly, they realized that different stages of sex life realize the unification of varied and frequently contrary elements in the psyche, at the same time that they help to "mediatize" social relations.

Among more civilized people, the bond between sex and the higher psychic functions is even more manifest. It is inseparable from love. Love, far from appearing as a simple disguising of the biological instinct of sex, belongs to an order that cannot ever be reduced to mere biology. We are not wrong in seeing love as the very essence of spiritual reality, once again touching upon the famous definition that John the Apostle gives of God.

Sexual desire, in psychically superior people, never has physical pleasure for its direct object — treating the partner in the sex act as a more or less active and skillful instrument. Communion of love with an individual is unquestionably the most imperious demand to which we feel ourselves bound in order to escape a sense of insecurity in the face of a world that is hostile on so many sides. For two people who love each other to think that they can realize their communion of heart at least partially, in sexual union, is obviously not foreign to their basic instincts. But the instinct has already ceased to be merely biological.

This is so true that most men and women, when they have heard of the solely biological demands of the sex instinct and sought their sexual pleasure without any spiritual element or expression of love, always experience a sense of degradation and decadence which is more or less vivid depending upon their sensitivities. It is precisely this search of such a degradation, this preoccupation with decadence, that motivates the sexual behavior of so many perverts.

Thus it is wrong to look upon sentiment and the need for love and affection as a mere disguise for a repressed sex instinct. Love is more than a mask thrown hastily over the otherwise shameful activity of the glands and ovaries. There are extraordinarily deep affections in which it is impossible to honestly discover even the least trace of sex. No matter what the disciples of Dr. Freud have to say about it, this is generally true of the bonds that join a mother and her child, or the affection that springs up between two exceptionally good friends. On the other hand, everyone knows that, in many cases, sexual relations can take place without either of the partners experiencing the least love or affection for each other. If we accept the hypothesis of Freud, says Karen Horney, according to which the search for affection comes from the unsatisfied libido (libido here in the Freudian sense of the term), it becomes difficult to understand why we should encounter this need for affection in persons whose sexual life is entirely satisfactory from the merely physical point of view[1]

II. *Harmful Consequences of Underestimating the Libido*

A misunderstanding of the true nature of love by psychologists and psychotherapists frequently leads to extremely serious consequences for individuals.

Jeanne suffered very much because of her husband's impotence (a malady he developed after their marriage); prior to this she had always enjoyed a perfect sexual harmony with him and she still loved him deeply. Following the doctor's advice, she took a lover in an effort to put an end to her suffering: she had no feeling of affection for this man at all, although she did find him physically attractive. She managed to have her physical satisfaction, but the neurotic troubles that had begun to show up since her husband's impotence, instead of disappearing, only grew more aggravated. Jeanne had a need for sexual satisfaction, it is true, but only with a man she loved.

---

1. *La personnalité névrotique de notre temps*, p. 101.

Roger suffered a good deal from the loneliness of his existence in a little village where he had neither family nor friends. His need for affection became so agonizing that he decided to consult a doctor. The doctor, imbued with all the prejudices described above, concluded that what Roger was suffering from was the result of his prolonged chastity and he advised him to pay a visit to a brothel. But after a certain number of such experiences Roger's anxieties only got worse. He decided that he was fundamentally incapable of finding the love he so desperately needed and as a result life appeared meaningless; he committed suicide.

* * * *

Opposed to the Freudian error which we have just denounced is another obstacle, almost equally dangerous, which consists in the conviction that love between man and woman is necessarily, and should necessarily be, of the purely spiritual order and any attempt at sexual union could only cheapen it. This is the mystique behind so-called "pure marriages." It was widely inculcated, in the period between the two world wars, by a certain famous Catholic university. A number of young teachers there believed and taught and actually practiced this type of marriage by taking a vow of perfect chastity within the married state. The disasters which resulted, in every case that ever came to my personal attention, are hardly less serious than those experienced by the other people who claimed to divest sex of every connection it had with human love. As for the original proponent of these "pure marriages," he married at an advanced age and had several children. Man, after all, is neither angel nor animal. As Charles Odier so well describes the situation, the repression of sexual love frequently leads to very serious consequences, such as the definitive abolition of the very faculty of love, and the correlative reinforcement of aggressiveness.[2]

---

2. *Les deux sources de la vie morale*, p. 145

III. *Deviations of Instinct*

There are many men who regularly visit houses of prostitution. Other men never turn down an opportunity to "have" a woman who is willing and available: maids, hotel women, girls they meet on their travels — it makes no particular difference. To all appearances, it is only physical pleasure that figures in this pursuit of women.

Still we observe that many of these men, among these expense-account lovers and connoisseurs of "occasional women," are not at all sexually frustrated. There are married men among them, completely happy and satisfied with their married life. Frequently they are even very much loved, in the most lofty sense of the term, at home.

The experience of psychology can only confirm the results of common observation. It teaches us that these men (and women) are at grips with an inner conflict, whose causes they themselves do not really understand. It is really the solution to these inner conflicts they are looking for in their concentration on the physical pleasures of sex.

John was an important industrial magnate: he holds a high place in society. His wife was a happy, beautiful, and distinguished woman; he lived in perfect harmony of heart and soul with her. Moreover, he was a practicing Catholic. Still, every week, embarrassed and humiliated, he paid a visit to the red-lantern district of the town and took the first girl he found to some cheap hotel. The physical pleasure was certainly never even roughly comparable, in intensity, to what he experienced in his sex relations with his wife, whom he loved. Often enough, he experienced no pleasure at all. After two sessions of psychological treatments, it turned out that John was laboring under a strong guilt complex, going all the way back to his childhood. What he was looking for in these prostitutes was not really pleasure, but self-punishment, humiliation. In going to confession after each of these escapades, to a priest who knew him very well and respected him for his contributions to the progress of the Church, he was looking not so much for pardon from God as his own masochistic humiliation in front of the priest he knew.

Janine told the psychologist that she was possessed by an "impure demon." She was 25, well educated, moderately intelligent, and the daughter of an excellent Catholic working-class family. She was still virgin and, as she told the story, up until two years ago she had hardly realized that she was sexed at all; there had been so few temptations in that area. At that particular moment she fell in love with her brother-in-law. Without even really being aware of it, she made several advances to him. One day, when her sister was away, she threw herself into the young man's arms. He embraced her and held her very close, then he took hold of himself and ever since he had been avoiding any occasion in which he would have to be alone with her. Janine suffered "humiliation and repentance" as she told the story, but whenever she was in the presence of "men of quality" — priests, doctors, respectable family men with very rigid principles — she could not help play the flirt, up to the point where she found herself actually in their arms. Still she always managed to "stop in time" so that their mutual intimacies never went beyond the stage she experienced with her brother-in-law.

Is it merely the repetition of sense pleasure, such as she first experienced it in her brother-in-law's arms, that she was looking for? It is obvious that this is not the case. What is more, even on that first experience, the specifically sexual excitation seems to have been at best only very superficial. It is also significant that Janine remained very reserved in the company of young people and resolutely rejected their advances. She flirted only with "superior men."

In the course of her treatment it came out that she had greatly admired her father. As a child, she always looked for him and wanted to be hugged. He was a nervous man and always preoccupied with his work, and he was seldom if ever very affectionate towards her. He frequently put her off and gave the impression that he preferred her more "reasonable" older sister. Janine was a very sensitive child and suffered a good deal from this coldness.

The attraction she experienced for her brother-in-law was at least partially motivated, it seems by her desire to get even with her sister. As for the "superior men" who were the objects of her attempts at seduction, these where obviously substitutes for her father. In letting them "go hungry" after she had managed to arouse them, she was not thinking primarily of preserving her physical virginity: it was rather that her unconscious, itself, had never really desired sexual relations as such with her father, the person whose place they took in her mind.

In the light of these examples, it is obvious that, even in the many cases of perverse sexuality, the properly psychological factors play a greater role than the biological. The primacy is still with love.

IV. *Animus and Anima*

I have had opportunity to verify for myself, and in very many cases, the perspicacity of Dr. Jung in distinguishing, in every psyche, a masculine element, called *animus*, and a feminine element, called *anima*. In the man it is generally the *animus* which predominates, and in the woman, the *anima*.

Still, if the man's psyche were nothing more than *animus*, we would have a person oriented exclusively towards the outside world, possessed of a very strong intellect, while his faculties of intuition and sensitivity would be completely atrophied; he would be hard and unyielding, incapable of understanding spiritual and esthetic values. Now, most of the male representatives of the human species are not like that, because, in their unconscious, there is an anima at work as well, effecting a compensatory function that is more or less vital. It happens that in some cases it is even stronger and more active than the conscious animus, to the point where we seem to be confronted with a natural freak.

The woman who is only anima would be completely incapable of adapting to the demands of the outside world. She would live in a perpetual dream world, and know things only by intuition, react only under the impulse of her sensitivity. Fortunately, in the feminine unconscious psyche, anima is always linked up with animus. Here too there are frequent anomalies: the "virago" does not give evidence of very much of the anima's femininity in her behavior.

* * * *

The compensation or regulations which animus and anima mutually effect upon each other in one and the same psyche are never complete. There does not seem to be such a creature as a pure "androgyne," either in the present-day world or in the history of the past. The normal thing is to be a distinct person which each of us hopes and aspires to realize in as human a way as possible.

In the desire to communicate with the one unique person, who alone seems able to complete our own self, there is something infinitely more far-reaching than the mere "animal" sex instinct. A young man who claims that sexual desire plays no role in the attraction towards the woman he loves is no doubt quite sincere. Even more frequently we see a young maiden looking forward ardently to her marriage, without experiencing the least carnal attraction or ever even dreaming of sexual union. Moral pre-conceptions and family training are obviously responsible for much of the "asexual" conception of human love. But it is still true that there is a need for specificially psychological comple-mentarity.

However, the sex instinct does play a preponderant role in every relation between animus and anima. Sex, in the broad sense of the word, here, as Freud himself admits of it. It implies the genital element, but is not reducible to it.

Our desire to emphasize the spiritual nature of sex relations must not, however, lead us into the toils of pseudo-angelism. In normal cases, even with people who are most spiritually developed, the communion of love between man and woman calls for sexual union in the strict sense of the term. Still, sexual pleasure itself is, in the man and particularly in the man who is spiritually more developed, qualificatively much different than that of the animal. The role of the spirit is much larger here, beginning especially with the choice of a partner.

Even on the lower stages of psychic development, this choice is not simply based on the more or less greater aptitude of the partner selected to procure physical pleasure. It is true that the psychic factors that enter into play here are egocentric, since they depend upon the demands and needs of the ego. The more developed the self is in the psyche, the more easily the choice of a sex partner will turn into a function of values that transcend the circle of the ego. The specific pleasure of sense is not ever done away with or even greatly reduced. Quite the contrary; it becomes a symbol and vehicle of higher communion, and it only gains in intensity. It is in this sense that we have a right to speak of a relation between sex and the higher activities of the psyche. They are not the product of repressed sex, but rather it is in the true development of sex that they have their real foundation. And, at the same time, they make sex more intense.

V. Perverse Sexuality

All practicing psychiatrists have observed, in almost all their mentally deviated patients, some anomalies of the sexual order. In some, the sex instinct has deviated from its proper object, in others from its proper purpose. Freud, in his work, *Three Essays on the Theory of Sexuality*, gives a detailed description of the different sexual preversions. His interpretation needs only partial correction.

In the catalogue of sexual deviation, *inversion* is the most frequent. Instead of going out towards the opposite, or rather complementary, sex, the sex appetite goes out towards representatives of the same sex (*homosexuality*). In the case of the complete invert, sexual attraction is felt only for individuals of his own sex. Frequently, such people are physically incapable of any heterosexual relations. But there are also, and more frequently than we would imagine, cases of hermaphrodism on the psychosexual level. Here the object of the sex attraction can belong, indifferently, to either sex. Finally, there are *occasional inverts*, who have recourse to homosexuality whenever heterosexual relations are temporarily impossible. This is obviously the case in prisons, in certain institutions, and, more generally, in any society which makes it difficult for men and women to meet together (for example, in the Islamic cultures).

Under the influence of the morality of the social group to which they belong, sex inverts sometimes consider their deviations as perfectly normal. This is true in the case of some artistic and intellectual circles, particularly since Andre Gide has spoken up in defense of "Corydons." Most of the time, however, inverts recognize their perversion as a sickness: they are ashamed of their anomaly and take pains to hide it.

On the other hand, there are some objective perverts who are attracted only by children, others only by animals, etc.

In the catalogue of perversions in which the *purpose* of sex is the object of perversion, Freud lists all the forms of sexual excitation which are found otherwise than through the normal play of the genital organs properly so-called. To this group belong *sadism* and *masochism*, perversions in which the sexual pleasure is bound up with the suffering that a person inflicts upon himself or others. But we cannot follow Dr. Freud when he extends his catalogue of perversion to include *kisses* and *caresses*, even when they do not explicitly tend towards sexual fulfillment.

* * * *

Our agreement with the founder of psychoanalysis is broken once again when he comes to offering a theoretical explanation of the deviations of a sexual nature. Freud refuses to admit that perversions are the consequence of disease or degeneration in the individual. He does indeed recognize the fact that certain perversions are so far from normal that we can have no choice but to call them pathological. Particularly those which incite the sex instinct by deliberately surmounting certain obstacles (such as shame, disgust, horror, pain) to accomplish abnormal and eccentric acts (such as licking or kissing human excrement, sexual relations with corpses, etc.).[3]

But even these eccentricities do not appear fundamentally different from the normal manifestations of sex in the eyes of Dr. Freud. The erotic pleasure that comes from caresses and kisses is certainly not procured by the natural use of the genital organs; and still no one considers them as a crime or a disease. Neither inversion nor any other deviation in the object or purpose of sexual relations seems to be "contrary to nature" in Freud's thinking, nor to deserve any moral condemnation.

Freud here remains faithful to his concept of the libido. The sex instinct exists independently of every object and every goal and is only a natural impulse towards pleasure. We might well believe that the sex tendency exists first of all independently of its object and that its full development is not determined by the excitation arising from the object.[4] Normal sexuality would thus be only that sexual practice which takes place commonly, and especially that which takes place in the interests of the social function of procreation. The shame and disgust which so frequently prevent "deviations" in sex, would be only a sort of railing around sex, invented by society in order to maintain the sex instinct within the limits of what is called normal.[5]

It does not take much speculation to recognize the fact that

_____

3. *Op. cit.*, p. 54
4. *Ibid.*, p. 35
5. *Ibid.*, p. 56

the sex instinct, like every other instinct, has a normal object and purpose. It is not by accident or under the constraint of the same "superego" that it is directed so strongly towards a person of the opposite sex. The erogenous zone extends well beyond the genital organs, of course; there is nothing unnatural in the pleasure that comes from caresses and kisses. But it would be a most serious error not to recognize the essential difference between such pleasure and the pleasures we normally speak of as perversions.

Perversions are not always "vices" which deserve moral censure, but they always are a clear sign that some order has been broken or set aside, and that the soul is sick. Quite obviously, the shame and disgust and horror they occasion are in a large part social in origin. But we are no longer in a position to look upon society as something artificial, something imposed on the human condition from without: human nature is as basically social as it is individual. It is precisely because the sex instinct in man is not only biological in nature that there is a possibility of sexual deviation; the purely biological instincts always act with mechanical precision. As a result, there is nothing more normal than for the psyche itself to invent a framework of feelings that are destined to maintain this biological instinct within the limits of normality.

VI. *Infantile Sexuality*

Psychoanalysts observe that, in most cases, sexual deviations date back to the childhood of the patient. Freud deduces from this that the child is a "polymorphous pervert." Perverse sexuality, he writes, is nothing more than infantile sexuality grown up and in a state of fixation on its particular tendencies. He also says that if the child has a sex life, that sex life can only be a perversion.[6]

---

6. *Introduction* . . . , p. 334

Infantile sexuality has no proper object or purpose as yet, and the child is thus in a position to become, with almost equal degrees of probability, homosexual or heterosexual, voyeur, sadist, masochist, etc. And since a person can only become in fact what he already is in principle, the baby is thus a polymorphous pervert. It is only under the influence of different causes, working at a later stage of his development, that his sex life will orient towards one particular object rather than others. Adolescent masturbation and various more serious perversions in the adult are only prolongations of one or another tendency of infantile perversity. In such conditions, the term "pervert" obviously loses its social stigma and does not function as a value judgment; it is no more than a concession to the common way of speaking. Freud even seems to regret the fact that, especially under the influence of family education, the sex instinct, in most adults, has to lose this polymorphism. Thus he considers the social stigma attaching to incest as the worst crime morality has ever committed against "love."

Obviously we have no awareness of our infantile perversion, but, as Freud puts it, we labor under an "almost total amnesia" with respect to everything that concerns our early childhood. He is even inclined to think that this amnesia is caused by the unconscious will of the social superego compelling us to forget our infantile sexuality in order not to contradict what "morality" admits as the only proper sexual orientation.

* * * *

There is little room for surprise in the fact that such speculations on sex in general and infantile sex in particular should have so violently shocked public opinion. Public reaction was all the more violent due to the fact that, under the influence of the Jansenist school and the "Cathari," the Christian world had come to look down on sex, considering it, in the most lenient of many hypotheses, as a necessary evil. Moreover, unmindful of the dogma of original sin, this same mentality regularly became quite sentimental over the so-called purity and innocence of the new born child.

And yet, Augustine, one of the finest psychologists of all times, had denounced this error which consists in treating the child like a "dear little angel." He maintained that all human instincts, and thus also the sex instinct, already existed in the child, but in a latent state.

In the light of unquestionable discoveries of modern psychology, there can be no thought of denying, or even seriously doubting, the reality of infantile sexuality. In very many babies, the excitation of the sex organ produces a pleasure that is noticeably more intense than the excitation of other parts of the body. Mothers and nurses are well aware of this fact; they frequently fondle the baby in just such a way to keep him from crying. But this still does not keep them from regarding every allusion to infantile sexuality as a sacrilege. Very many children of three or four (many more than would readily be believed) masturbate and sometimes even manage to experience orgasm.

But we do not follow the Freudian theory when he attributes all the child's hedonistic experiences to this infantile sexuality. Let us recall, for example, the famous stages of sexual development in Freudian psychology.

In the first, or oral, stage, the child experiences pleasurable sensations only through his mouth. Freud has not failed to recognize the biological purpose behind the instinct of nourishment. But since the child obviously takes pleasure in the very act of sucking — whether the object is his mother's breast, his own finger, or any of his baby toys — this is the clear indication of buccal eroticism. In this stage, the child is supposed to be strictly auto-erotic, the distinction between his own body and outside objects not yet having been clearly made.

In the *anal* stage, which succeeds the buccal, the pleasure-producing zone is situated in the region of the *anus*. Freud's proof: the child enjoys sitting on his potty chair, and has an interest in his own fecal matter. It is not until a third stage, towards the age of four or five, that the libido normally fixes on the genital organs and arrives at what is properly speaking a *sexual* stage. This is the age of curiosity about how babies are born, the differences between boys and girls, *etc.* Later, between the ages of 7 and 12 or 13, this instinct once again becomes latent, until it reappears at the age of puberty.

There is no denying the general overall correctness of these observations. But where is the evidence for using the term sexual — even in the broad sense of the term — to define the pleasure that the child gets from sucking his finger or sitting on his potty chair?

Rather than sexuality, the act of sucking seems to belong to the instinct of self-nourishment. Pavlov's theory of conditioned reflexes confirms this hypothesis. The child's nourishment, either at his mother's breast or from the baby bottle, takes on the form of sucking, and in the child's psyche the pleasure which results from satisfying his needs is intimately bound up with the sensation of sucking. There is nothing surprising about the fact that sucking should give him pleasure, even when it is not related to the process of nourishment.

To see the pleasure the child experiences through his anus as a form of sexual reaction, we would have to assume a position in which there could not be the smallest doubt regarding the full accuracy of Freud's theory about exclusive sources of pleasure. It seems much more probable that the extension of the child's pleasurable sensations gradually spreads from the mouth to other parts of the body. Thus, the appearance of anal hedonism does not put a stop to his buccal hedonism. If, as a matter of fact, towards the age of six months, the anal zone receives more attention than the other parts of his body, this is probably due to the toilet training that has already begun.

Once again, it is not our purpose here to question the existence of infantile sexuality. But, in most cases, it is not yet informed by libido and thus remains something diffuse, in a virtual state, something like the condition of his freedom, his intelligence, and all his other psychic functions. The transition to actuality takes place only gradually.

In some children, the sex instinct does, however, come to life at a very early age. Some babies experience erection before they are weaned, and we have already mentioned that there are some children of three or four who experience orgasm in masturbation. But such precocity, far from being a vindication of Freudian theory, seems definitely pathological, particularly since it is almost always bound up with symptoms of psychic anomaly. Under the spell of his excessive systematization, Freud tried to explain the normal by the abnormal, health by disease. Such a procedure looks most antiscientific.

In the case of the neurotic, no doubt, the libido almost always takes on a strongly sexual character, morbidly sexual. But we do not think that this is simply because the instinct of sex has undergone a process of "disguise," unless this were the case in every other human. It is more probable that the libido of the neurotic, by reason of his sickness, is prevented from the normal accomplishment of his other psychic functions and that he thus regresses to the sexual level. Jung says that it frequently if not always happens that this detour into sexuality serves to disguise the real problem. The patient tries to persuade himself and others that he is the victim of some sexual problem that has been poorly resolved for a long time, a problem whose causes lie in the distant past.[7]

VII. *Psychic Health and Chastity*

Psychology which is analytical in character has discovered the primary importance of sexuality in psychic life. As a result, not only laymen, but even specialists profess as a definitively established truth the principle that the use of the sexual function

---

7. *Metamorphoses* . . . , pp. 271-272

is indispensable for psychic equilibrium. This leads to an out-of-hand condemnation of chastity. Is there any basis for such dogmatism?

Andre, 45, married, as a virgin, at the age of thirty. A few weeks after his wedding night he became impotent. After long years of conflict with his wife, more and more tormented by the anxiety which made his life unbearable, he went to see a very orthodox psychoanalyst. Normally enough, this doctor concluded that the neurosis under which Andre was suffering was sexual in its origin. He even stated that Andre's impotence was due to the prolonged chastity he maintained throughout his youth.

Since this treatment produced no results, Andre came to me for advice. He admitted the explanation the doctor had furnished, but he felt a strong resentment towards the religious who had taught him in school; he held them responsible for his perfect chastity, and its unfortunate results. Little by little, I managed to discover that his neurosis was the result of causes other than his impotence. In fact, it was the neurosis that had actually produced the impotence, which had long been latent. Is there any point in mentioning the fact that neither the impotence nor the neurosis had any relationship of cause and effect with the chastity Andre had observed as a young man?

Another time it was a fervent Catholic mother who came to consult me about her son Louis, fifteen. He had been manifesting various symptoms of "nervous" disorders, and she had taken him to see a doctor. To the mother's great scandal, the doctor had advised the boy to have no qualms about masturbating whenever he felt the desire. There was nothing wrong in it, he said, and the boy was sick precisely because he had been forced into too many inhibitions in the area.

All Freudian psychologists obviously do not preach such a simplified approach to reality. This is not to deny the fact, however, that every constraint of the sex instinct seems dangerous to them, because it is contrary to biological laws — it being obviously understood that the energy of the libido is rigorously and exclusively biological.

* * * *

Every psychologist who agrees not to limit his observations to only sick psyches can observe the fact that many people practice complete chastity without the least disadvantage to their physical and psychic equilibrium. This is the case not only in the mystics, in whom we might speak of "sublimation," but even in very many quite "ordinary" men and women. In Christian environments, a large proportion of young ladies remain virgin until marriage, and the same is true, especially during the last quarter of the century, of their young men. There are adults, celibate or widowed, who live a life of voluntary chastity. Others are forced into it by circumstances (prison, for example). Obviously, not everyone can bear the constraint of prolonged chastity with equal ease. It appears to be particularly difficult and unbalancing for those who find themselves so obliged without their own assent. Even among those who are chaste by their own will, there are many who have a great price to pay for this practice and frequently there are nervous and psychic problems. In the case of young people, masturbation is more or less regular and widespread.

Still, there are young men and young ladies, virgins, who never masturbate. Others have masturbated, particularly between the years of fourteen and seventeen, and then completely stopped. Like almost everyone else, they might think that chastity is more or less difficult to bear, but in the far greater majority of cases it does not give rise to any serious psychic problems. "The reason for this," to quote Jung once again, "lies in the fact that every instinct and every function can be subordinated to some other function. Thus the self-instinct or the instinct to power can be put to the service of sex or, in reverse, it can submit sex to itself; the intellectual function can choke out all the others, or the affective function can absorb the intellectual and sensory functions, all depending upon the prevailing attitude in the subject."[8] In psychology, more than in the application of any other science whatsoever, it is vital to take individual differences into account. It is important here to recall our definition of the libido. By nature, it is undifferentiated affective energy. Chastity then might well provoke serious psychic troubles if the libido that is normally consumed in sex activity remains unemployed. On the other hand, it is perfectly safe in the majority of those who have learned to find another outlet for their libido. Intellecual or artistic work, sports, in a word, anything that is capable of turning into a center of interest can accomplish this proper displacement of the libido. It is a serious mistake, according to Jung, to suppose that a great number of married women are neurotic only because they are sexually unsatisfied, or because they have not found the man they are looking for, or because they have a fixation on some infantile sexuality.[9] To be sure, complete chasity or a sex life that does not give complete satisfaction, can well be causes of psychic trouble, but this is not always the case, and most likely it is not true in even the majority of cases.

It is true, however, that many of those who are proud of their chastity or who like to extol its merits seem to ignore the fact that true chastity as Mounier puts it, is a strong healthy chastity; it has nothing in common with the Arian dream that always has something unhealthy lurking in the background.[10]

Contrary to what Jansenists and other encratists might be inclined to think, sex is not the root and source of all evil, it is not the domain of the devil. And, on the other hand, chastity in itself, in its material elements, is not a sign of virtue either. It has no value, either on the psychological or the moral plane, unless it is subordinated to a higher human purpose. When it is only constraint, imposed from without by a static morality or from within by fear of the real or imagined dangers of sexual activity, for

---

8. *Metamorphoses* . . . , p. 435
9. *La guérison* . . . , p. 176
10. Emmanuel Mounier: *Traité* . . . , p. 154

instance, it will almost always have a bad effect on psychic equilibrium. If certain methods of sex education are debatable, the urgency of sex education, in principle, can surely not be called into question.

* * * *

Freud peremptorily condemns all the constraints that society has imposed on instincts in general and the sex instinct in particular. Those of his disciples who are more or less faithful to his inspiration have sometimes developed this teaching into conclusions which shock elementary morality and elementary common sense. With the dogmatic stubbornness that is so intolerable in the psychologist, they pretend to ignore the fact that the human psyche is not exclusively made up of instincts. Reason, moral and esthetic sense, the demands of social life, *etc.* — all make up a part of human living that is at least just as fundamental. The absolute freedom which is claimed for the sex instinct cannot be reconciled with the good of the psychic totality.

It does not, however, follow that instincts are bad "by nature," that sex in particular must be suppressed, that a man must live merely according to the laws of reason. Supposing, even, that such an undertaking were to succeed, the result would be comical; there would be no strength or dynamism to life. Instincts must not be suppressed, but educated. The ego must win as full a mastery over them as possible, without forgetting that this mastery will never become completely perfect in the present condition of humanity. Education, in particular, must never cast any discredit upon sex, no more than it has a right to make it something too wonderful. Prudery is not modesty, but neither does libertinism have anything in common with liberty.

6 families of souls

Modern day psychology, more than its predecessors, is conscious of the individuality of each soul. The good practicing psychiatrist, whenever he meets a new person, must in some manner forget what he has observed in any of his other patients: he must get rid of all his prefabricated ideas, all his outlines and presuppositions. He must act as if the present case is absolutely unique in its own right. The experience acquired from his contact with other souls will obviously be very useful, but only to the degree that it helps him to distinguish specifically original traits of the psyche upon which he is currently engaged. To a superficial eye, all the trees in a forest are the same, but the trained forester knows them as individuals. Whereas a stranger might see only a herd of cows or a herd of sheep, the shepherd, as the Gospel says, knows each of the animals by name. The same is even more true in the case of human beings. If so many psychoanalysts make mistakes and, in the last analysis, do as much harm as good, the reason might very well be their excessive allegiance to a given system, to a rigid procedure they learned in their books or from their teachers.

I. *The Psychic Universal*

The originality of each psyche is a well attested and well recognized fact, but experience teaches us that certain souls have common traits, that there are really families of souls.

A fundamental psychic kinship exists between all humans, no matter what their civilization, race, or religion. Its roots lie deep within the collective unconscious, in that common fund from which emerge all individual psyches. As we have said above, without this fundamental kinship we would not be able to understand anything written or said by, for example, a Chinese, even supposing we were able to learn the grammar and vocabulary of his language. Even less would we be able to understand the cultural heritage of the past. And psychology, insofar as it is a science, is possible only because there actually is a universal psychic element.

Among men who belong to the same civilization, to the same people, this psychic kinship is even more concrete. With many reservations, of course, but still with a certain underlying accuracy, we can speak of the "French soul," the "Russian spirit," etc. We can even recognize certain resemblances among peasants, workers, intellectuals, even when they belong to different nationalities. Finally, certain psychic characteristics are proper to men, others to women — we can speak of masculine and feminine psyche.

All these kinships and resemblances justify the scientific attempt to create a psychology of nations, peoples, classes, sexes, etc., in addition to individual psychology.

It is particularly interesting from the point of view of psychological practice, to note that there are traits common to a given category of individuals independently of their race, their culture, their social class, and their sex. Persons who belong to the same "family of souls" have the same reactions, the same attitudes in the face of existence and its problems. As soon as the psychologist has managed to classify the individual within such a family of souls, he has some extremely precious advance information for understanding the individual's psychic mechanisms. But we must insist once again on the fact that, notwithstanding their belonging to a given family, all souls are still unique in themselves.

II. *The Four Temperaments*

The writers of Greco-Roman antiquity had already divided individuals according to their "temperament." Up until the eighteenth century, it was universally admitted that the human race was divided into four temperaments. That this division was not without some objective foundation is proved by the fact that, even today, such theorists as Hartenburg and Carton are strongly in support of it.

Whether it is Hippocrates or Galen, Paracelsus or the Kabbala, or even certain doctors of our own day, everyone conceives of temperament as being biological in origin. They systematically ignore the spiritual unity of the psyche and attribute what is proper to the soul to some vital force instead. This does not keep many of their observations from being very valuable. What well informed psychologist of today could after all dare to cast doubt on, or even seriously minimize, the biological substructure of all psychic activity?

In speaking of temperaments, the ancients had recourse to a medical terminology. They distinguished *choleric, phlegmatic, sanguine* and *melancholic.*

Carton and his disciples prefer to call the *choleric* temperament the "motor temperament." The choleric individual is inclined towards hyperactivity, either physical or intellectual, frequently getting all stirred up in his work. Thin, sallow in complexion, they have a great resistance to physical effort. They are often dominating, irascible, vindictive. On the physiological plane, their liver has an overabundance of bile, although it still functions properly. They sleep little and poorly; they are predisposed to liver ailments and rheumatism. St. Vincent de Paul, as well as Richelieu and Napoleon are classed among the cholerics.

The *phlegmatics* are the diametrical opposite of the choleric. They are slow in work and reactions, in decisions, in word and thought. They eat a lot. Their complexion is pink, their flesh is soft and easily runs to fat. They evidence a tendency towards premature baldness; they are also predisposed to angina, bronchitis and enteritis. Their imagination lacks warmth, whereas their intelligence, though it lacks vivacity, might often be deep; they are excellent at scientific research. They are outstanding for fidelity, patience, and self control, but also nonchalance and laziness.

The *sanguine*, ruddy in complexion and coloring, are gay and optimistic. They love movement (more than activity); they have a lively sensitivity and imagination, but not always very profound. They are sociable and easy to like; they find it hard to bear loneliness, and this makes it difficult for them to be egotists. Whereas the phlegmatic temperament is generally found in the Northern countries, the sanguine is generally found in the South. They are predisposed to congestive disorders and fevers. They live well, they love life, have good imagination, adapt quickly, are successful in politics, journalism, *etc.*

The opposite of the sanguine is the *melancholic*. He eats little and does not care for strong or spicy food. Very emotional and impressionable, the melancholic is strong on activity, but accomplishes little. There are many artists among this number, and also many subtle thinkers. Such people are predisposed to mental disorders. They are especially frequent among the Oriental peoples.

"Pure temperaments" are obviously rare. It is rather a question of which temperament is predominant in a given individual.

III. *Character Families*

Classification according to characters partially overlaps the classification on the basis of temperament. Here, however, the accent is much more explicitly on psychology.

The word *character*, according to Mounier, is bound up with a happy sense of ambiguity. It can mean at once the complex of conditions which are given and more or less imposed upon us, and the more or less serious effort with which we learn to master this endowment.[1]

We speak of a "weak" or "strong" character, but we also say that a certain individual "has character." Rene Le Senne is supported by almost every characteriologist when he states that part of the psyche which is the result of the intersection of hereditary endowments in each individual can be called character. It is thus congenital, solid, permanent; it constitutes a sort of "skeleton of psychological life."[2]

We must thank the work of the Dutch, German, and English psychologists for the fact that characteriology is not based on vague literary considerations, but solid scientific foundation. They have gathered an enormous fund of statistical material which is indispensable for the classification and description of each different character type to have a really objective foundation. There are the now classic works of Heymans and Wiersma, Klages and Kretschmer. The French psychologists were opposed to this characteriology for a long time.

Only several years after the current had already begun did Emmanuel Mounier, Rene Le Senne, Gaston Berger, and several others, begin to devote important works to the subject, not only presenting the results of the work that had been carried on abroad, but offering an original contribution as well. But it is still very significant, or if you prefer, very "characteristic," that in France it is primarily the philosophers who are interested in the subject, whereas elsewhere the leading figures in the field have been recruited from all the ranks of the learned: doctors, biologists, experimental psychologists.

* * * *

---

1. *Traité* . . . , p. 52
2. R. Le Senne: *Traité de caracteréologie*, p. 10

The three properties that make up character are *emotivity*, *activity* and *"reverberation."* Those who have rapid reverberation are called *"primary;"* while those who have slow reverberation are "secondary." These three properties can blend together to make up eight distinct types: emotive-inactive-primary (melancholic); emotive-inactive-secondary (sentimental): emotive-active-primary (choleric); emotive-active-secondary (passionate); nonemotive-active-primary (sanguine); nonemotive-active-secondary (phlegmatic); nonemotive-inactive-primary (amorphous); nonemotive-inactive-secondary (apathic).

Within the limits of this chapter, we can only briefly indicate the dominant traits of each type of character. The reader who wishes a further and more detailed treatment is referred to any of the authors mentioned above. What we have said above about temperament is equally applicable here: pure types hardly ever exist as such. In the examples that follow, there is only a predominance of a given type.

The *melancholic* character lives in the passing moment; incapable of any real action, he spends himself in activity, following the impulse or impressions of the moment. His temper is uneven and he is not stable in his affections and enthusiasms, in his suffering and joys. His vanity is a veil for both his natural weaknesses and his self-satisfaction; the melancholic character is narcissistic. Women are more inclined this way than men, and many artists are of melancholic character. Baudelaire, Chateaubriand, and Byron are examples.

The *sentimental*, like the melancholic, is sensitive to what happens about him and undergoes many painful shocks. But, whereas the melancholic, because he is primary, reacts to the outside excitation impulsively, the sentimental, being "secondary," inhibits the impulse to react at all. He amplifies the effects of emotions and feels them very deeply. Not at all impulsive, he is always extremely vulnerable; he possesses a great capacity for suffering which more or less blunts his passivity. Meditative and introverted, scrupulous, timid, indecisive, individualist, and objectivist, he is sometimes also a misanthrope; he is inclined to keep a diary and loves to be alone. He is easily bored; he is ambitious, but not enough to realize his dreams. Rousseau, Robespierre, Kierkegaard are men of this type.

The *choleric*, like the melancholic, is emotive and primary, and thus almost as impulsive and excitable too. But since he is active, he seizes upon the impulses and excitations he experiences as a springboard for action. He has a way with words and easily adapts to all circumstances; he has great vivacity in both his positive and his negative opinions. He enjoys life, likes to eat and drink. He is very sociable, and espouses democratic and progressive ideas. He has a lively taste for initiative and novelty, and finds it hard to hold to one place or one occupation, or even one affection: he tends to be a "permanent revolutionary." He is optimistic and confident of the future, little inclined to contemplation, to painstaking and patient research. He seldom sins by default, almost always by excess. Peguy, Dante, Balzac are some famous representatives of this typically "Southland" character.

The *passionate* man belongs to an objectively richer character type. Emotive-active, he has all the qualities of the preceding type, but thanks to his element of secondarity, he manages to avoid most of the shortcomings. He is less impulsive, more likely to accomplish what he sets out to do, more reflective, more profound. He is also harder, it is true, more authoritarian, more calculating, but these very defects only add to his strength. He has no fear of obstacles, he has great working strength and generally follows through on his ideas. But he is very much attached to the past, he is conservative, little given to novelty, or change in the social order. On the religious plane the passionate man is more an ascetic than a mystic, more inclined towards morality than spontaneity. Some passionate type temperaments have been tormented men (Beethoven, Tolstoy, Augustine, Pascal), meditative (Michelangelo, Moliere), imperious (Foch, Richielieu, Napoleon, Lenin), intransigeant (de Maistre), methodical (Thomas Aquinas, Poincare, Descartes)....

The *sanguine* is recognized particularly by his eminently practical sense. Non-emotive, his activity and his social relations are almost always utilitarian in scope. As a result, his ambitions — for he is ambitious — are shortlived and he rarely accomplishes anything great. He is a good observer, with much intellectual presence, he wants success more for its money than for its glory. In politics, he is an opportunist, clinging to the radical party. His intelligence is more facile than animated, and generally shows little originality or depth. He is not inclined towards religion, because his positive mind cannot grasp the practical utility of religion. Women interest him little; his marriage is one "of reason." He is secretive and calculating and inclined towards diplomacy, where he generally achieves good results. Talleyrand, Voltaire, Mazarin, Metternich, Machiavelli, Anatole France, are all men of sanguine character.

The *phlegmatic* is characterized by his coldness, his lack of enthusiasm, his perseverance, his pondering attitude, his sobriety, his simplicity, and his great objectivity. The intellectual of this type will be a mathematician. He is a man of order, a skeptic, formal in his virtue; he is religious without fervor, because it is respectable to be so. He has some sense of humor and loves animals more than men. Englishmen are inclined this way, in general. Other examples include: Dalembert, Kant, Montaigne, Renan, Taine, Washington — these men were all phlegmatic in one degree or another and in different ways.

The *amorphous* and *apathic* are the two least enterprising character types. Objectively, they are the most impoverished. They are not energetic, they speak little, and they are not interested in anything very important. By reason of their primarity, men of amorphous character have a little more impulsiveness than the apathic character which is much more easily discouraged. It is not easy to find any really superior men of either type. Louis XV was amorphous, and Louis XVI was apathic.

IV. Typology

Depth psychology can only enrich the knowledge of soul families. Psychotherapy, as well as psychopedagogy, both have much to gain from the laws that are discovered in this area. Still the psychologist must beware of any generalization. He realizes that these theoretically pure types are very rarely encountered in practice — even less so than in the case of characteriology — and likely as not will never be encountered in their full purity. What is more, types interest him primarily insofar as they afford him a better understanding of the individual.

In the whole complex of Jung's thinking and method, typology occupies a primary position. For Jung and the psychologist who follow his line of thought, there is obviously no intention of wiping the slate clean of classifications according to temperament or character. Quite the contrary: there are many discoveries whose truth and usefulness necessarily force themselves upon the psychologist. But the psychologist's point of view will still be a different one. The characteriologist considers each character as fundamentally unchangeable, its strong points, shortcomings, and weak points all innate. Characteriology claims only to teach a person how to make the most of his natural endowments. The ambitions of the psychologist go further. Working on the conscious through the unconscious, he hopes to introduce some important modifications, even some significant and vital ones, into the depth of the psyche.

* * * *

According to the way in which people react in the face of external and internal events, Jung divides them into *extroverts* and *introverts*. These terms are not his own invention and he does not claim to have created typology in its entirety. In his work on psychological types, he demonstrates that, generally without being aware of the fact, the gnostics, some of the Church Fathers, and certain medieval theologians and poets and even some modern philosophers (William James, for example) are much taken up with this distinction between introvert and extrovert. Jung's typology, however, goes much farther than all the others; it is the first one that is based on really scientific observations.

* * * *

Psychologists have generally believed that the fact that some people are extroverts and others are introverts is a result of the conditions of their existence and the influences they undergo. This is no longer a supportable theory, since we have evidence of the fact that many children show perfectly "typical" reactions from the first years of their life. On the basis of all observable evidence, the identification with one or another type is something rooted deep in the most inaccessible strata of the psyche. The psychoanalyst discovers that typical reactions are not only the work of the conscious mind, but also, and primarily, of the unconscious.

Jung's typology is developed on the following observation of daily life: when we examine a man's way of life, he says, we notice that the destiny of one man is determined rather by the the object of his interests whereas that of another is determined more by his own inner attitudes, by the subject.[3] The word "determined" must be understood not in the metaphysical sense, but as a psychologist would use it.

Everyone has a natural tendency to understand things according to the structures proper to his type — and this is enough to demonstrate the practical importance of typology.

Jung defines introversion as an attitude which, in any given circumstance, seeks to give the ego and the subjective psychological processes predominance over the object and the objective processes, or at very least to uphold the subject in the face of the object.[4] Such an attitude puts more weight on the subject than on the object. The attitude of extroversion, on the contrary, as Jung describes it, subordinates the subject to the object, which then

---

3. *Types* . . . , p. 5
4. *Ibid.*, p. 7

acquires a greater value.[5] We must insist, however, from the very beginning, and in Jung's own example, that neither all introverts nor all extroverts are like peas in a pod. Individual differences are at least as important as typological resemblances.

* * * *

When we observe that a certain person habitually reacts, in his most frequent and most important decisions and actions, not on the basis of his own subjective ideas and theories, but lets himself be guided by outside events, we know that we are dealing with an extrovert. He thinks and feels and acts and lives in immediate accord with objective conditions and their demands. The extrovert is obviously not lacking, generally speaking, in opinions and ideas of his very own. But still his activity is based more on outside conditions than it is on his own decisions. There can easily be a conflict between his inner tendencies and the imperatives that come from outside, but generally he will follow the impulses from without.

Normally, the extrovert is thus more inclined to observe and study the world than to analyze his own feelings and ideas: he is not introspective. He gives evidence of a lively interest for other people and for other things. In recognizing the living conditions and human relations of the extrovert we are in a position to understand the reasons for his reactions with near certainty.

We must not suppose, however, that the extrovert is superficial, nor that he has forsaken his own ego. In adapting himself so easily to the outside world and its norms of conduct, he is not necessarily identifying with its personage. He is able to judge and even to condemn. Adapted to the outside world, he does not neglect his own needs and interests, but these are almost always satisfied by the concrete conditions of his situation. This is true in his choice of work, in his marriage, *etc.* Still it can happen that he devotes himself to the pursuit of social success to the point that

---

5. *Ibid.* . . . , p. 8

he neglects to pay the necessary attention to his own inner life and health. The extrovert might also happen to be less adapted to the world than he is "inserted" into it.

The attitude of the unconscious generally corrects and compensates for any excesses in the conscious behavior of the extrovert. The excessive attention that his conscious mind brings to bear upon the outside world threatens to deprive his activity, ideas, desires and demands of his ego, of all their vital psychic energy. Now, the extrovert's unconscious is almost always strongly oriented towards egocentrism. It is here that the ego must look for the libido that is necessary to those of its activities which are not social in nature. The unconscious is by definition "primitive"; as a result the spontaneous desires and ideas of the extrovert are often violent and anarchical, in opposition to his social behavior. We see men who are known for their sociability and altruism suddenly begin to give evidence of an almost brutal or even childish egotism. It is generally their friends and family who suffer.

* * * *

Together with Jung, we have distinguished four fundamental psychological functions in man: thought, feeling, sensation, and intuition. They all take on characteristics of their own, according as the subject is extrovert or introvert.

The thought of the *extrovert* will be directed by preference, towards objective realities, as furnished by sense perception. It will have little to do with the subject and unconscious sources. It is not necessarily pragmatistic; the extroverted intellectual can be profoundly idealistic. But the ideal that inspires him is almost always social. He has a passion for the ideas that are current in his age, and he is primarily a revolutionary. It is rare, for example, for an extroverted philosopher, in the middle of the twentieth century, to be a Thomist; he will be either a Marxist or an existentialist.

The solution to the problem of self holds no interest for him; what counts for him is the understanding of his times and his world. He is neither metaphysician nor logician, but rather psychologist, moralist, or sociologist. If he is a man of science, he will be oriented towards the practical applications of his specialty rather than pure research. The main shortcoming of extroverted thought is the fact that it seldom goes far enough: it is satisfied with the immediate. The intellectual of this type is also inclined to underestimate the importance of affective life, seeing it as an obstacle to the positive and creative activity of his thought.

His feeling, just as his thought, is in harmony with the social values: it conforms with objective reality. What counts for him is, primarily, for society to recognize the beauty or goodness of things; but he is incapable of admiring them himself. He must not, on this account, be taken for an opportunist or a hypocrite. Quite simply, the extrovert is so involved in the community that his feelings are spontaneously those of his environment. Whereas the intellectual extrovert is more typical of the male, the sentimental extrovert is more likely to be a woman.

Such a woman will love, and love very sincerely, "the proper way," that is, not primarily the man who is in a position to insure her fullest self-realization, but the one whose social and financial position and age, *etc.*, are most perfectly in conformity with the norms prescribed by society. She is generally a faithful wife, a good mother, but here too she demands that her husband and children all remain within socially admitted norms. This whole beautiful edifice can easily be overthrown by an irruption of the compensative unconscious, and then the extrovert will turn into an eccentric, and all her behavior and judgment will be in contradiction with the social norms,

The extrovert's feelings are so much determined by the object that the person in whom this type is dominant, is recognized particularly by his realism, which can turn into the most sordid materialism.

Intuition itself, a function of the unconscious perception, is turned towards external objects in the extrovert; he tries to grasp their inner possibilities. Linked with his thinking powers, this intuition can lead him to a certain interiorization and thus neutralize what is too objective in his thinking processes.

* * * *

The *introvert* lives in a subjective universe, even when he maintains his relations with objects and with the outside world. He lives in the world of ideas more than in that of men and things. Whereas the extrovert does not call attention to himself, the introvert is interested in practically nothing else. His practical behavior is rarely in tune with the world of reality; it is almost always the function of his own inner needs. He is not, however, any more self-centered than the extrovert. He is very capable of dedicating himself entirely to the service of others, but first of all he will need to feel a certain sense of identification with them, sharing their sentiments and sufferings. Instead of being an unconscious compensation, however, his fundamental subjectivism makes the introvert run the risk of actually breaking with reality, with the world of objects. Then the object takes on an obsessional character in the unconscious, and the result can be the neurosis of psychasthenia.

The introverted intellectual creates his theories and his systems in response to his own problems. He applies them to others by the simple process of extension, for he finds it hard to believe that other people and their world could be any different from himself. Facts as such hold no interest for him; he uses them not as proofs, but as simple examples. For this mentality, says Jung, reality has only secondary importance, whereas the description and development of the subjective idea, the initial symbolic image, which always remains more or less obscurely fixed in his inner eye, is the object of his primary interests.[6] If he is a philosopher,

---

6. Jung, *op. cit.*, p. 391

he will be a metaphysician and delight in "nominal" speculation. Immanual Kant can be considered as a perfect representative of the introverted thinker. If he is professor or priest, the introvert will have little personal influence, because those with whom he has his official business will not interest him as people and he will make no effort to adapt to them. The only thing that counts for him is the development of his own ideas and theories. He is looking for new depth rather than new breadth of thought, and he makes an excellent researcher, though he can easily become doctrinaire and dogmatic.

The sentimental introvert is quiet, hard to approach, hard to understand, melancholy; he likes to hide under an infantile or trite exterior. The real motives for his behavior are hard to grasp; they are not much connected with the world of reality. His coldness and indifference towards everything that is outside himself can reach the point of total insensitivity to the happiness or misfortune of other people. Other people, in fact, as such do not touch him. Moreover, he underestimates his own potential; hence his frequent oppressed and even persecuted feelings and attitudes. Just as in the case of the extrovert, the sentimental introvert is much more likely to be a woman than a man.

When sensation is the predominating type in an introvert, he will frequently lock himself up so securely in subjectivity that obsessional neurosis is a real and constant threat.

The intuitive introvert is a dreamer, a mystic visionary, but he can also border on fantasy, or be a real artist.

* * * *

Any pure type, introvert or extrovert, is necessarily excessive, a danger to the ego's sense of equilibrium. Fortunately, as we have mentioned above, the unconscious almost always plays a compensative role. Still, in order to keep this compensation from being anarchical and presenting a new danger of its own, it is absolutely essential to keep the existential communication between the two parts of the psyche from ever being completely interrupted.

The extrovert has a hard time understanding the introvert, and vice versa. Each type is inclined to consider his own typical behavior as the model of all human behavior as such. The former, however, is better equipped to understand the latter. The introvert's mistake, according to Jung, is that he always needs to explain the extrovert's way of behaving by his own subjective psychology, whereas the extrovert can only understand the introvert's inner life in terms[7] of external events.

The neurosis which most frequently threatens the uncompensated extrovert is hysteria, while the "family disease" of the introvert is neurasthenia.

V. *Typical Relations with Other People*

Karen Horney does not claim to have founded a new typology, in any effort to replace that of Jung. She is content with completing Jung's efforts by classifying men according to their habitual behavior towards other people. Relations with other people are, in her eyes, the fundamental psychological attitude. Even though it was established on the basis of neurotic attitudes, her classification does contain some precious material for understanding the normal psyche as well.

From this point of view, Karen Horney distinguishes three principal types: retiring, aggressive, and detached.

The *retiring* type are characterized first of all by their intense thirst for affection and approbation on the part of others. They cannot even live without support from someone else who will assume a maximum of responsibility for them, even conduct the major affairs of life for them. The person on whom they are dependent can be either father or mother, husband or wife, friend or teacher. If they find themselves deprived of this support, they

---

7. *Op. cit.*, p. 167

fall quickly into despair and anxiety. In an effort to escape these feelings, they are ready to abandon themselves into anyone's hands, no matter how obviously unworthy and incapable he is, provided they do not have to make their own decisions and act for themselves.

In order to avoid being rebuked by their teachers, they repress all their feelings and impulses that are self-assertive or vindictive or ambitious in character. But as generally happens in the case of repression, these feelings frequently burst their bonds with excessive violence. Then both the subject himself and those around him are likely to suffer very cruelly. Even the excessive need for affection that the retiring person experiences can be partially transformed into tyranny towards those from whom he feels he has a right to expect protection and friendship. Such a person is cured, or re-educated, primarily by freeing him from his unconscious aggressivity.

The *aggressive* type is the opposite of all this. Those who have this cast of character are firmly convinced that there are only hostile forces in the world outside them, without having made any effort to look for some objective proof to substantiate their conviction. In an effort to defend themselves against these hostile forces, the aggressive personality takes the offensive. Thus he is hostile to everyone, apparently without any good reason. He has to win on every count, and look brave in the eyes of others. He is ambitious, but often in a childish and simple way. In an effort to be reassured of his own worth, he likes to form close relationships with retiring people, whose only demand upon him is to be protected and even tyrannized. The aggressive person needs to be relieved of his unconscious inferiority feelings.

Detached people love solitude and shun society. When this inclination assumes neurotic proportions, a general break with the world of reality can occur (schizophrenia). They want to be self-sufficient in everything, not to depend on any person or any thing, and, primarily, to owe nobody anything. This need for independence can go all the way to self-destruction. They think they are unique, superior to everyone else, trust only their own judgment. Such behavior can only proceed from an unconscious feeling of extreme "fragility"; this is what the psychologist must concentrate on in effecting a cure.

7 self-ideal and superego

Drawing its psychic energy from the libido, the soul manifests itself in cognitive and affective, interior and exterior acts of all orders. It does not know where it is going nor what it will become. Theoretically, everything seems possible; the soul can be anything imaginable, the only limitations being constituted by the quantity and quality of psychic energy it has at its disposal.

A closer observation, however, reveals that our psychic growth normally takes place along a certain line, that even within the limits of our own libido we cannot be anything and everything we would like to be: at least within the limits of its broader outlines, the path of our development is, if not traced out for us, at least strongly indicated. We can, of course, approve of a given orientation, but can we take another if we will? It is obviously more exact to say that the soul realizes itself rather than that it makes itself or becomes.

In saying that the psyche realizes itself, we imply that it is already, in germ, in some manner, whatever it will eventually become. As the philosophers put it, the soul is in potency. It is in potency, however, in a radically different manner than the way the oak is contained in the acorn, or the month-old fetus is already the body of the adult to be. In the physical order, becoming is something mechanical; neither the oak nor the human body have a personally active part in this development. Then too, there can always be deviations along the course of the road, but they will come from outside factors. The psyche is a different case. The psyche and only the psyche realizes *itself*. If it does not arrive at its goal, this will always be at least partially its own fault.

I. *The Freudian Superego*

If we adopt the Freudian concept of psychic development, we would have to say that if it is so radically different from physical or biological development, this fact is due exclusively to the constraints which society, and particularly the family, exercises on the child. Without these constraints, the instincts would be the only dynamism with the psyche. They would function in the adult the way they do in the child. The only difference would be a more or less greater intensity or strength in the case of the former, just as his psychic power in general is stronger. If this is not actually the case in given circumstances, the reason is to be sought in the fact that the human being, from the first moment of his existence, is inserted into a society. This society has certain principles, certain ready-made ideas of good and evil, beautiful and ugly, what should be done and what should not be done, its laws, customs and habits. When parents teach their little child to behave, society has already begun inculcating one of its ideas. When the baby cries, he gets a slap, or else he is rocked: mother or daddy or brother or sister smile at him and do their best to bring back a happy smile to his face.

A young French girl who lived in Morocco was very much surprised to notice that her little brother's first indistinct words were in French, while the maid's little girl of the same age began to talk in Arabic. She saw something mysterious in all this, because she had not learned to understand what is meant by society or how the immediate social environment of the children was beginning to impose its own norms of speech. Differentiation in the majority of the other psychic functions is subject to the same general laws.

Why does the little boy want to be a doctor and then an explorer and finally an aviator? We are right in presuming that this ideal of life comes from outside influences. He has had occasion to see the doctor at work and admired him, either because of the healing power he seemed to possess or because of the fact that everyone seemed to respect him. He read about the adventures of the famous explorers: and he only needed to look out the window to observe the miracles of aviation.

* * * *

As long as it is merely a question of society consciously inculcating its principles and ideas in the child, there is no possible exception to the explanation given above. The only point on which we disagree with Freudian theory in this whole question is the Freudian *a priori* contempt for the influences of society (a contempt of which he seems not always to be aware). Only instinct, in all its biological purity, seems normal to him. Obviously even the most orthodox Freudian thinkers do not blame society for teaching the child toilet training or how to speak. But there is always a certain nostalgia about their references to instinct as following only its own immanent laws; and they have such a revulsion towards social restraint that we get the impression that it is only with great regret that they even admit its fundamental usefulness for the formation of the conscious ego. And society always remains an "outside power" in relation to human nature.

Freud's originality, in this respect, consists in his stress on the unconscious activity society exercises on the psyche. In the course of the ages, society has accumulated experiences, wisdom, memories. This heritage, without our ever being aware of it, contributes considerably to the formation of each individual's feelings and behavior. What we consider as "natural laws" of feeling, thinking, and acting, are really nothing other than the unconscious pressure of society on the individual.

We know that Freud and the Freudians are never completely free from the spirit of magic. They love to personify psychic functions. The unconscious influence of society on the individual has been christened "superego." This function exercises a constant censorship over the libido, which in the intrinsic logic of Freudian psychology, appears as an unpardonable crime. One of the primary tasks of psychoanalysis, in Freud's eyes, is precisely the destruction of this superego, this "heriditary enemy" of the individual.

The superego speaks primarily through the agency of moral conscience and thus it is not surprising that Freudian thinking wants to rid man of his moral preoccupations. Not that the individual must necessarily let himself be guided solely by the impulse of biological instinct. But the individual reason, the organ of the conscious ego, must be the only judge of what should or should not be retained in these objective social values. (We might note, in passing, that this offers a good insight into how Freudian thinking is bound up with a certain elemental rationalism, so popular in the nineteenth century.)

* * * *

The superego, such as it is conceived of in psychoanalysis, that is, as a basically maleficent force, can be effectively observed in the case of many neurotics. But it is their sickness that has impaired the functioning and made it regressive. To develop this fact into an out-of-hand condemnation of the superego as such is to imitate the behavior of people who speak, imprecisely, of their liver or prostate as diseases.

II. Self ideal

Psychologists who feel no obligation to subscribe to the Freudian conception of psychic life would no doubt do well to avoid using the term superego. Or else they should reserve it for describing an exclusively pathological function. The term "self ideal" seems much more indicated as an expression of this sort of inner appeal which the soul experiences in its more profound depths and which acts upon it as a dynamic force of attraction.

For my own part, I admit without hesitation that unconscious motivations have had their part in the formation of this ideal which serves as a sort of polar star for our psychic development. The young man whose ideal of manhood is a St. Vincent de Paul or a Napoleon, rather than a St. Francis of Assisi or a Talleyrand, is certainly not wholly aware of the motives for his individual preferences. In such cases, however, we are speaking only of the most superficial strata of the unconscious, the strata that are separated from the conscious mind only in a more or less accidental manner and to which conscious awareness has access under certain proper conditions.

There is something else, infinitely more fundamental, in our concept of the self ideal. What is the basic source of this call to go beyond the levels of biological nature? Who teaches us how to distinguish between good and evil? To say that it is society only puts off the basic solution one step further. It is true that, according to different civilizations and environments, the same concrete act can pass, sometimes for good, sometimes for evil. But we know that the distinction itself is anterior to this concrete judgment. It seems to be part of the deepest structure of the psyche. It goes back to the collective unconscious, as we have described it in Jung's psychology.

To make use of some notions that are dear to traditional philosophy, we might say that the libido plays the role of *efficient cause* in the psychic dynamism, whereas the self ideal assumes that of *final cause*. The energy for this self ideal comes from the unconscious, but this certainly does not lessen its originality.

III. *Ideal Self image*

The *self ideal* must not be confused with the self image. This last, according to Karen Horney, is not a goal towards which the individual tends, but a fixed idea which he adores.[1] A man who pursues his self ideal is very conscious of the fact that he has not yet attained the goal, that in fact he probably never will realize the goal, perfectly. Actually, the further we advance along the route pointed out by our ideal, the higher and more demanding this ideal appears to be. Thus the Christian religious image is always perfect resemblance to Christ. Whereas the mediocre believer easily thinks himself perfect, the saint and the mystic never stop lamenting the misery of their sinful state. That is because they have a clearer vision, acquired gradually and almost stealthily, step by step with their spiritual ascent, of what is still standing between them and their Ideal.

The self image and the Freudian superego have many common traits. It is narcissistic and focuses the individual upon himself, making him arrogant. The individual who has become its prey believes that he is what he wants to be. Instead of working towards perfection, he likes to believe that he is perfect. But since it is quite impossible, outside of pure psychosis, to be completely deceived as to one's own real identity, such an individual proves to be unsure of himself, extremely sensitive, always suspecting that others are refusing him the honors and attention to which he claims to have a right.

It seems certain that the self image is the product of the same psychological functions as those which give rise to the self ideal. Under the activity of various factors (we shall discuss them again in the chapter devoted to the diseased soul), the ideal has lost its energy charge, fixed upon a static image. Instead of bearing the psyche outwards, towards higher activities, it shuts it up within an infantile narcissism. In less serious cases, this gives rise to amorphous and mediocre people. When anxiety is added, the result is neurosis. In more serious cases, there might be psychosis, complete dislocation of the personality: the mental hospitals are crowded with people who think they are Christ or Napoleon.

---

1. *Nos conflicts intérieurs,* p. 79

IV. *Usefulness of the Superego*

The value judgment we pronounce on the self ideal, the superego, and the self image is obviously not the same. The first of these, unquestionably, is an authentic property of the psyche and no one could pretend to deny its necessity or value. As for the superego and the idealized self image, the psychologist and psychiatrist have a duty to fight against them. Still, we must not lose sight of the psychological function they fulfill. There could be no question of abolishing them and leaving the psyche without a guide, the helpless victim of its own instinctual impulses. The abolition of the superego or the idealized self image is justified only to the degree that the function they are performing so poorly can easily be transferred to the self ideal.

I had frequent occasion to observe cases in which the pure and simple destruction of the self image by psychoanalysis resulted in such a psychic disorder that I found myself wondering whether it would not have been much better to have left things alone in the first place. It is better for a man to live with his superego (in the Freudian and pejorative sense of the word) than to let his ego run headlong into exhaustion.

Therese, a young practicing Catholic, went to see the psychoanalyst because she suffered from agoraphobia. He quickly discovered the fundamentally inauthentic character of her religious life, which was strongly narcissistic. Instead of tending to surpass herself through the practice of charity, by a loving communion with God, Therese liked to compare herself, to her own advantage, with "unbelievers," and severely criticize the frivolity and wickedness of her neighbors. In order to give "good example," she felt obliged to great austerities in her dress; she never laughed or made conversation or jokes, she observed her "pious duties" with the exactitude of a maniac. It does not take a believer himself to realize that such a "religion," accompanied moreover by an abnormal and diseased scrupulosity, is not the Christianity of the Gospels. The psychoanalyst concluded, quite legitimately, that it was the work of the superego, in the pejorative sense of Freudian psychology. Therese was not at all embarrassed at her failings in the area of Christian charity; she thought herself perfect: even her childish scruples she attributed to the delicacy of her conscience.

Theoretically, there is no harm in destroying such a superego, and unmasking such a self image. The psychoanalyst in question set about this purpose with total success. But unfortunately he did not realize that religion in itself is more than a more or less pathological function of the superego. Thus he could not understand the need for putting an authentic religious life in place of the caricature of religion which he had just helped his patient to be free of. After this treatment, Therese might not have been a neurotic, but in many other important respects she was a perfect wreck. Is this progress? I hardy think so. False as her idealized self image might have been, and inauthentic as her superego inspired religion might have proved, at least she had some reason for living in them. At present there was nothing left at all, and, after several desperate attempts at finding something meaningful (they need not be discussed here at any length), she finally sought a final refuge in suicide.

Obviously this is not to be construed as a defense of neurotic religious life. But the psychologist who is not in a position to substitute the self ideal for the idealized self image must not attempt to handle such cases.

V. Collective Superego

Not only does each individual have his own star (self ideal, superego, or idealized self image), but there is also a guiding star for each human collectivity. Rene Laforgue, in many of his writings, but particularly in his *Psychopathology of Defeat*, has made a profound and thorough study of the evil influences of the collective libido when it is fixed on a pathological stage of the idealized self image. It is incontestable that, after actually undergoing centuries of persecution, the Jewish people, as a whole, bears the idealized image of the persecuted. This explains, in large measure, the refusal — or rather the impossibility — of most Jews to assimilate, the persistence of a certain number of particularisms which nothing can either justify or explain on a rational basis, but which all serve to provoke new persecutions on the part of anti-semites. Laforgue concludes that, by reason of his collective superego, every Jew unconsciously wants to be a victim of persecution, and thus provokes persecution.

We would not go so far as that. In the course of centuries, the Jewish people have lost their ancient religious ideals. As long as they were persecuted for the sake of those ideals, they had a right to claim the glory of martyrdom. But as so often happens, even though they had long since ceased to be a witness (martyr) to Yahweh, their unconscious still found some satisfaction in the prospect of martyrdom and persecution. Zionism has partially succeeded in putting things in better order.

I say partially, because the collective Jewish psyche has not yet managed to free itself from its ancient rancor, and as the history of the emerging Israelite nation clearly shows, the Jew has ceased to be a victim of persecution only to turn with equal vigor to the task of persecuting others.

The Jews are obviously not the only people to behave in terms of their idealized self image rather than their ideal. It would be easy to discover symptoms of this same practice in the collective behavior of almost any other people. In particular, the miseries and castastrophes recently provoked upon the German people were largely the doing of their collective superego. . . .

Laforgue also analyzes the evil effects of the collective superego on the social class. He sees it as the cause, particularly, of everything that is irrational in the actual class struggles of our day. It is because the social classes have formed fixed and unyielding castes that the self image has replaced the ideal. We must remember, in this respect, what we said in discussing Therese's case above. It is not the suppression of classes as a concept that will contribute a solution to the evils engendered by the class superego. The example of Russia is clear proof of that. Psychopolitics must fight against the tendency to lock class distinctions within a rigid caste system and try to revive a concrete historical ideal which could mobilize all the creative powers of every class in the service of the common good.

* * * *

The collective superego is not to be condemned in itself, no more than the individual superego. How can we miss the fact that it is the tendencies of one and the same collective German psyche that are at work in the terrifying adventure of Hitler's war, and at the same time in the music of Wagner and Goethe's *Faust*? On a less pretentious plane, these same tendencies have made the Germans one of the best working nations in the world. Under the pretext of keeping Hitlers from emerging in the world, must we destroy the chances of ever having another Wagner or Goethe? Must an effort be made to reduce the energetic German race to the lazy passivity of, say, the Neapolitan? An elementary grounding in psychopolitics teaches us that Hitler would not have been able to enlist the collective German energy for his work of destruction unless this psychic energy had been prevented from going to work in a creative manner.

We have already said what we think of the class superego which vitiates class consciousness. To speak of only the most differentiated of all the social classes of our day, must the conscious mind of the working class be liquidated simply because the superego of this same class frequently gives rise to revolt and revolution? This would be forgetting that this same collective consciousness can take credit for some of the most successful attempts at human solidarity, and that those who shared in these struggles resisted the idolatry of money more than many another modern man. Here once again psychopolitics must aim rather at eliminating the regressive superego and prevent it from standing in the path of the positive ideal.

Often in the course of this essay we shall have occasion to protest against those who want the psychologist to exercise only a negative mission. Quite the contrary; whether we are speaking of the individual or the collective, the psychologist must make it a sacred duty to channel the deviated psychic energy along some normal use, to enlist it in the interests of some constructive function. He will have to heal the sick, of course, but psychic disease, like any disease, represents only the *second moment* in the dialectic of existence.

VI. *Coexistence of Superego and Self ideal*

The difference betwen the conscious self and the unconscious superego cannot be called into question. Still the logic of the distinction must not be pushed too far, to the point of creating an irreducible opposition between the two. There are not, and must never be, any closed compartments in the life of the psyche. The ideal self, like the ego itself, constantly draws new strength and nourishment from the unconscious sources of energy, and thus necessarily communicates with the superego. For the superego to fail in accomplishing this positive function and actually turn the libido towards a static idealized self image, some pathological factor must always intervene. Thus there is no question of destroying the superego, for the psychologist, but rather healing it, that is, putting it back into communication with the self ideal.

We have said that the progressive conquest of the unconscious by the conscious is the normal path of psychic growth and maturation. It is essential here for the self ideal to integrate as fully as possible all the energy that had been monopolized by the superego. Still the self ideal will never succeed in completely draining the superego of its psychic energy, any more than the total unconscious mind can ever become conscious. We have conceived of the libido, in Jungian terms, as being, by nature, a neutral and undifferentiated psychic energy. It seems to me that we must conceive of the superego in somewhat the same way. It can exert influence, according as the case predisposes it to be, on the self ideal as well as on the idealized self image.

We see no disadvantage in admitting that the superego is social in origin. But the ideal we have of society and its role is considerably different from that of orthodox Freudianism. This last sides with the extreme individualism professed by so many intellectual circles of the nineteenth centry where the naturalism of Rousseau's philosophy still survived. A psychology less in sympathy with prejudices and *a priori* postulates finds itself more comfortable in the company of the old philosophers who define man as a "social animal." He is not so by any accident, by any chance miscalculation, but by essence and of his nature.

Nothing is more normal than for the psyche to receive some of its most fundamental structures from society. The superego obviously belongs to that number; but in the self ideal the role of society is also not inconsiderable. There is, moreover, as Freudian psychology points out, the important activity of the family, natural intermediary between the newborn individual and society. But some of the individual's most primitive and strongest tendencies come from far, far off, borne along the course of centuries as they are by the collective unconscious.

8 complexes and symptoms

After the word "libido," of all the notions that are dear to psychoanalysis, the word "complex" is perhaps the most popular; although people are not too well informed, in every case, as to its real meaning and application. We have only to allude to something more or less irregular in a person's conduct or behavior and we hear the answer: "Oh yes, he has a real complex." We speak of complex as if it were a more or less hypertrophic organ the way we say that something has "crawled over his liver" to mean that someone is angry without a particularly good reason.

I. Psychic "Bundles"

We have seen that the psyche, conscious as well as unconscious, is animated by instincts or tendencies that are more or less charged with affective energy. These tendencies form a continuous network. But this network can contract in a given area and form what are called "bundles." These bundles are what we call complexes. But we must not lean too heavily on the terms we borrow from the world of physics; complexes are "bundles" only analogically. The whole framework of psychology as a science was established long after the natural sciences had attained a high degree of maturity, and thus psychology could not help borrowing many of its concepts from the sciences of nature. There is no particular disadvantage in any of this provided that we never lose sight of the fact that the realities studied by psychology are infinitely more moving than those of physics and even the same words cannot possibly have precisely the same meanings in each of the sciences.

Since they form a network, the various tendencies of the psyche should not be cut off from each other. In most cases, the complexes themselves are not tied together to the point that all communication between them is broken off. Only by accident do they become more or less autonomous, forming those "little independent psyches" of which Jung speaks.

As long as a complex is not cut off from the current of energy which unites it to the other tendencies of the psyche, there is no sign of neurosis or mental illness. It even seems that complexes are something indispensable in the mental life of most people. Theoretically, it is possible to conceive of all the tendencies in the psyche as sharing the libido equally between them, the libido freely circulating from one to the other, and thereby effecting a perfect harmony in the soul.

Existentially, this ideal is never attained. All men, without exception, have complexes. Freud is convinced of this from his study of inadvertent acts, slips of the tongue, and other more or less important disturbances in everyday living. He is wrong, however, when he refers to such phenomena as the "psychopathology of everyday life." There is nothing properly speaking pathological about it at all. Jung, Baudouin, and other psychologists have greatly advanced the study of complexes in normal people. They arrived at the conclusion that such symptoms are necessarily not a sign of sickness, nor even inferiority.

II. *Autonomous Complexes*

Every complex implies the accumulation of affective energy on one particular point, which thereby takes on a dominating role in the whole of psychic life. The fact that a given person has one kind of complex rather than another depends on his individual dispositions and also on the more or less chance events of his experience.

The idea of complex always implies an element of conflict, an unbalance of forces. As the tension of the libido weighs upon a particular tendency, a person systematically gives a preponderant position to that tendency, in accordance with the nature of his complex. Such a concentration of affective energy even seems to be necessary for every effort that is beyond the ordinary, for every success and for every act of creativity. The "normal" man who has no dominant complex, would necessarily also be mediocre. Taking sides and a more or less partisan attitude often seems to be indispensable. Every genius that ever lived and every superior person have all had their complexes; most of the time the complexes even operate with an excessive vigor; this generally makes them more "original."

Still it can happen, under the influence of causes which we shall discuss later on, that this "bundle" reaches such a stage of development that the complexes are almost completely autonomous. Each one of them then behaves like an independent psyche without paying any particular attention to the other tendencies of the psyche. The victim of such an autonomous complex thinks and judges and acts solely in terms of the complex. Neurosis and even serious mental disorder can easily be the result.

Complexes are formed in the unconscious, and it is in the unconscious that the whole danger exists. Psychic activity can be disturbed to the point of madness, without the subject knowing and being in a position to take steps to remedy the problem. What we see on the outside is not the complex itself, but only the symptoms. It is a mistake to confuse the two, as so frequently happens. Still there is a close and essential bond between the two. Dreams, for example, are symptoms that are produced by complexes.

A complex rarely exists in an isolated state. It is bound, in a network, to other complexes. The symptoms of the various complexes all interlock in practice.

Each person's predominant complex is generally the occasion of some suffering for him, precisely because of the excesses to which it gives rise. Still, such suffering is not a disease. It is only in the case of sick people that the autonomy of a complex is such that the subject no longer believes that it actually exists within him. He has the impression that some outside force is acting within him, making him respond in an automatic and stereotyped manner.

The psychologist must do everything he can to combat this excessive autonomy in a complex, since it is the cause of suffering. But he must not expect to completely abolish every complex. Supposing that he does succeed in such an ill-advised undertaking, the person concerned would be absolutely without resources, without the least psychic skeleton. The undeniable disadvantages of complexes are the exact counterpart of the services they always perform for the psyche.

Thus there are no grounds in the claim (so often publicized) of certain psychoanalysts that they have no complexes. It is precisely because no one is ever free of complexes that the choice of a doctor or a teacher or a psychologist is so very important; it is actually a choice between different and more or less autonomous complexes.

III. Oedipus Complex

No one knows how many complexes there are, in himself or in the psyche of a given individual. But psychologists have had a chance to study a certain number of them, with more or less precision, particularly those whose symptoms are more frequent among neurotics, that is, those which manifest a more marked inclination to autonomy. Here it is possible to describe only those which seem to have most importance from the psychologist's point of view.

* * * *

In the perspective of the Freudian system, the Oedipus complex is the most important of all. It is supposed to explain almost all neuroses, and normal psychic activity as well. Without being categorical, non-Freudian psychologists also recognize the existence of this complex.

Let us briefly recall the Greek legend. Oedipus, son of Laius, King of Thebes, is condemned to death by his father because an oracle had foretold that Laius would one day be killed by his own son. In order to escape his destiny, the father orders Oedipus to be hung from a tree by his feet. But shepherds take him down, carry him away from the wicked man's power, and bring him to Corinth, where the king brings him up in the royal household. Oedipus never knows that he is the son of Laius. One day he meets Laius, quarrels with him, and kills him, thus accomplishing the substance of the oracle. After delivering Thebes from the Sphinx, Oedipus becomes king. He marries Jocasta, Laius' widow, without knowing that she is his own mother. When a second oracle reveals this fact, Jocasta hangs herself. Oedipus, after putting out his own eyes, goes away from Thebes, guided by his daughter, Antigone. He disappears mysteriously in the groves of the Eumenides in Attica.

Freud sees this legend of Oedipus as the symbolization of a psychic drama common to all men. On the conscious plane, it is only by accident that Oedipus kills his father and marries his mother. But the unconscious, which is really controlling all this behavior, knows very well what is really going on. Deep in the uttermost depths of his soul, Oedipus loves — sexually, that is — his mother and hates his father as a rival. The same thing is true of all other men. In most cases, this love obviously never arrives at the point of incest, nor does the hate go so far as parricide. But this does not modify the fundamental terms of the problem in the eyes of the founder of psychoanalysis.

When he is still a child, Dr. Freud writes, the son begins to experience a particular affection for his mother. He looks upon her as his own possession and sees his father as a sort of rival disputing his claim to that possession.[1] Presented in this simple fashion, this statement can be verified by the constant experience of observation. The passionate attachment of almost all little children for their mother is a sort of proof in itself. It is also an undeniable fact that the attachment is more exclusive in the case of the little boy than in that of the little girl. The daughter, for her part, at a more or less tender age, frequently grows attached to her father in the same exclusive way. Frequently enough, too, we can observe that the child will experience a certain jealousy, or even hostility, towards the other parent.

Freud's originality consists in taking this attachment of the child for his mother as sexual in orgin. It is specifically a rivalry in love that pits son against father and daughter against mother. Only their moral taboos, interiorized by the superego, keep them from the incest towards which their libido would "normally" tend. The terrible censure to which the Oedipus complex would submit a person is thus supposed to be the origin of almost all neuroses.

Such a theory should not surprise anyone who is familiar with the Freudian theories of libido. Since by definition, the libido is identical with the sex instinct, all affective attachment must necessarily be sexual.

* * * *

In certain cases, which are manifestly pathological, the love between mother and son, and between father and daughter, is really incestuous. But even this fact does not prove that, in all incestuous sexual relations, there is really a primitive impulse or

---

1. *Introduction* . . . , p. 226 (French edition)

instinct at work. In fact it seems, at least in many cases, that these relations proceed rather from an unconscious identification of the parent with a stranger. Whatever the case may be, in keeping with every sound principle of scientific methodology, as Roland Dalbiez so well describes it, the Oedipus complex has to be proved and not presumed.[2] To conclude, on the basis of the reality of incestuous love in the case of neurotics or degenerate people, that the affection between all parents and all children is incestuous is, from the point of view of scientific methodology, a logical monstrosity. Since there is absolutely no evidence for the incestuous character of this love in normal people, it would no doubt be closer to the truth to consider the Oedipus complex, in the proper sense of the word, as a mounting degeneracy, a morbid deviation of filial love.

The notion of an Oedipus complex, as such, must not be rejected out of hand by psychology. It does offer a fairly accurate explanation of certain psychic facts. But it must be kept within the perspectives of the better developed and much richer theory of libido as explained above.

It is perfectly normal for the child to show a preference for the parent of the opposite sex. In many cases, this preference is merely a response to the predilections of the parents themselves. Neither the one nor the other, however, is normally a case of sexual attraction, or repressed incestuous love. What, then, is the real substance of this Oedipus complex? And what is its psychological usefulness?

We recognize the Oedipus complex in a case when the child's fixation on one of his parents becomes so exclusive that it results in an inhibition of his whole normal affective evolution. When he becomes an adolescent, the child with an Oedipus complex always acts as if he were still a child, that is in absolute dependence on his mother's (or in the case of a girl, her father's) will. It seems inconceivable for such a person to undertake any enterprise,

---

2. *La Méthode Psychanalytique et la Doctrine Freudienne II*, 280

particularly to marry, without the authorization or approbation of the parent who is the object of his fixation. Often he will remain celibate, so that he can live with his mother.

If he does marry, his wife will be a very motherly woman, older than he, and his unconscious will be looking for a mother's love rather than a wife and lover. Even if his mother is dead, he always tries to act in a manner that "would not have displeased her." He is always trying "not to cause her any pain." There is something very childish about his behavior in the face of concrete living: he is timid, awkward, and generally an introvert.

In the case of the young girl who is exclusively attached to her father, we most frequently encounter a rejection of femininity. She wants to be "like Papa," and shows a particular leaning towards those vocations which have a social character. Just like the young man with an Oedipus fixation she also will find marriage difficult, but for different reasons. Whereas the young man is too dependent on his mother to ever experience any real feeling for another woman, the girl will be too independent to submit to any man, particularly because she considers them all inferior to her father. Some authors, remembering how Agamemnon's daughter avenged her father's death, have called this Oedipus complex in the woman the "Diana complex."

With only rare exceptions, there is nothing properly sexual about the Oedipus complex, no more than the baby's attachment to his mother is sexual. In most cases that I have been in a position to observe, the fixation is the result of education errors. A mother who is not completely happy with her marriage will turn all the affection her husband does not want, towards her son. She is a real "mother hen"; she surrounds him with all kinds of attentions, always afraid that he will make a mistake or hurt himself; she keeps him from the progressive emancipation which is only normal. The girl grows exclusively attached to her father especially when she sees that her mother has an obvious preference for, let us say, her little brother. Then, too, an "Oedipus complex climate" exists almost solely in families where there is some lack of understanding between husband and wife. Frequently such a complex is hereditary.

IV. *Ego Complex*

The ego complex, also known as the "will to power," plays almost as important a role in Adler's psychology as the Oedipus complex does in Freud's

The subject of the ego complex has an exaggerated idea of his own worth. He feels that everything is coming to him, and he acts and lives for prestige; he shrinks from nothing in an effort to assert his domination over other people. It might sometimes look as if he is trying to make himself loved, but generally even this area of his activity is oriented towards dominating other people and thus reinforcing the good opinion he has of himself. He never listens to advice, follows only his own lead.

The ego complex is much more predominant in the Western psychology than in the Oriental. We are too much taken up with the prestige of the "active virtues."

As long as this complex does not become completely autonomous, it can be a very positive element in a person's psychic life. The feeling of power can be based on intellectual power or physical realities. In this stage, the word "complex" is an abuse. It begins to appear only if a man attaches a disproportionately large degree of importance to his progress towards social or business success, when the search for prestige and domination over others becomes the principal or even the only goal of his activity.

Those who have a very strong ego complex are incapable of real communion with other people. They are excessively authoritarian; they demand a submission and respect that they themselves are in no way inclined to give in return. They frequently humiliate others without apparent reason, particularly those who are dearest to them. Their unconscious mind seems to see this as a new assertion of their natural dominance.

It frequently happens too, that in order to exercise this domination more positively, the will to power hides under a disguise. A woman, for example, might better succeed in tyrannizing her whole circle of friends and acquaintances, not by her excessive crying or throwing a fit of temper, but rather by her excessive amiability and softspoken tenderness. Generally she will not realize that it is the ego complex which is behind her apparent sweetness; like every complex, the will to power is most often unconscious.

Men in whom the ego complex is dominant show a marked preference towards political and military careers; but they can be equally as successful in the business world. The complex can thus serve ends that are socially and objectively good. But if the conscious mind does not succeed in asserting at least a partial control, the complex will pursue its objective with an inhuman harshness, like a psychic Machiavelli.

In pathological cases, the ego complex remains completely unconscious. In such circumstances the will to power is not based on any real values. It is born of hate, desire for vengeance, inferiority feelings. Hitler is no doubt one of the best examples of the disadvantages that come from a neurotic ego complex. Since he had completely identified his own complex with that of the German people, he shrank from nothing in an effort to overextend his own power and that of the German nation. The hold that the complex had on him was so great that he lost all his aptitude for objective judgment, all his ability to evaluate the real force and position of either himself or his adversaries. As a result, he could only destroy himself and lead his country to catastrophe. The same thing might be said of Stalin and many other dictators.

In the neurotic, the quest for power is generally a means of protecting himself against his own insignificance, against the weakness he faces in his own unconscious mind.

V. Inferiority Complex

This complex is probably one of the most frequently encountered problems in practicing psychology. It might equally well be referred to as a superiority complex; in practice the two are so correlative that it is almost impossible to distinguish between them.

There are many timid and awkward persons who can adapt only with difficulty to new situations, who succeed only very poorly in life. When their inferiority feelings are conscious, it is relatively easy to help them. But here, too, the complex is, most often, totally or partially unconscious. Consciously, the subject does not believe that he is the least bit inferior to other people. He might even have an excellent opinion of himself and believe that he is very superior. But this does not keep him from acting in a way that results in a *de facto* inferiority situation. . . . In his book on the psychopathology of defeat, Rene Laforgue gives a remarkable analysis of the inferiority complex disguised as a feeling of superiority.

At first sight, we might be astonished to learn that the author chooses the case of Napoleon as an illustration of this thesis. Laforgue shows, however, that the Corsican's need for some spectacular success, his radical incapacity to choose the opportune moment for putting an end to his military undertakings and settling down to a constructive work, proceeded not from an exceptional will to power, but from his unconscious feeling of inferiority. Waterloo and St. Helena appear not as untoward accidents that plague the career of an exceptional man, but rather as the logical result of his behavior. We might say the same thing with even greater objective truth in the case of Adolph Hitler.

As we have said above, a complex is rarely an isolated factor. The feeling of inferiority and the will to power can very well go together, to the point that it is not always so easy to tell whether a given behavior should be attributed to one or the other complex. This is true both of neurotics and more or less normal men.

When the inferiority feeling goes hand in hand with a real objective inferiority, the complex functions as a force that inhibits the subject from making the necessary efforts to surmount his inferiority, to make him say that he "can do nothing more," and that he regards himself as once and for all condemned to mediocrity. But this complex can often make a man believe he has inferiorities that he does not really have. Now, unfortunately, a man who starts out believing that he is inferior, without any good reason, will, in time, actually become inferior.

The ego complex leads many people to form an excessive and unrealistic idea of their own worth and thus gives rise to ambitions that are out of all proportion to their real capacities. After meeting with a check in their ambitions, they are discouraged and believe that they are inferior to everybody and everything. Once the psychic bundle of inferiority is well established in the soul, a person is no longer in a position to determine what, in his reversal, is the result, essentially, of simple external circumstances and what is really the result of his own insufficiencies. More and more discouraged, he becomes envious and surly; he considers all superiority and all success as a personal offense.

VI. *Mutilation Complex*

Freud, faithful to his pansexualistic inspiration, makes much of the castration complex. According to him, from the time the little boy first becomes aware of the difference between the sexes, he considers himself very superior to his sisters and all other women. He believes that women do not have any penis, because they have undergone mutilation, castration. He is terribly afraid of becoming victim of a like mutilation, losing the attributes that permit him to assert his superiority. Some ill-considered threats on the part of parents and nurses greatly contribute to reinforcing this terror, turning it into a real complex, which might well inhibit the subject's whole psychic existence.

The little girl's reactions, again according to Freud, are correlative to those of the boy. From the first moment she is aware of her femininity, she thinks of herself as incomplete, mutilated. This is supposed to be the reason why she envies the penis, desires to be a man, feels a deep sense of inferiority.

The castration complex is the basis of many neuroses, both in women and in men. Some psychologists have gone so far as to explain the whole feminist movement, the whole literary output of George Sand and Simone de Beauvoir, on the basis of castration complex. By defending their rights to exercise the same professions as men, women are supposed to be refusing to be second-rate people: but actually they are only symbolically revindicating their right to the penis whose absence is supposed to be, in the eyes of their unconscious, the cause of all their weakness and inferiority.

* * * *

Many psychologists who are not Freudian in any respect have observed that the complex described by Freud does actually exist in some people and does play a very unfortunate role. But it is still far from being a universal fact. The observation of many children is evidence of the fact that most boys do not really believe that their sisters have been mutilated. If they do believe it, the reason is that they themselves have been threatened with castration for having "been naughty."

In the case of some little girls, there actually is an envy of the penis. They see its absence as a sign of inferiority and their whole existence can suffer from the consequences. Women who have no femininity and try to ape male conduct at every opportunity, up to the point where they develop into active homosexuals, belong to this category. Still, the majority of young girls, after they have become aware of the physiological differences between themselves and boys, do not experience any feelings of inferiority, and never get the idea that they have been mutilated.

VII. *Frustration Complex*

The most far-reaching reproach that most children can have against their mother, according to Dr. Freud, consists in the fact that she has given them too little milk — a fact which they interpret as a lack of love. The child, and later on, unconsciously, the adult, attribute all their maladies and all their miseries to weaning. Since weaning takes place at an age in which the child is oriented exclusively towards buccal pleasure, the result is a feeling of universal frustration. Most children resign themselves to this situation without too much difficulty and are willing to be satisfied with the suppletive pleasures that are afforded by the baby bottle, but some children still do suffer and refuse to accept any other form of nourishment. This first feeling of frustration makes itself felt through their whole life and is the cause of all the reversals they encounter.[3]

This complex which can be found in a certain number of individuals can sometimes result from the psychological shock occasioned by the weaning process. At other times, the child believes he is no longer loved by his parents because they leave him home alone, especially when they want to go out and have a good time in the evening, or when they send him off to school, particularly a boarding school — that is, submit him to a prolonged separation. Contrary to Freudian psychology, all complexes in all individuals are not so bound up with early childhood, and the frustration complex can result from several successive separations, all more or less painful to experience.

VIII. *Cain Complex and Some Other Complexes*

We must be content with merely mentioning some of the complexes that we do not have room to discuss in any great

---

3. See chapter five of *Nouvelles leçons de psychanalyse*

detail, and which, moreover, partially overlap the phenomena already described.

The *Cain complex* is marked by the hostile attitude of certain children with respect to younger brothers or sisters. This hostility does not always disappear in the adult, but from a conscious feeling it passes over into the unconscious.

The *destruction complex* is characterized by a network of instincts that express themselves in cruelty and pointless vandalism.

The *exhibitionism complex* is the cause of the disordered tendency to show oneself, childish personal vanity, and sometimes goes on to the point of childish crimes, or even spectacular crimes and perversions.

The *guilt complex* appears to be one of the most important complexes in the eyes of most psychologists; it has been much studied as a result. We pass it over with only brief mention here, because we shall have occasion to discuss it at greater length in the chapter devoted to psychology and morality.

We have already mentioned that no intelligent psychologist can claim to liquidate every complex. Most men live very comfortably with their complexes, and moreover the complex lends a certain something to their personality, the basis of their originality and charm. It is only when a complex becomes autonomous to the point of dangerously threatening the psychic equilibrium that it is necessary to consult the psychologist.

9 dreams, the language of the unconscious

1. Universal Belief in the Meaning of Dreams

What we know of "primitive" civilizations inclines us to think that, since the first stirrings of consciousness, man has been both astonished and intrigued by his own dream activity. Some very poorly evolved tribes in Africa and Oceania seem to believe that what happens in a dream is just as real as the events of waking life and that a man thus leads two different existences. The same feeling of double existence is to be encountered in many psychically ill people. We have known some persons who maintained that there was a real continuity between their dreams from one night to another, and obstinately refused to believe that this was not "true." More generally, however, the primitives do not believe that dreams are real. They are said to come from gods, from spirits, from jinnis.

All the peoples of antiquity attributed a profound meaning to dreams. They did not believe dreams could be taken as literally true, but they always looked behind the dream images for a hidden meaning, frequently as a key to the future. Moreover it was understood that the dreamer himself could never decipher his own dream and learn what the gods wanted him to learn: the profession of oracle was everywhere honored, and frequently identified with the priestly office.

There is little point in citing lengthy examples from the mythologies of Greece and Rome, nor Egypt for that matter. We need only recall the very important role that dreams play in the Bible. It is through a dream that God speaks to Abraham, Isaac, Jacob, Job, Moses, Samuel, David. Joseph's success in Egypt was due to his gifts as an interpreter of dreams. In the New Testament, it is a dream that leads Joseph, Christ's foster father, to understand God's wishes with regard to his Son. Nor is it impossible that certain of Christ's visions, as, for example, the encounter with Satan in the desert, are also the product of a dream.

The Greeks, Romans, and Etruscans never undertook a war without having first consulted the interpreters of dreams, the most famous among whom were always to be found in the personal service of the kings.

The Christian Middle Ages remained faithful to this tradition. There is hardly a saint's life in which dreams do not play some role as a vehicle of profound and mysterious religious truths.

II. Modern Skepticism

It was not until our own time — the age which is so aptly called the "modern age" — that people of some education refused to place any credit in the language of dreams. The dream did not fit in with their materialistic conception of the reality of psychic life. Only supersitious and uneducated people continued to look for meaning in their dreams, to consult "dream analysis keys."

Still, however great their official contempt for dreams might have been, educated men could not help attempting some explanation of dream activity. What are the mechanisms of dream life? Why does one dream contain more images than another?

Considering the psyche as a simple biological function, the psychologists for a long time attributed dream activity to bodily excitation. Some still maintain it today. Binet, in 1879, treats the dream as a material process which is always useless and very often morbid. Clinical experiments were conducted in an effort to prove that the dream is the product of bodily excitation. Here is a dream recounted by Hildebrandt — he attributes it solely to the sound of the alarm clock.

"I was out walking one spring morning and I wandered through the fields to a nearby village where I saw people all dressed up heading for the church, their prayer books in their hands. . . . The service was just starting. I decided to join the crowd, but since it was very hot I went out into the cemetery beside the church. I was just starting to read the various tombstone inscriptions there, when I heard the bellringer start up into the belfry and I saw the little bell far overhead which was just about to announce the beginning of the service. It was still silent, immobile, for some few moments, and then it began to move, and suddenly its tones became clear and piercing, to the point that they broke my sleep. It was the alarm clock that made me have that dream."

Another time, it is the same alarm clock that puts an end to an equally complex dream, but the noise heard in the dream is that of little bells. Still another time, it is the tinkling of a broken glass.

Let a sleeping person smell some Cologne and when he wakes he will tell you how he dreamt of romantic adventures in the Orient. Pour some water over his forehead and he will dream of a banquet where the choicest wines are being served.

In the light of these and many other experiences, we can speak of a definitely established relation between the external excitation and the development of the dream. But all these experiments teach us very little about the real nature of the dream. Is the excitation to be considered as the adequate cause of the dream? Why, then, should the alarm clock sometimes simulate the echo of the village bells, sometimes the tinkling of small house bells, and sometimes the tinkling of broken glass? What is the source of all the more or less coherent images which make up this dream world drama?

These are the real questions that must interest the psychologist. It is obviously impossible to hark back to the theory of external physical excitation, that the Cologne only *happens* to plunge one dreamer into his adventures in an oriental harem, whereas it might lead another dreamer deep into the spring woods of his boyhood.

Some psychologists have claimed that the dream issues from the excitation of internal organs. You eat too much at night and you will dream of monsters chasing you. But the same questions must be asked all over again: why this terrifying image rather than some other? Why, and from where, do we have all this complicated context of the dream?

Just as insufficient is the statement that the dream is more or less an absurd reproduction of elements drawn from the experiences of the recent past. Here again, we must ask why some elements are preferred to others?

III. *The Language of the Unconscious*

The distinction of having reestablished the psychological meaning of the dream unquestionably belongs to Dr. Freud. Since his day, all depth psychologists have continued the exploration he had begun over fifty years ago. None of them who have seriously considered the problem, has ever had the slightest doubt that the dream always has a hidden meaning whose discovery can be of a sovereign importance for understanding the psyche or, as the case may be, curing it. The only disagreements among the psychologists bear on the interpretation and its laws, each of them obviously thinking in terms of his own conception of the psyche. Jung recognizes only "important dreams" in this respect.

Since modern psychology has studied dreams with the maximum of scientific rigor, we can definitely establish that dreams are not produced by excitations from within or without — a rather absurd hypothesis in the light of any strict scientific methodology — but rather that they are the manifestation of psychic activity during sleep. In the sleeping person, conscious psychic activity is suspended. The control that the ego normally exercises over the imagination, the ideas, and the feelings, no longer operates. If there were only conscious activity in the psyche, the explanation of dream activity would be well nigh inconceivable. But we know that this is not the case.

It is precisely when the conscious mind is suspended in a state of sleep that the unconscious psyche is freed to exercise a much more intense activity. No longer embarrassed by the controlling power of the ego, it can come and go almost at will. I say "almost" because we shall see that this freedom is never completely total. It is always true, however, that the interpretation of dreams is, as Freud puts it, the royal road to the knowledge of the unconscious, the surest basis for our research, and it is the study of dreams, more than any other study, that will convince us of the value of psychoanalysis and make us appreciate its usefulness in practice.[1]

Most dreams are quickly forgotten, generally even before the person wakes from sleep. Other dreams can be remembered next morning, but they die out gradually in the course of the day, until they have completely disappeared from the memory by evening. Yet there are other dreams that we can remember for years. This is frequently the case with the dreams of childhood, and with those which occur during a period of psychological treatment.

Whereas the same dreams do not generally keep coming back, some of them can repeat over more or less regular intervals, during a person's whole life or as long as a given psychological situation lasts. Sometimes it is the same dream reappearing in precisely the same way; sometimes only the principal theme remains the same while the details change. A young woman, who found herself in a difficult love situation, regularly dreamed, each Friday night for several years, that she had gone out of her house with-

---

1. *Cinq leçons sur la psychoanalyse*, p. 147

out realizing, until she had got out onto the street, that she had forgotten to put on her skirt. She did her best to cover her nakedness, but there was nothing much she could do and the passersbys all laughed at her.

Louis, who had never been in prison, often saw himself, in his dreams, in the position of a prisoner who had just been released from jail and didn't have a penny to his name and didn't know what to do with his new found freedom.

Obviously the insistence with which dreams recur is not without its meaning. In children, there is a frequent repetition of dreams in which the dominant motif is either a fall through empty space or a sense of flying in the air.

Such periodic dreams generally cease in keeping with the changes that occur in the psychological situation of the subject. The woman who dreamed of being undressed in the street will no longer have this dream once her love-life is better organized and ceases to embarrass her. Louis will no longer see himself as a penniless beggar fresh out of prison after a long psychological treatment has managed to adapt him better to the conditions of his existence.

IV. Manifest Content and Latent Ideas

The oracles of antiquity already knew how to distinguish between the manifest content and the latent ideas in the dream. Thus the Pharaoh dreamed of cows and sheaves of wheat, and Joseph interpreted them as years of abundance and years of famine to come. Psychoanalysis has developed a technique which might be termed *scientific* for determining the latent meaning of the dream. But the psychoanalytic interpretation of dreams must not be regarded as a universal key to dreams; the personal role of the interpreter and the dreamer always plays an important part.

As the language of the unconscious, the dream might be expected to express what the unconscious wants to say in the clearest possible manner. Since this is not actually the case, Freud deduces the presence of censorship in the unconscious expression. There are affective situations which are absolutely contrary to what is admitted by morality and the principles and attitudes which are inculcated by education. Rather than a function of the conscious ego, this censorship is a function of the unconscious superego. During sleep, when the control of the ego is relaxed, the unconscious is still not in a position to express its needs entirely without restrictions. Thus it has recourse to a symbolic language, in the dream. The images that the dream uses can be borrowed from the more or less recent experiences of real life, from reading, etc.

Here, by way of example, is the dream of a young lady as Freud describes it: She was with her husband at the theatre; one section of the orchestra was completely empty. Her husband told her that their friend Elise and her fiance had wanted to go to the theatre too, but had been able to find only rather poor seats that they preferred not to take. She was thinking what a shame that was.[2]

The manifest content of this dream is drawn from real life experiences of the recent past. Her friend Elise has recently become engaged. What is more, the lady who had the dream had been to the theatre a short time before, although a good many other patrons had been missing on the occasion — a fact which had caused her to wonder why they had not canceled their reservations.

But this is what Freud interprets as the latent meaning of the dream: "It was most foolish of me to marry so early in life. I can see from Elise's example that I would have lost nothing by waiting a bit longer." The hasty marriage is symbolized by the image of the location of the seats; marriage itself, by going to the theatre in the company of her husband. Freud also notes that all the other manifest elements of this dream are also the expression of latent

_____

2. *Introduction . . . ,* p. 136

ideas, more or less connected with the central theme as interpreted above.

In most dreams, we can recognize a principal latent theme and several secondary themes. Still the former does not always occupy the most important place in the manifest content. The psychologist must use a good deal of patience and great skill to discover it among the welter of secondary themes. According to Freud, these last appear with greater precision than the former, largely because of the element of censorship inhibiting what the unconscious would really like to say.

V. *Satisfaction of Repressed Desires*

The easiest dreams to interpret are, in Freud's thinking, those of children. Censorship is not yet at work here and there is little objective difference between the manifest content and the latent ideas. Often, the dream plays the role of guarding the child's slumber. It permits the realization of desires experienced in a waking state and not yet arrived at satisfaction. If the desires remained unsatisfied during the child's sleep, the sleep would easily be disturbed. Thus the child who has been refused a piece of candy he was asking for and who was disturbed at this refusal will dream that he is eating giant Hershey bars.

Even in the adult, the dream can fill this same role as guardian of sleep by giving satisfaction to the instinctual needs which went unsatisfied in the waking state. The person who eats too many spicy foods and then is thirsty in his sleep, will likely enough dream that he is drinking.[3] The chaste man regularly dreams of sex relations and the result is ejaculation.

But most of the time, under the influence of censorship, it is only in a disguised manner that the satisfaction of instinctual desires, particularly when it is a question of sex desires, takes

---

3. *Introduction* . . . , p. 148

place in the dream. Here is Freud's retelling of a dream that a respectable lady of fifty once had:

She went to the military hospital and told the man at the desk that she wanted to speak with the chief doctor: she had come to offer her services. But she emphasized the word "services" so strongly that the man at the desk understood immediately what kind of "services" she had in mind. The lady made her way into a large and dark room where there were a number of officers and military doctors seated about a table. She repeated her offer to a doctor who understood her meaning immediately. "I, and several other of the ladies and girls of Vienna are ready to be of service to the soldiers, officers and enlisted men alike, without any distinction as. . . ." At these words, she heard (in the dream of course) a murmur which prevented her from finishing her sentence. But the embarrassed and still smirking expression that came over the officers' face let her understand that they knew precisely what she meant. She continued her message, but each time she was on the point of expressing the sexual idea in some more precise way, the murmur interrupted her once again. Freud sees this as the activity of censorship, suppressing the passages that the lady's superego considered to be indecent.

Censorship, according to Freud is rarely manifest in such an open way, so naively, we might say, as in the dream just recounted. More generally it is at work in a more subtle way, imposing a series of attenuations and approximations and allusions to the real thinking. . . . Omission, modification, regrouping of materials; these are the effects of censorship and means by which dream messages are deformed.[4] A certain young person who makes much of his "purity" might well be prevented, by censorship, from satisfying his sexual needs, even in a dream. He can satisfy them only under a form that is so disguised that nothing short of analysis can unveil the fact that it is still a question of sexual satisfaction.

---

4. *Ibid.*, pp. 152-155

Many psychoanalysts, following the example set by their master, have come to look on all dream imagery as sex symbols. All elongated or pointed objects — canes, unbrellas, trees, knives, daggers, lances, sabers, guns, bayonnets, crayons, hammers, and also jet airplanes — are supposed to represent the genital organs of the male. The female genital organs are symbolized by anything that more or less closely resembles a receptacle: mines, ditches, caves, vases, bottles, boats, rooms, churches, etc.

We might well ask whether it is really experience that led Freud and the Freudian school to such pansexualism or if it is not rather their complex on sexualism that makes them attribute a sexual meaning to all dream imagery. In any case, once we admit such a long and disparate list of symbols as really being sexual in meaning, how can we help but find sexual conflict in the raw materials of every dream?

VI. *Laws of Dream Composition*

Freud believed that he could discover four laws at work in the elaboration of the dream. A knowledge of these laws is thus necessary for interpreting the dream. We must understand first of all that a dream can draw its important materials from anywhere, but it never does so without good reason. Thus it is not difficult to observe that a given dream image has been borrowed from a situation recently experienced by the dreamer; but it might very well be transferred into some distant time or place. We can discover persons we have known for a long time and places very far apart, geographically, all united in one and the same dream. The unconscious has established a bond between all the disparate elements: psychology has to find out what it is.

The *law of condensation* describes the fusion of several distinct images into one single image. Such a dream, in itself, is brief, poor, and laconic, compared with its breadth and richness of thought, says Freud. The person who appears in the dream has A's features, B's mannerisms, is something like C, and still he acts very much like D.[5] The same thing applies to a condensation of several localities or objects. In the process of interpretation, the problem is to discover what these persons or objects or localities all have in common. Condensation is effected under the influence of censorship, to make the dream more obscure in content: it is the psychologist's task to make it clear, to "decondense" it.

The *law of replacement* explains how censorship has substituted a secondary and more accessible image in the place of a latent image of great importance. The affective charge has been detached from its real object and replaced on a secondary object. It happens rather frequently that what is essential in the drama that is unfolding in the unconscious is hardly even represented in the manifest content of the dream, whereas the details that have no particular bearing on the real meaning frequently occupy a very important place. A man dreams that he is being attacked by a big dog whom he is trying to choke. Analysis reveals that this dog is more or less similar to the dog that belongs to a certain person whom the unconscious considers as an enemy and would like to get rid of. The superego cannot approve of homicide, and thus it is the dog that is being strangled instead of his owner.

The third law Freud calls the *law of dramatization*. It means that ideas and abstract sensations have been translated into concrete images. The dream actually contains only visual images, even when it is involved with theoretical questions. Let us take, for example, the case of a young man, torn between his moral principles that are very much a matter of family honor and his passionate love for a married woman. How will his dream activity translate this moral and psychological activity? The young man will dream, for example, that he is at a crossroads. One of the roads leads back towards his family home, while the other leads towards a neighborhood which, as he remembers it, is closely bound up with something erotic. It might be a farmyard, where

---

5. *Ibid.*, p. 190

as a child, he first saw animals mating, an experience which has long departed from his conscious mind, but still remains vividly in his unconscious memory. The dream almost never represents any really logical relationships. In this respect it is like painting or sculpture, which both give a picture of what is experienced.

Whereas dramatization explains the passage from abstract to concrete, the *law of symbolization* explains how a concrete image can take the place of another equally concrete image. In dramatization, it is impossible to set up any fixed rules. The conflict of the young man described above is expressed by a crossroads. But it could just as well be translated into any other image that is equally adapted to expressing the concept of duality, the obligation to choose, hesitation. Symbols, on the other hand, seem to be the same among all men and all nations. Jung, more than Freud, has contributed much to discovering a universal symbolism, such as is encountered in popular language, legends, folklore, etc. This symbolism can never be reduced to the rigid sexualism of Freudian symbolism.

* * * *

We might very well ask why the dream does not speak in a clear, Cartesian logic. Why does it have to have recourse to such obscure symbols? In order to understand this we have to recall that the thought process of those who are called "primitives" do not function according to the rules of formal logic; in fact Levy-Bruhl and other sociologists have developed a concept of "prelogical thinking." These people express their thinking very naturally, without effort or artifice, in symbols and images. Something very much the same is true of many of our best poets and painters. And the most symbolic of all, in our civilization, is the language of music. We can thus consider that clear speech, in conformity to the rules of rational logic, is the work of the ego in an already well developed stage.

We have admitted that Freud was not wrong in considering the unconscious as a "primitive," provided of course that this term is understood to have no pejorative connotations. During sleep when the ego has ceased its activity, the psyche normally reverts to the language of image and symbol. How can we help but recognize that this language is frequently much richer than our more civilized ways of speech?

We have two forms of thinking available to us, writes Jung: directed thinking and dream or fantasy. The former works in view of communication through the elements of language; it is hard and exhausting. But the second one works effortlessly, spontaneously we might say, through means of a material which it finds ready-made, and guided by unconscious motives. The former creates its own new acquisitions and adaptations and imitations of reality, at the same time making an effort to react upon them. The latter, however, turns away from the real, setting free all its subjective tendencies and never producing anything that can serve as adaptation.[6]

VII. *Compensation*

Having observed that the child's dream is presented as the realization of an unsatisfied desire, Freud, with his habitual sense of system, deduces that every dream expresses a desire that has been repressed by censorship. Whereas in children the repressed desire is manifest in its full clarity in the dream, the adult psyche expresses the real message under a disguise.

There are not many psychologists today, even among the Freudians, who have remained faithful to this over-simplified idea of the dream. Moreover, the master himself, in the later years of his life, was obliged to recognize that not all dreams have this satisfaction of repressed desires for their object. In saying that the dream tends towards either the satisfaction of an impulse or the liquidation of a conflict, or the statement of a doubt, or the

---

6. *Metamorphoses* . . . , p. 67

realization of a project, Freudianism of later years is much closer to the truth.

For Adler, the dream reveals the innermost personality of the dreamer. It reveals his deep-seated attitudes with regard to others, as well as the traits of his character and his neurotic deviations.

Jung while preserving the essential points of Freud's and Adler's teaching, believes that there are two primary functions in the dream: compensation of conscious attitudes that are too unilateral, and what he calls "prospection."

* * * *

We can never insist strongly enough on the fact that the psyche is an indivisible totality. Conscious and unconscious, far from being two independent universes which meet only accidentally, are mutually complementary; they compensate for each other's insufficiencies. It is no mere chance that the unconscious chooses to express itself in dream imagery. This is moreover not a question of some radically autonomous function of the unconscious mind. The dream almost always implies some elements that are complementary to the conscious psychic situation.

The ego is generally oriented towards the outside world, towards some tangible project to be accomplished, and thus frequently something short-range. In the heat of activity, it can easily forget its own limitations and almost completely identify with the personage, the "mask." In an effort to vindicate its rights as the neglected party in this real objective psychic situation, the unconscious intervenes by way of dream imagery. The compensation which results can often consist in the satisfaction of a repressed desire. But it can also be something quite different. As Jung puts it, it is not easy to determine which of the laws is at work in dream compensation. Compensation, in its essence, is intimately bound up with the entire nature of the individual. The number of possible compensations is beyond reckoning, inexhaustible, even though experience permits us to crystallize some of the fundamental principles.[7]

Here, by way of example, are two dreams, cited from the repertory of Carl Jung. The dreamer is a man of high social position and very ambitious. The son of poor peasants, he is very gifted and managed to achieve a rapid and brilliant social success. But he is not satisfied; he wants something more.[8]

1. I found myself in my home town. On the street was a group of little peasant children with whom I had gone to school. Pretending not to recognize them, I passed them by. Then I heard one of them saying, "It's not too often that he comes back to the town."

2. I was very busy because I was about to go on a trip. I tried to get the baggage together and couldn't find a thing. Time was running short; the train was ready to leave. Finally I did manage to get everything together and dash out onto the street. But I noticed there that I had forgotten my briefcase with its important papers. I went back to look for it, running and out of breath. I finally found it and started running to the station, but could hardly move one foot ahead of the other. Finally, in a supreme effort, I threw myself past the station door, only to see the train already leaving the station.

It was a long train, and it made an S-shaped picture along the track, I was thinking that if the engineer did not pay attention and gave full steam before the locomotive reached a straight stretch of track, the rest of the cars would still be on the curve and the acceleration would derail them. As a matter of fact, the engineer did give full steam; I tried to scream at him, but the cars still on the curve began swaying back and forth terribly, and finally did derail. It was a terrible catastrophe and I awoke trembling all over.

The images in the first dream are easy to understand, pro-

---

7. *L'homme* . . . , p. 239
8. *L'homme* . . . , pp. 284-285

vided that the interpreter is familiar with the individual's life and history. The dream is reminding him of his humble origins, which he himself wants to forget as far as possible.

The second dream is more complex and demands a more attentive analysis. The dream describes the excessive precipitation which impels the dreamer in question to rise constantly higher along the social ladder. Just like the engineer who pays no attention to the cars behind him, the dreamer was paying no attention to his own inner psychic structures. The derailment symbolizes a warning: in going too fast he is courting catastrophe.

It is very significant that no symbolism of sexual origin is to be found in these two dreams. On the other hand, it is obviously impossible to interpret them correctly without a thorough knowledge of the conscious situation of the subject. Dream symbols are frequently the same in the case of extremely different individuals. But there is a good deal of suppleness about them. That is why the most experienced psychologist cannot honestly play the role of drawing room oracle in dream interpretations. His experience teaches him that a given dream image symbolizes a given psychic situation. But it is almost always indispensable for a really correct interpretation to have an acquaintance with the dreamer's conscious situation, with all the details of his personal individuality.

VIII. *Prospective Function*

We know that the ancients were interested in dreams primarily because of their prophetic perspectives. Even today, there are many people who look to dreams for a knowledge of the secrets of the future. Depth psychology does not completely frustrate these hopes. The psychology of Adler in particular stresses this role of the dream and claims to find frequent reference to future events in dreams. Jung's theories are not essentially different, though they are better developed. The "prospective function," as he describes it[9] presents itself under the form of an anticipation, rising up within the unconscious, of future conscious activity; it conjures up a preparatory sketch, a broad outline, a working blueprint. Its symbolic content occasionally involves the solution to a conflict.

Certain possibilities, certain chances, certain dangers seem to be recognized in the unconscious before the ego is aware of them. Thus the dream of the social climber discussed in the preceding paragraph obviously contains a warning. If the dreamer does not moderate his ambitions, which are going far beyond the real potential of his libido, he will derail, just like the wagons in the train that accelerated too rapidly. As a matter of fact the individual in question did not listen to the warning, and thus he became the prey of a psychic exhaustion which put a brutal end to what looked like a brilliant career.

Still in the "prospective" dreams studied by psychologists, we never encounter a real prophecy, a prediction, properly so called, of future events, especially events that do not have a direct bearing on the subjective situation of the dreamer. The conscious ego is in a position to discover other solutions to the situation than those that are presaged by the dream. By changing his conduct, the social climber discussed above could very easily have escaped the catastrophe that was "predicted."

Still it is probable that telepathic phenomena, whose reality seems incontestable, do exercise their influence on certain dreams. I have had frequent occasion to verify the fact that the dream can represent, with great profusion of detail, events that take place at the same moment, some distance away. As for the future, we have no valid proof for claiming that it can be predicted by a dream. Supposing that such proofs do exist, we would have to conclude that there were processes in play whose nature is still unexplored by psychology.

---

9. *L'homme* . . . , pp. 241-242

IX. *Reduction Function*

People are sometimes astonished by the fact that virtuous and pious persons can have dreams of such shocking obscenity. Men who are very concerned with their respectability see themselves, in their dreams, in particularly humiliating situations. A person who recognizes only rational principles, and claims to be completely atheistic, sometimes has dreams that are manifestly mystic in content. There can obviously be no question here of concluding that the conscious attitude of virtue, respectability, or irreligion is false, or that the dreamer's "true nature" is obscene or vulgar or mystic. That would mean claiming that only the unconscious always houses the full truth — and this is an indefensible position.

Freud has very properly observed that, in such cases, the dream exercises a "reductive" function, which partially overlaps what Jung calls the "compensatory" function. The subject is being reminded that he is living in an illusion by trusting only in his conscious attitudes. The obscene dreams of the rigorously virtuous person do not reveal his hypocrisy: they only point up the fact that he has neglected to integrate sexuality into his adult personality. This sexuality is thus repressed and can make known its demands only through a series of images that are particularly foreign to the personality as he wills it to be. In the case of the atheist, his mystic dreams are a sign of the repression of the religious function in his psyche.

X. *Rules for Interpretation*

No dream is ever the result of the unconscious mind alone. It always draws a more or less important part of its materials from the conscious situation of the individual, for which it tends to compensate. Thus it is never advisable to undertake the exploration of an individual's unconscious mind without first having made a thorough study, together with the dreamer, of all the conscious elements he is aware of. Sometimes, the conscious elements themselves are enough to reveal the meaning of the dream. Still, in more important dreams, the role of the unconscious is largely preponderant, and the greater this role, the more difficult the interpretation. Only an experienced psychologist, well versed in the archetypes of the collective unconscious, can successfully undertake such a task.

We must never forget that every interpretation is, in the last analysis, only an hypothesis which needs to be confirmed by the analysis of other dreams, which equally reveal the same unconscious situation. Thus Joseph interpreted two of the Pharaoh's dreams, before he could predict what was going to happen. It is important to realize, too, that the dreamer is never simply a passive transmitter in the service of the collective unconscious. He always assumes an active role; and this makes it indispensable to understand his personal situation, before attempting to interpret any of his dreams.

How, practically speaking, is the interpretation of a dream to proceed? Obviously it is never merely a question of consulting some list of symptoms and images. Even the most universal dream symbols, those which are encountered most frequently, can never be interpreted without extreme caution. The psychologist, moreover, must not tell the dreamer himself what the real meaning of the dream should be until he is in a position to understand and profit from it. Not infrequently a premature awareness of some deepseated unconscious situations will give rise to serious traumas in the subject, sometimes even more serious than those which were to be remedied.

In his theory of associations, Freud has discovered the method which all modern psychologists now use, with more or less individual application.

Plato and Aristotle already observed that secret relationships existed between words, images, and ideas. Locke, Condillac,

Hamilton, Stuart Mill, Taine, Ribot — these men took such relationships as the central point of their psychology. Considered first of all as a simple mechanism, the bond of associations, thanks particularly to the work of Ribot, gradually came to assume the faculty of revealing affective relationships. If a given word or image easily evokes another word or image, apparently without any real resemblance to the former, this is not the result of chance; it argues the existence of an intimate bond between the two on the affective plane.

The psychologist asks the dreamer what, in his mind, a given dream image evokes. The answer to this first question is obviously not the key to the hidden meaning of the dream. The process must go on from image to image, until it seems probable that the keystone of the dream's whole construction has been arrived at, that is, the unconscious source of the dream. The image which occupies the preponderant place in the manifest content of the dream generally does not reveal the essentials of the latent content and thus frequently the series of associations, so elaborately constructed by the psychologist, ends in no results. Then it becomes necessary to analyze all the other elements of the dream in the same way, even those that are apparently most insignificant. Frequently only the analysis of other dreams will reveal the real meaning of a dream that is, for the moment, undecipherable.

Freudian psychologists generally practice what is called free association, the individual under analysis being free to take his dream images as the point of departure for any other direction he sees fit. This process is necessarily very slow; only after many painful impasses is there generally any chance of finding the right road. In an effort to alleviate these problems, many psychotherapists believe they must assume a more active role. They try to direct these associations towards what seem to be their essential elements. In acting thus, they cannot, obviously, exclude all possibility of deception. The psychologists might easily take something for essential that is really only secondary: the unconscious never yields its secrets without a struggle. Still it does seem that this last method, applied by many careful and experienced psychologists, is more workable than the practice of free association. But no matter which method is being used, it is important to avoid hasty results.

10 psychic conflicts

The psyche is not like the stagnant water of a pond, or a dead sea. It is like the mountain torrent, a sea in storm. But it is best compared to troubled waters, the crossroads of many contrary currents.

I. Divisions and Discord

The ideal would obviously call for perfect harmony between conscious and unconscious, among all the different tendencies of both of these sources of activity, among all the various complexes. But this is, unfortunately, a purely abstract ideal, impossible to realize in the concrete conditions of humanity. The most surprising factor, at first sight, is the fact that these discords between the different components of the psyche are not only inevitable, but even necessary. As Jung describes it, it is not until a person "enters into collision with himself" that he can have the reassuring impression that he is really himself.

Still, there are no grounds for complacency in this state of internal division. Conflicts can be a great blessing for the soul, but only if a genuine effort is made to surmount them. If an individual is passively resigned to them, they degenerate into neuroses such as hysteria or schizophrenia. For them to be a worthwhile stimulus in the process of self-realization, the ego has to be strong enough to dominate and direct them, and to control the anxiety to which they give rise.

It is always most important to understand that neurosis, the disease of the soul, is not a particularly "strong" psychic conflict, but a conflict that has become static, because it remains unresolved. There is no paradox in the observation that while there has to be conflict we must do our best to stop the conflict, realizing full well, in advance, that there will never be any authentic existence, in the present condition of humanity, without new conflicts immediately coming in to take the place of those we have succeeded, not in suppressing, but in transcending.

II. Conflict, Cause and Result of Civilization

If the psyche were free of conflict, man would never have risen above the level of animal life. Hegel is right in saying that, phenomenologically, what distinguishes man from animal is the immensity of his desires, which are never content with the immediate satisfaction of his instinct. But the materialists are wrong in concluding that this distinction is a very fine one, so very fine that human transcendence is almost denied. It is only because the animal soul is without conflict, that is, static, that it is not susceptible to progress and creativity — the twin sources of civilization.

Civilization is not only the result but also a source of conflict. The more civilized a man becomes, the more aware he is of the deep-seated lack of unity within the innermost depths of his psyche. Civilization involves a more and more perfect mastery and control of whatever is primitive within the soul; but the primitive element never yields without a struggle. Particularly in a hypercivilized society, this conflict threatens to be more dangerous. Any attempts to chain something primitive, completely and once and for all, inevitably involves the almost certain prospect of violent revolt.

* * * *

Practically speaking, psychic conflict can take on the most diverse forms. A certain individual feels an attraction towards a life of prayer and meditation that is to be found only in the monastery. But he also experiences strong urgings towards a "normal" sex life. Another person wants to devote himself wholly to music, but he would also like to earn enough money to support the woman he loves; he realizes that he has very unlikely prospects of doing this as an artist. For very many men, attachment to their mother or love for their wife are factors in a painful conflict. For modern Christians, it is often most difficult to reconcile a strict fidelity to their Church with the equally imperious obligation of keeping up with the present-day world. It is never an easy matter to serve eternal and temporal interests with a like generosity.

In eras of greater stability, conflicts are not generally so numerous and acute as they are in our own tormented and frantic civilization, where every set of values is called into question and men constantly face new and brighter prospects for bettering their position. The values of the civilization of tomorrow are a source of worry and frequently of fascination, even though their general outlines are not yet too precise. We can feel that many of our traditional values are enjoying only a momentary reprieve before being once and for all relegated to the storehouse of history.

Still we do not know what will be rejected and what will survive in our new civilization. But what is most confusing of all is the fact that among the values which we believe or know are destined to disappear, many are still indispensable for our present society. Whether we like it or not, we are rooted in this agonizing civilization. In wanting to be emancipated prematurely, we run the risk of being fatally uprooted. Lack of orientation in time is much more harmful than lack of orientation in space. But, on the other hand, those who hide before the breath of the new way of things, clinging fast to traditions that are about to die, expose themselves to the danger of sclerosis.

* * * *

The conflict under question here is not purely of the rational order, nor is it a purely theoretical speculation. In discussing this conflict, we are standing, from the outset, at the very heart of the existential drama. Man sees himself involved personally with everything about him. Unfortunately, it is not always possible for him to resolve this conflict once and for all, by a final and definitive choice.

Towards the age of twenty, John was strongly torn between his aspirations towards the contemplative life and his love for a young lady. He chose love. But his need for contemplative solitude was always there and it became even stronger as the routines and monotony of everyday living began to wear upon his married love. Thus there was a more or less permanent conflict between his aspirations and his professional and family obligations. Had he chosen the monastery, the conflict would probably have been just as intense: he would have always had a more or less compelling attraction for a woman's tenderness and affection.

Suppose that such an important and enthusiastic choice could actually mobilize the affective energy to the point where the other alternative would begin to lose all its attractiveness, even cease to be the source of any regrets. This actually happens, let us say. But even then it would be a mistake to suppose that the individual was free from all psychic conflict. John would no longer experience any nostalgia for his contemplative aspirations. But very probably he would have to face new conflicts, for example, in the area of his various family and professional obligations.

More to be pitied are the weakhearted and overcautious people who, from fear of renouncing one of the alternatives, refuse to make a choice. They make up the greatest part of the psychiatrist's clientele, because their conflicts, instead of being resolved, have simply been repressed in the unconscious.

III. *Unconscious Conflicts*

For conscious conflicts it is relatively easy to find adequate solutions. At least, the better developed personalities will succeed in this respect. They do not shrink before the obligation of making a positive choice. They do what they can to safeguard, as far as possible, the valuable elements of the alternative that is eliminated. Without too much difficulty, they keep the conflict from shunting over to a siding and degenerating into a neurosis. Things are not so simple when the conflict takes place in the unconscious.

The very existence of an unconscious conflict is revealed only through the conscious symptoms. Here is a man who cannot decide whether or not to accept a position offered to him. Another young man has been courting a young lady whom he loves, but he can see a thousand reasons for not proposing yet. Is this always a conscious conflict? Pehaps. The psychologist, before concluding that there is an unconscious conflict, must always consider this possibility. Certain characteristic traits will quickly show what the problem really is.

Faced with a conscious conflict, the subject experiences a sense of uneasiness or anxiety that is more or less intense because he must choose between several possibilities, each of which offers certain attractions. This uneasiness becomes particularly painful when the attraction of the various possibilities is approximately equal in force. But things are very much different when it is the result of unconscious conflict.

Marcel would like to marry, but he cannot decide to take the step; still he does not feel attracted to any other vocation that cannot be reconciled with the married state. Frances abandons her position as a social worker in which she had been enjoying considerable success. Her decision does not come from the fact she has found, or hopes to find, another job somewhere else, better adapted to her tastes and capabilities. It is rather that an indefinable anxiety haunts her in the performance of her present work, and it is this anxiety she hopes to avoid by leaving the job. She takes another occupation: the anxiety persists. It is clear that this anxiety has its source within the psyche, and not in the external conditions of her work.

Apparently, the anxiety of unconscious conflict is without any motive, that is, the motive is not known to the ego. In mild cases, education, or even self-education, can surmount the obstacles that this unresolved unconscious conflict engenders. But if the problems are handled poorly or not soon enough, the conflict grows worse and threatens to turn into neurosis.

IV. *Fundamental Conflict*

It sometimes seems that, underlying all the particular conscious or unconscious conflicts, there is a "fundamental conflict" within the soul. The primitive religions, in which experiences of a psychological nature always play an important role, all speak in terms of a combat which is going on in the soul, between the forces of light and the forces of darkness. The same insight is to be found again in the various Christian heresies inspired by dualism and, with many more nuances, even in orthodox Christianity. The Apocalypse of John offers several particularly majestic tableaux of the combats between Christ and Antichrist. We are certainly not incorrect in seeing them as an image of world history. But the Fathers of the Church already understood that the symbols used by the Evangelist are a much more faithful representation of the history of the individual soul.

Freud, very legitimately, is looking for a psychological explanation to the conflicts which upset the depths of the psyche. He sees the origin of this fundamental conflict in the constraint which the superego (that is, the social constraints which have become unconscious) claims to exercise over the instinctual impulses which will not tolerate any such control. We have already spoken of the superego; there is no point in repeating our opinions of it here. We believe, with Karen Horney, that, in many neurotics, there actually is such a conflict between the instinctual impulses and the social superego. Still this is not a question of the fundamental conflict, but rather of a secondary phenomenon, bound up with the neurosis.

In explaining this fundamental conflict, Jung uses the symbols of animus and anima. In human beings, these principles of masculinity and femininity coexist. Normally, in the conscious psyche of the man, animus is predominant, whereas in the woman it is anima. The presence of anima in the man's unconscious, and animus in the woman's, helps to reestablish a sense of equilibrium. The result, among other salutary functions, is the possibility of a mutual understanding between man and woman. Animus and anima always remain distinct in an individual, and thus there is a permanent conflict in the psyche; this is the source of the existential dialectic. Instead of being a dialectic, the conflict can, however, become static, and thus neurotic, if the man becomes too masculine or the woman too feminine.

Karen Horney thinks that the fundamental conflict, which she calls the basic conflict, results from the opposition between conscious and unconscious attitudes towards other people.

* * * *

Freud, Jung, Horney, *etc.*, all present an excellent analysis of certain deep-seated conflicts. Still, their theories are far from being verifiable in every detail. This leads us to believe that none of them has actually discovered the real fundamental conflict. Philosophy, in its turn, has a right to go beyond mere psychological experience; philosophy can, it seems, look into the nature of the soul and see its basic lack of unity as the real fundamental conflict. And in this lack of unity, the Christian might easily enough recognize the consequences of original sin.

V. Conflict and Anxiety

Contemporary philosophers who are more or less faithful followers of Kierkegaard, tend to credit anxiety with a very important function in any really authentic existence. They do not always distinguish explicitly enough between neurotic anxiety and the anxiety that arises from what we would call normal psychic conflict. The former, like neurosis itself, is more destructive than creative.

For Kierkegaard, man suffers anxiety because he is a sinner "by nature." Anxiety and sin are thus two correlative notions. Sin holds an attraction because of the pleasure it holds out to him and the apparent assertion of his personal freedom that it seems to offer. But at the same time it terrifies us by all the disastrous consequences it involves, by the disorders it gives rise to, by the opposition and enmity it establishes between man and God. Torn between two alternatives by the attraction and the horror of sin, man experiences anxiety.

Kierkegaard, obviously enough, could not dream of the discoveries of the new psychology, three quarters of a century later. In his analyses he never refers explicitly to the unconscious mind. But it is obvious nonetheless, at least for the modern day psychologists, that the conflict which results from the attraction and horror of sin does not generally take place on the plane of consciousness. Many people who suffer this anxiety, neurotic or otherwise, have no conscious sense of sin, and even deny its existence. But the unconscious mind is equipped with sources of information that go back much much farther than the "positive morality" of the nineteenth century. It is primarily among those who deny the existence of sin that existential anxiety generally turns into something neurotic.

* * * *

The answer to this anxiety is obviously not resignation, any more than in the case of psychic conflict. Nor must we hope, as some priests and psychoanalysts want us to hope, that we can put an end to this turmoil within by suppressing one of the terms of the conflict from which this anxiety has sprung.

In referring to the "classic" case of conflict between flesh and spirit, too many spiritual directors advise us to master the flesh, so that the spirit will acquire a full freedom for the pursuit of its own proper objectives. The only real result of such tactics is to divert a conflict that is developing in the conscious mind, into the unconscious, and thereby considerably aggravate it.

The behavior of certain psychoanalysts is hardly more intelligent. Their doctrinal prejudices make them see biological instincts as the only natural dynamics of the psyche; if these instincts enter into conflict with morality or the other demands of the "spirit," and thereby give rise to anxiety, the analytic technique can restore these instincts to their full freedom. They hope thereby to suppress whatever is contrary to "nature." But the spirit cannot be chained, or suppressed any more than the flesh can be.

Andre was a young man who had been brought up according to strict Christian principles. Very early he had been taught to see sex as one of the worst dangers and occasions of sin. As a seminarian, he made a conscientious effort to follow all the advice of his spiritual director to subdue the flesh. The director was very satisfied with the results, since his charge no longer experienced any specifically "sexual" temptations and could even practically forget that he was sexed at all. But then the young man grew more and more distracted, incapable of fixing his attention on either study or prayer; his professors and classmates all considered him as "terribly lazy" and made fun of him. Next came doubts of a religious nature, which increased his feeling of uneasiness, and this turned into a real anxiety. Andre was sent away from the seminary. Acting on a friend's advice, he went to see a psychoanalyst, a very orthodox Freudian. This doctor had no difficulty in discovering that, not only the distractions, the lack of energy, and the great indecision that Andre suffered, but also his religious doubts, were a direct consequence of repressing the libido. Interpreting this in a strictly sexual sense, he set about liquidating the religious superego which was inhibiting his patient. When the process of liquidation seemed to be far enough advanced, he recommended masturbation, then a "go" at a prostitute. The final result of this liquidation process was hardly less lamentable than the problem itself.

A few months later, when according to the psychologist, everything was "back in good order" the young man fell prey to a new anxiety more violent than all his former psychic conflicts, manifestly and seriously neurotic. Later psychoanalysis, conducted by a different psychologist, was to reveal that the conflicts Andre had experienced in the seminary were the result of a "superego" oriented religion, but that his whole spiritual life and morality had no connection with the superego. The psychoanalyst who had recommended that he listen only to the voice of his instinctual impulses had seriously thwarted the spiritual functions of his psyche. This time, it was the spiritual functions that underwent the repression and demanded some abnormal satisfaction. Andre's new anxiety actually led him to observe some obviously superstitious rites and ritual practices that were absolutely contrary to the promptings of his conscious ego. It is a serious mistake to believe that instinct alone is capable of repression. The higher psychic functions are just as susceptible.

VI. *Repression*

The time has come to make a brief investigation of what depth psychology understands by repression. In everyday language, the the repressed person has become synonymous with the inhibited, the over-reserved, the man who is "bent back upon himself." Since the time of Freud, psychology has found a more "technical" meaning.

Repression is a psychic process which prevents certain facts from penetrating into the conscious mind; it rejects them, "represses" them in the unconscious. We can voluntarily repress memories, things we have seen or experienced, that are disagreeable to us. Such a repression is always more or less superficial and it takes only a slight impulse, from within or from without, to bring these repressed memories back into the plane of consciousness.

Real repression, the repression that plays such a big role in Freudian psychology, is unconscious. The superego, through the medium of censorship, rejects certain psychic facts into the unconscious, without the ego being able to intervene or even be aware of the process. There is thus no room for surprise in the fact that, for Freud, the primary object of repression, properly so called, is the sex tendencies, particularly the infantile sex tendencies.

As in all of Freud's sexual speculations, there is a large element of truth in this conception of repression. There is no denying the fact that sexual impulses are frequently the object of repression. This will be true even more frequently in sociological milieux that are characterized by a narrow and rigid moralism in sex matters, based on fear of sin or on taboos that have no underlying connection with any mystique.

Still, the other tendencies of the psyche can also be repressed. Thus, for example, a tyrannical mother who, in order to keep her child close to home, turns into a mother hen, frequently succeeds in repressing her child's ego instincts. Repression always results in a regression to an infantile psychic stage. We shall place great emphasis, in chapter XVI, on the serious consequences of repressing the religious tendencies.

* * * *

Contrary to a rather widespread prejudice, we feel that repression is not to be condemned out of hand. The ideal would naturally be for all the tendencies and all the instincts to be mobilized as a group, by the process of sublimation, in the service of the higher human aspirations. But, unfortunately, we know from experience that such an ideal is rarely to be attained. Many men do not have the necessary psychic resources for effecting a real sublimation. And it seems that no man is in a position to sublimate all his instinctual impulses. Now, both in the interests of the individual and those of society, it is certainly not desirable to give absolute freedom to all the instincts that we have not succeeded in sublimating. What can we do then, except repress them? Despite all its disadvantages, repression in many cases still appears to be the lesser evil. Only when it gives rise to a real neurosis must we attempt to liquidate it any at any price. As long as it is only a normal psychic conflict, we need to weigh the pros and cons, then decide upon liquidation or repression.

VII. What to Do

Concretely, what can and ought we to do when we are faced with a psychic conflict.

We have already said that, under pain of a progressive dislocation of personality, we cannot recommend passive resignation. Every conflict calls for an appropriate solution, even if we are sure beforehand that the solution we find will, in its turn, become a factor in a new conflict. This, after all, is the fundamental law of the existential dialectic.

In many cases, particularly when it is a question of persons whose ego is very strong, conflicts can be overcome without outside help, by a succession of proper choices and decisions. Stimulated by existential anxiety, a person will pass from one psychic conflict to another, and this is the only way he can actualize all his potential. Neither saints nor sages can live in an Olympian serenity which spares them every sense of anxiety, every interior conflict. Quite simply, their conflicts situate them on a higher plane, incomprehensible and inaccessible to the common run of humanity.

In many cases, however, the individual is too much bound up with his conflicts to be able to surmount them dialectically by his own power. Without effective help on the part of an educator or psychologist, the unsurmounted conflict might easily become fixed and thus degenerate into a neurosis. If it is an undeniable fact that a soul in conflict is not necessarily a neurotic soul, it is just as certain that every conflict that remains unsolved is raw material for a neurosis.

We cannot, unfortunately, advise all individuals who are incapable of solving their own conflicts, to visit their psycho-analyst or undergo some other form of psychotherapy. This is always long and costly and must necessarily remain the therapy for neurotics in the strict sense of the word. To escape the danger of neurosis, a particularly acute danger in our poorly oriented civilization, we must generalize the profession of the psychologist not as a doctor but as a teacher. Our home and school education is directed almost exclusively to the rational side of the soul, whereas only a training in the affective life can put the psyche into a situation which will allow a man to develop fully and live a happy life. And it is important, too, for every educator to acquire at least some rudimentary knowledge of depth psychology.

The psychologist can be of great help in discovering the real nature of the conflicts which inhibit the individual and isolating their unconscious components. He can help to find a more fruitful use for the affective energy that has gone unused; he can teach the subject to live with his conflicts, to make them dynamic instead of static.

Frigid women, lazy and easily distracted children, the timid, the awkward, the unpredictable — these people are not generally so sick that they need to be treated. They are people who are subject to a psychic conflict that is poorly resolved, and whose libido needs to be educated.

11 the sick soul

In beginning the study of the sick soul, let us say once again that the soul in a state of conflict is not necessarily sick. It is rather the absence of conflict which should cause concern to the psychologist, whose first objective is not the cure but rather the promotion of the normal psyche.

Still, diseases of the soul do exist and they are at least as frequent and as serious as those of the body. In relatively uncivilized societies, only madness and "being out of one's mind" are considered as mental diseases. These are generally attributed to the maleficent influence and activity of demons, to "possession." But still, at least in our civilization, there are numerous psychic diseases — and they can be very serious — that cannot possibly be considered merely as "madness." They are called "neuroses." It even seems that they are becoming more and more frequent, gradually, as Western civilization advances along the paths it has been travelling for the past two or three centuries.

In the last decades of the nineteenth century, when the triumph of materialism in the scientific domain could no longer be contested, doctors and psychologists looked upon mental sickness as merely a disease of the brain. This was the era in which thought itself was considered as a "secretion of the brain." It took the developments of psychoanalysis to establish the specific character of psychic malady.

I. Real Neurosis

Materialistic as the *philosophy* of Freud might have been, as a scientist he was too ingenious an investigator into human behavior to miss the specificity, in fact, the quasi-autonomy, of psychic life. Quite logically, he was forced to recognize the psychogenetic character of neurosis as well. In our day, there are only a few backward-looking thinkers who still question what is clear evidence in the eyes of the great majority of psychologists.

Neurasthenia, anxiety neurosis, and hypochondria Freud calls "real" neuroses. None of the three he claims, is really psychic in origin, but all of them result from "real" physiological troubles in the sex instinct. Thus, anxiety neurosis is supposed to be caused directly either by sexual continence or by the practice of *coitus interruptus*. Neurasthenia is supposed to result from any of several sexual abuses, particularly excessive masturbation. Hypochondria, which is characterized by the indefinability of its symptoms in different organs, is supposed to be due to a poor regulation of the sex function. A true child of his age, Freud went so far as to presume the existence of "sexual chemical substances."

Today, even among Freud's disciples, there are only a very few who would profess the existence of actual neuroses such as the master conceived them. And naturally no one believes in the "sexual chemical substances." It is biology itself which, thanks to its own remarkable progress, has furnished the proper antidote for much of the dogmatic biologism of past ages.

For our part, we believe that there are some neurotic troubles whose cause is "real," but the cause is always psychological in nature.

II. Psychoneurosis

Freud studied particularly two psychoneuroses: hysteria and obsessional neurosis. In the logic of his system, these also take on a more or less sexual character, but much less openly than those he calls "real" neuroses. Psychoneuroses are supposed to be the consequence of repressing the sex instinct, the libido being bound up in complexes. Whereas the "real" neurosis can generally be cured by reestablishing the normal sex activity, the psychoneurosis demands psychonalysis, properly so called.

In reality, as we have said above, all neuroses are psychoneuroses. But their psychological causes can be either really present or dating back to a more or less distant past.

$$* \quad * \quad * \quad *$$

The symptoms by which obsessional neurosis is most frequently recognized are an irresistible impulse to gestures or acts which the subject can neither explain nor rationally justify. The obsessed person is preoccupied, or even haunted, by ideas which have no real interest for him. He is obliged, against his will, to scrutinize and investigate, as if these trifles with which he is obsessed were the most important and vital business of his whole life.[1] It does no good to advise him to stop thinking about it, to get interested in some more reasonable things. He is perfectly convinced of that himself, but he cannot do it.

A certain person, before retiring each night, has to turn off the bathroom faucet fifteen times. If he happens to forget this, he cannot get to sleep. Another person, in dressing or undressing, has to follow a strict order, as if it were a sacred rite: first the left sleeve, then the right sleeve, etc. Without being able to say why, he feels that even the slightst modification in this ritual would be followed by some terrible personal catastrophe, something he could not bear to face. Educated and intelligent people find themselves totally incapable of crossing the street, for instance, generally some particular street.

Frequently the obsessed patient will begin to doubt even the most obvious decisions he has made.

---

1. Freud. *Introduction* . . . , p. 280

Here is Freud's description of a case of obsession which he observed.[2] A young lady of thirty would keep rushing out of her bedroom into the adjoining room, several times a day. In the next room, she would stand at a predetermined spot on the rug, always the same spot, right in front of the table which stood in the very middle of the room. Then she would smile at the maid and give her an order of some kind, or simply send her out of the room. Then, she would rush headlong back into her bedroom. When she was asked why she acted this way, she invariably answered that she did not know, that it was something stronger than her. Only psychoanalysis could uncover the secret motives behind such bizarre behavior.

The characteristic trait of obsessed people, and for that matter of all neurotics, generally is that, excepting for the area affected by their neurosis, they can behave in a perfectly normal fashion. This marks them off from the real cases of "madness."

* * * *

Hysteria is the first of the neuroses in which psychiatry became interested. It was on the basis of psychiatric studies that Dr. Freud first elaborated his system, little by little.

The characteristic note of hysteria is a preoccupation with "an imaginary sickness." Its symptoms are actually produced by suggestion, particularly autosuggestion. There is no question here of any deliberate malingering, since the process of autosuggestion in the hysterical patient, takes place entirely within the unconscious, and thus he is the first to believe in the objective reality of what he feels within himself.

The symptoms of hysteria are most often somatic: epilepsy, stigmata, and other lesions, acute headache, choking, cramps, etc. Professor Lhermitte, a strong Catholic, has devoted a remarkable book to the study of hysteria in the false mystics.[3]

---

2. *Introduction*, p. 283
3. *Vrais et faux mystiques*

The anxiety neurosis is distinguished from the normal existential anxiety described in the preceding chapter, by its more diffuse character. The neurotic no longer knows why he is terrified — the reasons behind his anxiety. A very intelligent young lad, all of a sudden one night, is afraid to go to bed. As soon as his mother takes his hand to lead him to his bedroom, his heart begins to beat violently, and he is terrified. It does no good to threaten him with punishment; there is no point in reasoning with him. He tells the doctor that he is afraid to go to bed because he is afraid to die — but he cannot explain this fear.

Lisa's anxiety — she is a very sensitive and well educated young lady — makes her fear the sudden death of her husband or children — without any valid reason at all. She wakes up in the middle of the night, convinced that one or the other is dead. It is not enough to see them breathing when she goes to check; she has to wake them up, hear them speak, and have them get angry with her for interrupting their slumber. She knows that it is perfectly ridiculous, but this does not keep her from experiencing the same anxieties again the following night.

*   *   *   *

The list of neuroses is a long one. Jung speaks of the neuroses of youth and the neuroses that belong to maturity. The first are characterized, in the causal order, by the abnormal dependence which the patient feels upon his parents, real or imaginary, and in the final order, they give rise to disproportionate fictions, that is, to an intentionality and volitions that are not adapted to reality.[4] The "neuroses of youth" can also attack an adult, even an old man. The neuroses of maturity, no matter what their symptoms, all make their appearance at a more or less advanced age. Whereas, in Freudian thinking, every neurosis dates back to childhood, Jung claims, and with good cause, that this is not always the case. It is not at all necessary, in every attempt at

---

4. Jung: *Psychologie de l'inconscient*, p. 120

curing the neurotic, to take the case all the way back into the patient's childhood.

III. Character Neuroses

Traditionally, neuroses are classified according to their symtoms. But little by little, psychiatrists and psychologists are noticing that there are neuroses, or rather neurotic states, which are not characterized by any particular symptom. It is the general behavior of the individual that appears pathological, or at least bizarre. This is the so-called character neurosis.

Many psychologists, today, have a tendency to consider all neuroses as character neuroses, no matter what their symptoms might otherwise indicate. It is always the person as a whole that is sick, and it is thus the whole personality that must be treated and cured.

Among the neuroses that are very specifically character neuroses, we must include the *defeat neurosis*. The actions and behavior of the individual who is subject to this neurosis unconsciously tend to doom all his undertakings to premature failure.

Since the character is, at least partially, the product of civilization, it follows that the neuroses which affect it take on a different form in different civilizations. Some civilizations seem more susceptible to neurosis than others. The American civilization, for example, is a good case in point, probably because it lacks any deep roots in a land and in a history.

IV. Psychoses

Neurosis, as we have seen, does not totally vitiate the autonomy of the ego. But there are psychic diseases which disturb the functioning of the psychic totality, seriously disturbing judgment, reasoning, and even perception. Here, the contact with reality is more or less completely abolished, and not merely disturbed, as is the case with neuroses. These serious mental afflictions which imply a real alienation of the personality, are called psychoses.

Commotional psychosis results from a serious emotional shock (a railroad accident, outbreak of war, loss of a loved one, etc.).

Hallucinatory psychosis implies the existence of a more or less systematized delirium. It frequently involves affective apathy and intellectual weakening.

In *schizophrenia* the patient has lost contact with reality; he lives in a closed universe which is his own artificial creation. Many doctors see this as *the* psychosis *par excellence*, and refer to it as *dementia precox*.

Paranoia is the name given to interpretative psychoses, characterized by phobia of persecution, attributing thoughts and intentions to other people without the least objective grounds.

Finally, there is the *manic-depressive* psychosis, etc.

In itself, a neurosis is not a "little psychosis," and it is wrong for neurotic people to fear that they will go mad. Still, certain neurotics do exhibit marked schizoid and paranoiac tendencies. In these cases, psychosis can easily follow a neurosis, even a neurosis that has been cured.

V. Psyhcosomatic Illness

In their gross ignorance of Christian philosophy, the positivists thought they could put an end to Christianity by denying the dualism of soul-body. It was not difficult for them to prove that at the basis of all the functions traditionally attributed to the soul there is a bodily stimulus, that the "sicknesses of the soul" were, at least in many cases, only afflictions of the body. In reality, the body-soul dualism is not particularly Christian. It is Cartesian in inspiration. Christian doctrine has never ceased to profess a substantial union between soul and body; and this goes much farther than a simple functional bond.

To return to our subject, if we consider neurosis as a sickness that is psychic in origin, we never mean to cast doubt on the fact that it is almost always a bodily disease as well. But contemporary medicine goes further still, in asserting the existence of a substantial union. It is an almost universally recognized fact today that many diseases which affect the body have a psychic etiology. This is true in particular of pulmonary tuberculosis, stomach ulcers, and probably also cancer. These are psychosomatic sicknesses. Thus, not only does the body make the soul sick, but the sick soul can also make the body sick.

These distinctions are still rather artificial and lean heavily on Cartesian dualism. When we, as psychologists, speak of psychosomatic sickness, we understand that every sickness is psychosomatic to some degree. It is never the soul or the body alone that is sick, but always the person in his radical and indissoluble totality, body and soul. It can be said, obviously, that certain diseases affect the *psyche* primarily, and others the *soma;* they take root in a trauma that exists in one or the other component of the human person.

VI. *The Neurotic*

Every neurosis, as we have seen, is characterized by an unresolved psychic conflict, in which one of the conflicting tendencies is unconscious. Seen from without, only the intensity of this psychic conflict distinguishes the neurotic from the healthy person. Neurosis, according to Jung, is an existential disunion of the person as such.[5]

An important difference exists, however, between the healthy person and the neurotic; whereas the former *acts*, the latter is *agitated*. This is because in the former the conflict is dialectical, whereas it is static, or even mechanical, in the latter.

5. *Psychologie* . . . , p. 50

The neurotic is almost always a nervous person. Still it is not his nervousness that causes his neurosis, but rather inversely. Many nervous persons, however, are not at all neurotic, and there are some neurotics who are not nervous at all.

The neurotic is unhappy. He is unhappy because his obsession or excessive sense of insecurity keeps him from really enjoying the tangible pleasures of existence. If the dinner table is laden with food, he is inclined to fear for the day on which he will be wanting the bare necessities of life. In the arms of his beloved, he trembles at the thought of some imaginary accident that, perhaps tomorrow, will take her away from him forever. His suffering is very different from that of the healthy person, even if we suppose this healthy person to be seriously at grips with his conflicts. His suffering is always proportional to its real causes, whereas there is no proportion at all between the intensity of the neurotic's sufferings and its apparent cause.

This leads us to believe, even before a thorough case study, that the apparent causes are not always the real ones. Not infrequently, moreover, an apparent cause is completely lacking in the suffering of the neurotic patient. This has a very strong resemblance to the "strange pains" some people complain of, but can never discover any adequate reasons for. A certain neurotic patient of my acquaintance localized her anxiety feelings in a precise area of her chest: they kept her from breathing properly at times. There is no point in mentioning that the radiologists could find nothing wrong with her. But still we must not conclude that the sufferings of the neurotic are to be treated as "imaginary." Even in the case of hysteria, which is, more than any other disease, a creation of the imagination, the results are no less really painful.

Activity, especially the exercise of his profession, is never a source of joy for the neurotic. It always takes on the appearance of a painful labor, to which he is passively resigned, unless perhaps he revolts against it like a child. He wants to be doing something different from what he is doing, and to be somewhere else than where he is. What he does not realize is that his unhappiness and suffering is within himself, and he prefers to attribute it to outside conditions. He is like the children who blame the chair or table that they have run into. But if he does change his location or his work, he very soon experiences just as much suffering as before, and he wants to change again. In every neurotic, under somewhat different forms, this same instability is to be found, with various modifications — this same inability to adapt to a concrete situation.

We have already alluded to the feeling of insecurity which is another trait common to all neurotics. They cannot have any real trust in anyone, especially in themselves. It is precisely because — and in this they are quite correct — they cannot have trust in themselves that they lean so heavily on others. But their unconscious is well aware of the fact that they cannot get everything they want from others. The infantile logic of the neurotic leads him to conclude then that these others do not deserve *any* trust. His attitude towards the future is extremely pessimistic, with respect to both his personal destiny and that of the community.

Neurotics can revolt, but they will never turn into true revolutionaries nor even active reformers. They are not capable of undertaking anything unless *something* or, preferably, *someone* forces them to it. Even though they generally have an unbalanced mistrust towards other people, their feeling of insecurity makes them extraordinarily docile towards a teacher, whether it is a doctor, spiritual director, or boss. The reason for this is that they are trying to discharge the whole burden of existential responsibility, which weighs too heavily on their own shoulders, onto someone else. Meeting with a strong personality is not likely to reassure them. They are afraid that they will be crushed by such a personality and they offer a childlike resistance. No one is ever so jealous of his own autonomy as the neurotic who really has no autonomy to speak of.

The habitual reactions of the neurotic in the face of persons, events, and things, are all strongly stamped with infantilism. Even if he is hypercivilized and possesses a superior degree of education, we are not too incorrect in considering him as "backward," emotionally backward. It is because he is not really adult that he is afraid to assume responsibilities. Still we do not need to probe the depths of his unconscious to discover the fact that the neurotic lives infinitely more in the past than in the present to which he is unable to adapt, and even less in the future, which he greatly fears. He has forgotten that, even when this so unfortunate past was the present time, he was just as miserable and unhappy as he is now. But, at this moment, the past is something he knows, and therefore something solid, something from which there can be no threat. He idealizes it and leans on it.

Unreconciled to the world that is, the neurotic flees reality and hides as much as possible within an inner dream. It is there he creates his "masterpieces." He will not easily admit how fragile they are. In fact, it is precisely this feature that lets him often exercise the most extreme severity in his judgments of the past and present accomplishments of other people. He compares their actual accomplishments to the beauty of his imaginary creations, and naturally finds them far inferior.

VII. *Collective Neuroses*

Certain civilizations are obviously markedly more susceptible to the spread of neurosis than others. This is particularly true of civilizations in which men have collectively lost their sense of security. Thus, Jung has observed that, in Europe, neuroses are proportionately less frequent in solidly Catholic cultural milieux.

Protestants, especially those who live in a Catholic country, are much more susceptible to neurosis. Neurosis is almost general among the Jews, who are almost a type of the people without roots. On the other hand, many psychologists and doctors observe that nuerosis is much more widespread in the United States than in most other countries. This is probably because the population of America was built up of immigrants of many nationalities and ethnical groups; also because the American way of life has not ever managed to promote a feeling of being solidly rooted in any historical situation.

Still, it is not only the individuals, however many of them we might consider, who suffer neurosis in the midst of a given civilization. We are forced, by the unmistakable light of experience, to recognize the existence of truly collective neuroses. Rene Laforgue speaks of family neurosis. But this once again is really nothing more than a number of individual neuroses among the various members of one and the same family. Much more symptomatic are the real maladies of whole civilizations, of which contemporary history can furnish many striking examples.

It does not seem that all Germans, (1925 to 1945) nor even the majority of Germans, were neurotics. Moreover, it would be childish to blame Adolf Hitler's personal neurosis and those of the other Nazi chiefs for everything Germany experienced, actively or passively, between 1933 and 1945. If Germany, vanquished and humiliated, managed to transform itself so rapidly, since 1925, into a terrifying apocalyptic monster, this fact is largely due to the enslaving of the libido that had accumulated in the collective unconscious of the people. The whole merit of the Nazis, if merit it is, was to organize the energy thus set free. We must not be too surprised, consequently, that the inability of the whole mass of the German nation, including the butchers and torturers of Dachau and Buchenwald, found it so difficult to admit their guilt for the crimes in which they were the docile and frequently even enthusiastic instruments of execution. In saying that they "did not want any of this," they are perfectly sincere. As individuals, they certainly did not want it, and we might easily enough admit that, as such, they did not commit these crimes. Just like personal neurosis, in collective neurosis too, the complex has become autonomous: it seems to act all by itself.

Another very typical example of collective neurosis is to be found in a certain phobia of Communism. It shows up in the United States under the form of McCarthyism. It became absolutely impossible to hold a rational discussion on Communism with almost any American. The collective unconscious, seized with a great insecurity, had found an excellent outlet in the phobia.

We could easily enough discover a collective neurosis, more or less serious, in any civilized people. To speak only of France, the Frenchman is easily convinced that the whole world loves his country, that everyone admires him, even that they are jealous of him. Now, this is a well developed superiority complex. But we must not forget that, in chapter VIII, we saw that such a complex frequently goes hand in hand with an inferiority complex. The way the French lost Syria, Lebanon and Vietnam, the way French politics mishandled affairs in North Africa and provoked political reversals in the Saar — this all points to a strong defeat neurosis. The collective unconscious of France was driven to act in such a degree that its own best intentions could not help leading to these astonishing setbacks.

The resurgence of aggressive national feeling which we observe in almost all the present-day world is another form of collective neurosis. The "national fact" has, after all, completely gone beyond the plane of economics, politics, and cultures. Still we find great resistance to the indispensable — and inevitable — integration of some peoples into broader communities that are more adapted to the reality of our times. In this affective attachment to a past that is no more, it is not difficult to discover a form of regression to the infantile stage which is perfectly characteristic of all neuroses.

VIII. *Neurosis and Sex*

In Freudian theory, there is always a close relationship between sex and neurosis. The founder of psychoanalysis was first led to elaborate his various theories on the basis of his activity as a practicing psychiatrist. Actually, in the neurotic, the psychic functions generally manifest themselves with a degree of acuteness that is never found among "normal" people. It is easy to understand how Freud was tempted to deduce that neurosis is only a projection of the normal psyche's ordinary irregularities.

Many of Freud's observations, and those of his disciples, relative to the sex function in the neurotic, are incontestable; they have been verified a thousand times by psychologists of all different schools. Thus it is true that, in almost all neuropathic individuals, there are unconscious tendencies to inversion. The majority of such people obviously never practice homosexuality, nor even experience any conscious desire for it. But their general attitude with regard to persons of the other sex and the nature of the difficulties they experience in facing marriage are enough for the experienced psychologist to recognize the symptoms of a latent homosexuality, even without recourse to analysis.

It is true that almost all neurotics have remained in an infantile state of sexuality. Even supposing that they have managed to get beyond that stage at some given moment, under the influence of their neurosis they fall back into it. However the infantilism of the neurotic is not limited merely to the domain of sex. It is his general behavior that is similar to the child's. Therese, the mother of several children, a character neurotic, is fundamentally incapable of behaving like a mother towards her children — like an adult. She gets angry over nothing and punishes her children; she cannot keep from "joining the game" with them. She knows that such an attitude is not in the best interests of their education and upbringing, but she cannot help herself.

It is also certain that, in almost all neurotics, the first stirrings of the sex instinct were very precocious. Many of them had begun to masturbate at the age of three or four. Others have always experienced a lively curiosity towards their own sex organs and those of persons who were close to them, and at an age in which "normal" children generally pay no attention to such subjects. As we have said, it was the observation of sexual precocity in sick people, a precocity that was almost always somewhat perverted, that led Freud to his hotly debated theories of general infantile sexuality. Now it does seem that precocity and sexual perversion are closely bound up with neurosis. Sometimes they appear to be the cause, and sometimes the consequence.

Freudian thinking has a tendency to consider every neurosis as a consequence of constraints imposed upon the sex instinct. Under the effects of *censorship* the desires that proceed from this instinct, instead of leading nomally towards the satisfaction that every instinct demands, are repressed into the unconscious. There they are still at work, always trying to break down this barrier. Since a frontal attack seldom accomplishes this effect, the libido sets out to find a detour into the conscious mind. Neurotic symptoms thus appear as a substitute satisfaction, according to Freud, destined to replace what has been refused in the normal life.[6]

In every neurosis, moreover, the Freudians think they recognize the famous Oedipus complex. Social morality, fixed within the super ego, condemns incest, and thus the sex instinct which "naturally" tends towards incest, is sidetracked into the complications which are characteristic of Oedipus complex behavior. Whether this is inversion or any other sex perversion, it is, fundamentally, the Oedipus complex that is at work.

* * * *

In strict logic, we would from the Freudian premise, have to conclude, that the best way to prevent neurosis from getting a start, would be to give full freedom to the sex instinct. If its impulses lead naturally towards incest, homosexuality, or any other kind of perversion, we must never dare to contradict or repress its activity. In proclaiming that this interdiction against incest is

6. *Introduction . . . , p. 324*

"the worst crime against love," Freud seems to be taking just such a stand.

Still, and despite these characteristic quirks of his thinking, the founder of psychoanalysis always refused to carry these theoretical conclusions to their practical extremes. He recognized readily enough that most men are perfectly at ease in their normal sex life and they do not experience, consciously or unconsciously, any inclination towards perversity. He even admits that certain persons seem to renounce all sexual satisfaction, without the least damage to their psychic equilibrium.

In order to explain this apparent illogicality, Freud postulates that the libido of the chaste man — libido in the Freudian sense, of course — has set out upon other paths, and has found other "substitute satisfactions" outside neurosis.

Obviously there is no question here of rejecting, as false, the whole Freudian theory of neurosis. As in all the other theses of psychology, exact observation can be allied with erroneous interpretation, and, most dangerous of all, with abusive and ill-founded generalizations.

IX. Etiology of Neurosis

In many cases, neurosis is the result of an emotional shock, sometimes very unimportant objectively, but always very serious subjectively. On the very day that she learned her husband was a victim of polio, Louise began to show clear signs of obsessional neurosis. Both she herself and her friends considered her husband's condition as the cause of this neurosis. But a more precise psychological exploration revealed that, for some time already, Louise had been struggling with unconscious conflicts that had remained unresolved. Her life appeared to have been calm and happy up to that time, and thus she was not aware of any disorder. The shock, or trauma, in the language of psychology, disturbed the order that the ego had been able to maintain up to that time. The defenses were broken, and the neurosis had a chance to show itself.

Still, many neuroses appear without being precipitated by any traumatic shock. These are called spontaneous neuroses.

It is extremely rare for a neurosis to appear as suddenly as some physical disease. It first undergoes a more or less lengthy period which might be compared to the period of incubation of certain bodily diseases. During this time, the future neurotic feels uncomfortable and uneasy "without knowing why"— he is in a painful state of insecurity. He is worked up without any reason and he gets angry over nothing; his behavior starts to become bizarre and capricious.

Louise, whose story was just discussed, did not turn really neurotic until three years after her husband fell sick. Meanwhile, she had moved four times, whereas prior to that day she had been living in the same apartment for fifteen years. She thought she had to move "because the apartment reminded her of the days when she was happy." But she always felt just as uncomfortable in her new lodgings. Up to that time she had been rigorously faithful to her husband and experienced only slight sexual urgings; but six months after the dread disease struck her husband, she fell passionately in love with a young dandy who made her his mistress. She had read a few popularizations of psychoanalysis and thus she attributed her falling in love and subsequent adultery to her previous continency which had been "contrary to her temperament."

But after some weeks of this first illicit love affair, she experienced a new pang of love for someone younger: this time she explained it as due to the insufficient virility of her first lover. During the three years, without manifesting any specifically neurotic symptoms, her inner instability grew in leaps and bounds. Finally, she began giving herself, sometimes even offering herself, to any man she happened to meet and who seemed to show any interest in her at all.

Lack of sexual satisfaction, so it appeared, was really not one of the factors involved in her behavior, nor did she really appeal to it to excuse herself in her own eyes. When, finally, the first symptoms of obsession began to appear, Louise believed that she had already recovered her equilibrium, because for several months she had been faithful to her first lover.

* * * *

Only rarely is the constraint imposed on the sex instinct the real cause of neurosis. Neither for Louise nor for many other cases we have personally observed was this ever the case. Quite the contrary, it is an undeniable fact that neurosis always spreads in an affectively poor "climate." Children who are deprived of parental love (orphans, products of broken homes, children who are brutally treated by their parents) are much more predisposed to neurosis than those whose first years were spent in a normal affective situation. Louise's parents were very puritanical, excessively austere. She never recalled that they had ever embraced her or used endearing terms: they only told her what she had to do.

The love or friendship that a person experiences during adolescence or youth, outside his home and family, can repair, at least partially, the ravages caused by the affective privations of childhood. But if the love or friendship are not there, there is no other refuge than neurosis. The situation is even more serious when we realize that many of those who have been thus deprived of love have lost all faith in love and no longer want to make the necessary effort to bring it to life within themselves. Such people might be blamed for their hardness of heart, when in reality their hearts are desperate, not hard.

Still, a childhood spent in an atmosphere of affection must not be confused with a pampered childhood. In no other country of the world are children less brutally treated and more sheltered from any material privation than they are in the United States. The freedom of their instincts is respected more than anywhere else. Still, there are not many other countries that have so many neurotics. Real love, the love which is indispensable for the development of the soul, is, obviously, something very different.

* * * *

As for the "civilization factor" in the etiology of neuroses, it seems that it is bound up primarily with a lack of real spirituality. In the "desacralized" civilization of the modern Western man, existence is cut off from transcendency and thus seems to be deprived of all justification. Death, the inevitable sufferings and checks of life, all appear as absurdities and can give rise to nothing but panic. A successful struggle against neurosis could not rest content with efforts on merely an individual plane; it also requires work towards the transformation of neurotic civilizations.

* * * *

Some people speak of the benefits of neurosis, attributing a positive role to it, if not in the destiny of the individual himself, at least in that of civilization. In reality, this is a grossly erroneous way of looking at the problem.

Even some psychologists, actually, do not make sufficient distinction between psychic conflict and neurosis. Psychological conflict is, after all, the condition of all higher psychic activity. As for neurosis, it cannot construct anything, it can only destroy. If there are great artists among neurotics — and there are — they do not create their masterpieces because of their neuroses, but in spite of them. Sometimes even, it is true, they succeed in mobilizing the neurosis in the service of their creativity, as in the case, for instance, of Salvador Dali.

12 cure of the soul

Depth psychology is not the result of philosophical speculations which have been put to practical use as an afterthought. Freud, Adler, Jung and all the other pioneers and masters were practicing doctors and psychiatrists. They built up their general theories on the basis of their therapeutic experiences.

It is thus not impossible, at least *a priori*, for these theories to be false in some respects, without there being any reason to deny or cast any doubt on the general effectiveness of their method. Such is, in fact, the apparent paradox of Freudian psychology. As an excellent doctor and scientific observer of rare genius, but completely lacking in philosophical insight, Freud deduced very incorrect and even invalid theories on the basis of his very rich experience. Thus it is a mistake to turn to the unquestionable therapeutic effectiveness of some of Freud's methods for an argument in favor of his doctrine. On the other hand, the rejection of Freudian doctrine does not ever justify the condemnation of the method and technique of his psychoanalysis. There are more and more psychoanalysts who, like Roland Dalbiez,[1] profess this necessary distinction between the doctrine and method of Freudian psychology. The method is scientific, and never subordinated

---

1. *La méthode psychanalytique et la doctrine freudienne,* 2 vol.

to the postulates of his doctrine. Thus it can very well be applied — just as it is, or more or less adapted, depending on individual cases — without the psychologist feeling obliged to subscribe to the doctrine of the libido, nor believe in the universality of the Oedipus complex.

Paradoxical as it might seem to the laymen, it even seems that psychoanalysis is more effective when it is applied by men who use the method without being too much concerned about the theories. The majority of the failures that I have had an opportunity to witness in this respect seemed due, in the last analysis, to the analyst's obsession with finding an Oedipus complex or establishing a "transfer," or doing his best to verify some other theoretical presupposition.

There must never be any rigid orthodoxy in the area of psychotherapy: proof of this is the fact that Freudians, Jungians, and many other psychologists who do not belong to any school can all point to very obvious and incontrovertible results. It is childish to claim, as some doctrinaire psychologists and other thinkers like to do, that the cures effected by Jung's psychology, for example, or that of some other "heretic," are not so deep-seated or thorough as Freud's. The psychologist's job is not to refashion the personality of the patient according to the psychologist's own preconceived ideas; he is rather to do his humble best to make possible an existence for his patient that is really in conformity with the patient's real potential. It is because certain psychoanalysts do not have enough basic respect for the individual personality of their patients and believe that they must liquidate their every complex, that many of their patients end up looking so haggard and listless and even lifeless after the analysis is completed, and seem even less adapted to real life than the neurotics themselves.

In order to successfully combat the problem of neurosis, the psychologist needs a method, but it is never possible, in all honesty, for him to claim that his is the only effective method.

I. The Fight against the Causes of Neurosis

Long before Freud, people have tried to cure the diseases of the soul. We shall say nothing here of exorcisms and other prescientific "techniques," although some of them do contain intuitions and insights of real psychological value.

On the plane of scientific therapeutics, we know that Janet achieved excellent results through the use of hypnosis. Freud himself used this technique in the beginning. Even today, not everybody is thoroughly won over to specifically psychological theapeutics. Psychiatrists and neurologists use either electric shock, or narcoanalysis, or lobotomy or some other surgical process. They certainly achieve results. As we have repeated so many times, no psychic activity, no matter how profoundly spiritual it is, can ever exist without a certain organic support. There is nothing surprising in the fact that treatment of the body achieves results in diseases whose psychological etiology is manifestly evident.

Still, in the light of the observable facts, it does seem that electroshock, narcosis, lobotomy, etc., are able to remove only the symptoms of neurosis. The cure is thus only provisory. Later on at some time, the neurosis will reappear under the form of other symptoms and these are generally more serious than the earlier set. The same pattern holds here as in the case of any disease that is approached on the basis, not of its underlying and fundamental causes, but solely of its apparent symptoms. Still, there is one general justification for such treatment, and that is the fact that it is generally applied only in cases in which every other procedure has proved to be without effect.

* * * *

Since neuroses are almost always caused by some unconscious conflict there is no way to really cure them without resolving these conflicts. Once this truth is admitted, the only important problem that faces the psychotherapist is to know how he can have access to the unconscious. But a thorough explanation of the process of psychoanalytic methodology is not within the scope or purpose of this book; it is enough for our purposes to examine it as it has been worked out by Freud and is commonly applied today, more or less faithfully, by the majority of psychologists.

The repression of instincts is, according to orthodox Freudian psychology, the origin of all neurosis, and thus the psychologist's task is to unravel them. In order to achieve this goal, the decipherment of dreams, the language of the unconscious, appears to be the most effective means. Convinced that dream images are a disguised and symbolic manifestation of unconscious activity, psychoanalysts try to discover, or rather to make their patients discover, the reality these dreams express. We have seen that the method followed is that of free association. Taking any point of his dream as a springboard, the patient is invited to talk about all the ideas and all the images that come to his mind. This same procedure is then followed with all the other elements of the dream: persons, places, objects, events, colors, etc.

Sometimes the analysis never does arrive at any certain results. Other times, it meets with *resistances* which it then needs to unmask and overcome. It is generally only after the analysis of many dreams, dreams that extend over months and even years, that the unconscious conflict is fully revealed.

Freudian analysis lasts even longer when the analyst is more scrupulous in observing the principle of really free association. From fear of influencing the subject by questions that might act as a form of suggestion, the analyst allows him to go in any direction he pleases. The chances of the patient automatically setting out in the right direction are about one in one hundred. In order to eliminate this disadvantage, many psychologists prefer to guide the subject. No doubt there is some danger of suggestion here and the unexperienced psychologist will not always be able to avoid a series of pitfalls and blind alleys; but with experience the proportion of error will greatly diminish.

Still it is always true that the man who directs these free associations must possess not only a solid grounding in scientific psychology, but also be an "accomplished psychologist" in the current sense of the term.

* * * *

No matter how necessary for a final cure dream analysis proves to be in exploring the patient's unconscious, it is far from being the only available route. Nor is it always particularly effective as a method. There are, after all, neurotics who do not ever dream, or at least who do not regularly remember their dreams. There have to be other paths into the unconscious source of their neurosis. Thus Jung relies greatly on the use of "leading words," as a basis for his analysis. Other psychologists use "daydreams" for the same purpose, and others work with "psychodramas."

No matter what method is used, the analysis ideally results in the subject's being aware of the unconscious process which has given rise to the neurosis within his psyche. Obviously, this is never a case of mere intellectual knowledge: it is not the psychologist who teaches the patient the meaning of his dreams and the cause of his problems. Still it is rather frequent for people who go to the psychologist to think they know the causes of their neuroses. They have read psychoanalytical works the way other people read their medical dictionaries. From the date of their very first session, they inform the psychologist that they have an "Oedipus complex" or that they have a fixation on the "anal stage." It is not impossible, of course, *a priori*, for this personal diagnosis to be correct enough in the main. But this rational knowledge is not equivalent to a cure, and generally, it does not even help it greatly. The awareness that is indispensable to the dissolution of the neurosis is an awareness of the affective and vital order. It is only in the course of a well directed analysis that the subject will succeed in arriving at this knowledge.

Obviously there could be no question here of transforming

the whole unconscious mind into the conscious. Anyone who could even conceive such a foolish ambition would quickly experience the most painful setbacks. No human consciousness ever has the potential breadth it needs to accept and assimilate the whole content of the unconscious, even supposing that the whole unconscious mind — and this is certainly not ever the case — is capable of becoming conscious. It is enough, for the purposes envisaged by psychotherapy, for the *pathogenous* part of the unconscious to be transformed into consciousness. Once this result is accomplished, the neurosis is dissolved.

II. *Transference*

As long as the treatment continues, a very particular relationship is established between analyst and patient. We call this relationship the *analytic situation.*

In Freudian psychology, this analytic situation is characterized primarily by the psychological process of transference. Transference is supposed to consist in the patient's projecting certain more or less neurotic feelings onto the analyst, feelings which prior to his treatment had been directed towards other persons. Max felt hate and contempt for his father whom he accused of having preferred his older brother. After some weeks of treatment, he begins to have a violent hatred for the psychologist. He blames him for not spending enough time with him, for preferring his other patients, who are richer or better educated or better looking. Among his friends, he speaks of the psychologist with contempt, saying that he is incompetent and poorly trained. We call this procedure *negative transference.*

Jeanne was very attached to her father. This attachment prevented the full development of her own femininity; it made her very bitter and she gradually developed into an active Lesbian. In a word, she began to manifest all the symptoms of the famous Oedipus complex. The psychologist quickly took the place of her father. Gradually he turned into the exclusive object of Jeanne's affection: this is *positive transference*.

The patient is ignorant of the true nature of these feelings towards the analyst. He believes that it is really the analyst whom he hates or loves. Frequently, the negative transference of the first period of analysis gives way to positive transference. A certain woman who, at the outset, hates her husband in the person of the psychologist, eventually transfers to that same psychologist, the real affection she had always felt towards her brother.

* * * *

Most Freudians are convinced of the therapeutic necessity of transference. If there is a negative transference, the analyst must act in such a way that it is transformed into positive. Then he will have to help the patient discover that his "love" for the analyst is only a *step* in the therapeutic process. Generally, it is only after the liquidation of this positive transference that the neurotic can be considered as really cured.

Still the analyst can let himself be drawn into the problem. Instead of treating the transference coldly and objectively as it fits into his therapeutic goals, he can himself begin to experience hostile or tender feelings towards the patient he is analyzing. This is known as *counter-transference*. This type of transference can seriously harm the therapy and even completely defeat its purposes, if the analyst himself is not well aware of the real nature of his feelings. It is primarily in an effort to keep their members on their guard against these dangers of counter-transference that societies of psychoanalysts all demand that their future members first undergo a thorough analysis themselves.[2]

Still it is only too easy to observe in the light of experience, that didactic analysis does not succeed in liquidating all complexes any more than therapeutic analysis does, and thus it is

---

2. This analysis of future psychoanalysts is called *didactic*. It follows precisely the same pattern as therapeutic analysis, but with more thorough explanation of the doctrine and method of psychoanalysis.

not a perfect safeguard against counter-transference. We know eminent masters who have all been analyzed by doctors even more eminent still, and whose behavior towards some of their patients still takes on all the characteristics of counter-transference.

An over-dogmatic faith in the inevitibility and absolute necessity of transference for the success of analysis sometimes gives rise to really grotesque situations. Analysts will go out of their way to provoke such a positive transference, but they are not always in a position to resolve it in turn. They are, perhaps, not all sufficiently detached to really want such a resolution of the transference; they find a certain degree of satisfaction in playing the role of idol, which the transference complex accords to them in the eyes of the subject. On the other hand, since certain psychoanalysts, even very famous ones, find it sometimes very difficult to admit that the neurosis has been resolved, that the moment has come for the subject to take a step beyond the analyst, the non-resolution of the transference appears to be perfectly justified. Proof of this is to be found in the fact that, despite their mastery of the techniques and despite the didactic analysis which they themselves have undergone, they are unconsciously victims of counter-transference. This is particularly clear in the case of those psychoanalysts who are surrounded by a veritable court of admirers and hangers-on. When positive transference does not take place in one of their subjects, they conclude that he is putting up some unconscious resistance, or that he is negatively transferring, and they unduly prolong the analysis.

* * * *

Together with some outstanding masters of depth psychology we think that it is not always necessary, for therapeutic success, for transference to take place. And the fact is that it is not always produced. Moreover, as Jung very properly points out, such a transference is in itself a sort of neurosis. In provoking such a transference, the psychologist merely substitutes one neurosis for another. Is it never possible to liquidate the neurosis for which the analysis has been introduced by some more simple and direct method? Many psychologists have succeeded in doing so, and the result is almost always an appreciable reduction in the duration of the analysis.

* * * *

Still, the analytic situation does imply certain characteristics which are specifically proper to it. There is something childish in the claim of some psychologists that they exercise no personal influence on their patients, that they apply their technique with a total scientific objectivity. This is a leftover from the nineteenth century; the attitude of the learned man with respect to the object of his studies. Today, the doctor himself recognizes that he is much more prone to subjectivity as a researcher. As for therapy, the physician who is concerned with bodily ailments alone already goes beyond the mere objective application of his science. Or if some doctors fail to do so, it is probably for that very reason that so many sick people have begun to turn to healers of one kind or another instead. The doctor himself is the one to effect a cure, much more than technology and pharmacy. The same thing is true, *a fortiori*, in the case of mental disorders.

The psychologist and the neurotic whom he treats do not form two abstract entities. They are two human persons who, by the the force of necessity, are cast into a very intimate relationship. The neurotic tells the psychologist the most intimate secrets of his soul, secrets that he himself did not even know existed before. How can the psychologist remain absolutely and coldly objective? The psychologist's indispensable desire to give real help to his patient could not help but create an atmosphere of sympathy. When the psychologist, for any reason whatsoever, finds it impossible to experience any such sympathy for his patient, he cannot help the patient very much either; the best he can do is to recommend him to another specialist. This is one of the reasons why the choice of a psychologist is so very important.

As for the neurotic, he is necessarily a weak person, like all sick people. He experiences an acute need to trust someone, to lean on someone who is stronger than himself. Normally, he looks to the psychologist for the help he so desperately needs.

The existence of such circumstances in the analytic situation makes it obvious that the psychologist's profession must be exercised only by persons who are deserving of other people's confidence, and extremely respectful of their individuality of soul. It is ridiculous to claim, as some doctors do, that psychoanalysis excludes all possibility of suggestion. It is obvious, for anyone who is better acquainted with the situation, that this is never the case. The most dangerous suggestion is the one that the psychologist exercises unconsciously, all the while living in the illusion that he is objectively applying the scientific method. It is in this area that he always runs the risk of imposing his own complexes, his own prejudices, both theoretical and practical, on souls who are already weak and disturbed, and thus more than usually receptive to anything their psychologist tells them. Thus, it seems an incontestable fact that if Freudians recognize an Oedipus complex in all their patients, the reason behind this "discovery" is their own unconscious suggestion.

It is much better for the psychologist to recognize, in all honesty and simplicity, the extraordinary influence he exercises in the analytic situation. This influence is nothing to be ashamed of; quite the contrary, it is often most useful in the therapeutic process. Thanks to this influence, the receptivity of the subject is always much greater and the resistances to formal treatment are more easily overcome. But it is important for the psychologist to know what his duties are in this area and that he has a perfect right to suggest things to a patient who is confiding in him. This he can do only when he is fully aware of his power.

III. *Medicine or Pedagogy?*

In certain cases, it is obviously desirable for the psychoanalyst to be a doctor. This is particularly the case when the psychological etiology of the disease is not immediately evident. Still, the diploma of doctorate of medicine does not, in itself, confer any of the qualifications or capabilities that are essential to the good therapist.

Even in the case of serious neurotics, the psychologist's task is education much more than medication. It is unfortunate for psychoanalysis that some analysts, often for reasons which are no deeper than a desire for publicity, claim to practice medicine as well. The result is much misunderstanding and jealousy on the part of the medical profession, and, in the last analysis, it is always the patient who has to pay.

The psychologist needs to have a deep understanding of the soul, to be able to direct, counsel, educate. No matter how useful the techniques and empirical knowledge of his profession are for the psychologist, there is no really valid and effective psychology that is not at the same time a philosophy.

The psychologist obviously does not have the right to impose his own metaphysical, scientific, political, or esthetical convictions on any of his patients. But he must be able to fully understand those of the patients who confide in him, so that he can help them become free and achieve self-fulfillment in the light of their own existential authenticity. Now, experience has shown that such deep understanding can be achieved only by a man who has some solid convictions of his own. His psychological maturity must be strong enough for his faith to be without sectarianism: he must be able to admit that all human beings can search for the one Absolute along paths that are different from his own. I never hesitate to recommend, for example, that a fervent Catholic consult a Jewish psychologist or a believing Protestant, rather than a skeptic or an agnostic. I myself have had occasion to deal with people who do not share any of my metaphysical convictions; I did everything I could to help them to a more authentic realization of the goals towards which they aspired.

Thus, when it is not a question of therapy for really serious neuroses, but rather a question of helping the individual to resolve his own psychic conflicts which, for lack of solution, might eventually lead to neurosis, the psychologist's mission is much more obviously one of education.

IV. *Psychosynthesis*

It is impossible to speak of a genuine psychological cure as long as the person involved is not in a position to freely live up to his most lofty aspirations. Certain Freudian psychologists believe that they can and must liquidate the religious faith of their patients: what they thereby produce, however, is not a superior person, as they like to suppose, but a psychic wreck. The claim of some American psychologists, who say that Communists could be "cured" of their political and economic ideologies by simply being psychoanalyzed, is inadmissible, and, what is more, stupid. A person, no matter whether he is Catholic, Protestant, Communist, or agnostic, could not have perfect confidence in the services of the psychologist unless he were absolutely sure that there would be no violence done to his ego and that once the affective energy in his psyche was unblocked, he could put it to use in keeping with his own personal aspirations.

The goal of psychotherapy is not the liberation of the instincts. Man being what he is, mastery, or as it frequently must be, repression of instinct is a practical necessity. What is really important is to surmount those inner divisions of the psyche which keep a man from full self-realization. Before undertaking the exploration of the unconscious, it is important first of all to make a thorough inventory of the situation on the conscious plane. It is not at all impossible for the conflict to be resolved by simply dealing with its conscious factors.

When the resolution of unconscious complexes becomes necessary to make it possible for the affective energy to penetrate further into the consciousness, the psychologist must act with great discernment. Not only is the suppression of all constraints on the instinctive forces not desirable, but it generally appears to be very harmful for the subject. It is certainly not good, for most patients, to know everything the psychologist thinks he can read in their unconscious. First of all, there is always a risk of reading something there that is the projection of his own prejudices or theoretical postulates and thus exercising an influence on the patient that is not always good. But even supposing that he knows for certain what is going on in the unconscious of one of his subjects, the psychologist must still ask himself whether or not the subject is in a position to bear this knowledge, and whether the knowledge will really prove useful to him. There are some things that must be revealed only progressively, gradually, when the structures of the ego have grown strong enough to support the knowledge. There are other things that are better not to be ever known at all. I had occasion to deal with the case of a young man, 45, who was suffering from sexual impotence. The analyst's brutal revelation of the cause for this condition — an incestuous fixation on his mother — plunged the man into terrible mental disorder. Life seemed suddenly so ugly and meaningless that suicide was the only way out.

* * * *

Classic psychoanalysis could not ever be enough for the psychologist who is aware of his duties and the dignity of his mission. It is astonishing to note that practitioners of some standing still believe that it is enough to discover the unconscious causes of neurosis or conflict for mental health to be reestablished.

It is not to be denied that neurosis almost always disappears as soon as the conscious mind has taken possession of the repressed complex, by resolving it. Theoretically, the former neurotic should thus be immediately in a position to live and act like a free man, an adult. But this is forgetting that he does not have the habit of acting this way; a serious retardation has affected his development during the time of his neurosis. How many former neurotics once they have completed their analysis at the hands of a Freudian doctor, are still very far from being well adapted and normal people. They are well aware of their psychological mechanisms. They think they are no longer neurotics, and perhaps they really no longer are. But seeing the way they live, we are tempted to ask if it might not have been better for them to stay neurotic. The neurosis gave them a reason for living, even if it did involve a lot of suffering. At present, they no longer have any such reason. Their psychic energy has been set free to work, but no one has taught them how to use it.

The indispensable resolution of conflicts can be considered as only the first stage of psychotherapy. The next problem is — and here we are touching upon an essential objective — to help the subject reestablish his personal synthesis. From the very first session, moreover, the psychologist must be attentive to the problem of reestablishing this synthesis, or in certain cases, of establishing it for the very first time, when the subject has not ever managed to arrive at a synthesis. It was in an effort to underline this primacy of synthesis over analysis that I have called this work of psychology, not *psychoanalysis*, but rather *psychosynthesis*.

In order to reestablish, or establish, the personal synthesis, it is generally almost indispensable to use the reductive, analytic method. Still, this is not always the case. We constantly appeal to the conscious resources of the ego, to the free will of the subject being analyzed. Analysis is necessary only when the ego is too weak or too enslaved to act, and then only in the measure of that weakness; it puts us in a position to fight against obstacles which are the result of psychic determinism. The constructive, synthetic work depends on the individual's free will, that is, his conscious mind. Our duty is to teach the ego to make use of all the determined elements in the psyche.

V. Problems of Adaptation

Not withstanding their regular denial of the fact, the conception many Freudians have of their mission as psychotherapists is tightly bound up with their general philosophy of man. What is so regrettable about this is the fact that most of the time they are not aware of this philosophy and that, consequently, it acts, in an irrational manner, similar to the activity of what Freudian psychology refers to as the superego.

These psychologists generally do not want to be satisfied with curing the disease for which the patient has come to see them. They claim that they can liquidate everything that makes the individual in question depart from the "normal man," everything that keeps him from being perfectly adapted. Obviously such a conception of their mission is fraught with danger.

The neurotic certainly is not well adapted. But there is nothing so aleatory as the concept of human normality. It depends on each individual civilization and, within each individual and strongly differentiated civilizations, it depends on the ideologies particular to a given group. The partisans of private property and free enterprise, for example, tend to interptret hostility towards this system as emanating from an inferiority complex or jealousy. The collectivists, on the other hand, have a tendency to interpret the "bourgeois" attachment to a concept of ownership (which seems historically outmoded to them) as a "sado-anal" fixation, to put in it in Freudian terminology. The atheistic psychologist sees religious faith as a neurosis to be liquidated, whereas the believer considers lack of faith as an anomaly. In an effort to "normalize" the individuals who come to see him, must the psychologist, following his own theoretical bent, make an effort to abolish the private ownership complex in one patient and the collectivist complex in another? Must he work to destroy the faith of one client and to convert another? Merely asking such questions is enough to demonstrate the inadmissability, in psychology as it is practiced, of the criterion of the normal man.

The very same thing is true of adaptation. In America, a Communist is necessarily poorly adapted. In Russia it is the liberal democrat who is out of step. Public powers are frequently blamed for treating socially maladapted persons as criminals. But is it any more legitimate to consider them as sick?

Moreover, almost all creative geniuses — Baudelaire, Dostoevski, Einstein, Picasso — have been poorly adapted to a greater or lesser degree. Even supposing that a Freudian approach might succeed in reducing all maladapted and original persons to "normal," we would then find humanity freed of neurosis perhaps, but still frighteningly mediocre. Those who fear that in submitting the superior neurotic to psychological treatment we will take away his creative gifts together with his neurosis are not entirely wrong in their fears. But this fear is justified only with respect to one particular category of psychoanalytical procedure.

VI. *Individuation*

Rather than this inadequate conception of normal man, we must prefer the therapy of *individuation*, originally connected with the name of C. G. Jung, but rethought and adapted by every other psychologist on the basis of his individual practice.

The psychologist must refuse to have any *a priori* ideas about normal or adapted men. He does not forget that the person who has come to see him has done so because he felt ill and was unable to realize himself. The psychologist has to understand, with the active cooperation of the patient, what the patient is in the depths of his psyche, what are the obstacles which prevent him from existing as he really is. Psychosynthesis does not violate or change the individual: it merely helps him develop his true personality.

Psychosynthesis obviously demands intellectual training of its practitioners, but even more so, respect for other people. Still I would not dare to claim that it is equally effective in every case. Thus, I gladly concede that the Freudian method is indicated in the case of neuroses which can be presumed to be the result of sexual conflicts. Other neuroses are better treated by Adler's methods. But whenever the patient is a person who is in any way out of the ordinary and whose neurosis seems due to causes and motivations that are more complex, Jung's psychology, or psychosynthesis which is inspired by Jung's psychology, seems better equipped to understand the patient. The same thing is true whenever the patient does not have a well defined and recognizable neurosis, but a more or less acute psychic conflict. Baudelaire and Oscar Wilde could have been treated by just such an approach, without their natural genius suffering the least risk.

* * * *

Psychosynthesis is not aimed at freeing a man from psychological mechanisms that are well regulated, but rather at removing the shackles on his human freedom, letting him act and live not as a well oiled machine, but like an individual who is in full possession of his faculties. Thus it is impossible to speak of a cure until the subject has acquired a sense of his own responsibilities and the strength to assume them properly. What is more, it is not enough for him to feel responsible only to himself; this might be nothing more than a simple narcissistic complex, taking the place of the other complexes that have been resolved. Individuation, such as it is envisioned by psychosynthesis, implies that a man assume the concrete responsibilities of husband and father, for instance, or citizen, member of the human race, etc.

The sign of the soul's return to a state of health is the patient's ability to get interested, with more or less real passion, according to his psychic makeup, in something higher than himself. Existence, as we have said above, is authentic only when it is bound up with transcendence. It is impossible to consider a definitive cure in the case of a patient who is still incapable of any enthusiasm, any strong passion, who claims to live according to the simple "pleasure principle."

VII. *The Proper Therapeutic for the Case*

Psychic conflict obviously cannot find any really effective solution outside psychology. It is wrong to accuse Freud of having recommended sexual indulgence to the neurotic patient, who is, by definition, a sexually repressed individual. The advice to live sex life to its dregs, he writes, has nothing in common with real psychoanalytic therapy.[3]

Unfortunately, not all his disciples, or those who claimed to be his disciples, have been able to understand their master's hesitancy or real intentions in this respect. In practice, they act as if the Freudian theory of "real neuroses" explained every neurosis, even those that Freud himself considered as psychoneuroses. Thus, in strict logic, they are led to believe that a rejection of sexual inhibition is indicated, if not as an outright cure, at least as a stepping stone towards the cure of neurotic conditions. One doctor once advised a young man to have no qualms about masturbating when he felt like it. Another doctor told a married woman who had been frigid in her relations with her husband, to take a lover. The two patients each followed the doctor's advice. The results were most unfortunate. Each of them wound up in a very serious and deep-seated conflict with his own moral conscience. The psychoanalyst, always inclined to be doctrinaire, merely concluded that the moral principles that were the basis of this new conflict and which were bound up with the patients' religious faith, were neurotic in character and thus needed to be resolved and removed.

This is how the neurotic patient is robbed of even what

---

3. *Introduction* ..., p. 463

strength he has. Any psychologist worthy of the name, whether he be Freudian, Jungian, or "independent," knows that no one ever has the right to separate one symptom or function from the psychic totality of the individual. Since the cause of neurosis is a psychic conflict, only a psychic remedy can effect a cure.

Many diseases, as we have seen in the preceding chapter, affect both body and soul; we call them psychosomatic. In these cases, the psychological therapy must go hand in hand with the organic treatment. In many other cases, the doctor can accomplish very little in fighting against a disease because the psychic state of the sick person is opposed to the cure. Cooperation between doctors and psychologists appears to be indispensable, in order for each of them to accomplish what they are setting out to do.

* * * *

Frequently, a doctor will recommend a psychologist for a mentally estranged patient, that is, a sick man who no longer has any control over his mental faculties. The psychologist can do very little for such people. The methods and techniques at his disposal are really effective only in the case of sick people whose sense of self-criticism and responsibility is still intact, whose ego still possesses a certain minimum of freedom to collaborate actively in the analytic and synthetic processes.

Some psychiatrists, however, have been successful in applying properly psychoanalytic procedures and techniques to these mentally estranged patients, but always adapting them in such a way that the patient's ego had no active role to play.

* * * *

We have seen that, in the etiology of most neuroses and psychic conflicts, the factors of civilization have a large part to play. It is obviously impossible, in such cases, to arrive at any satisfactory results without acting at once on both the interior and exterior motivation of the neurosis.

Let us suppose that enforced solitude is one of the dominating factors in a given patient's psychic conflicts. It is difficult, if not impossible, to remedy his conflict without finding a solution for the real causes as well. The psychologist has to help his patient find human contacts that can put an end to this solitude.

The psychologist's task becomes even more difficult when it is the social order itself which is opposed to his patient's psychic health. He cannot therefore afford to ignore the economic, political, and cultural conditions of the world in which he has to exercise his calling. Obviously he cannot make any particular progress, as an individual, towards changing the path of civilization. But he can at least teach his patient to fit as well as possible into the structures, not to run afoul of the established order.

* * * *

Modern medicine of organic disease tends to be more and more preventive in character. The same thing should be happening in the field of mental health. The psychologist's mission, rather than merely to heal sick souls, ought to be the prevention of mental disease. This means that his primary patients would be not the sick people themselves, but parents, educators, "heads" of businesses or communities, in a word, all those whose intelligent behavior and administration could contribute to the creation of an "atmosphere" in which neurosis would have the least possible chances of developing.

Take the case of a young woman who is highly strung and somewhat frigid, unable to really enjoy life; it is true she shows no specifically neurotic symptoms at the moment; but if she goes to see a psychotherapist at about the age of thirty, there is a good chance that she will immunize herself, within the space of three or four months' treatment, against the serious neuroses that will threaten her when she turns forty. But above all, she will be in a position to help her children harmoniously resolve the psychic conflicts which threaten them, making for a happier and more expansive home atmosphere. The businessman, the manager, the politican, with the help of an experienced psychologist who would unblock their inhibited affective energies, would not only become better organized in their private and professional lives, but would help to create an atmosphere of understanding and joy all around them, an atmosphere which could only increase the effectiveness of their fellow-workers, their pupils, their subordinates. When the psychologist's position begins to take on such an individual and social usefulness, becoming as thoroughly "demystified" as that of the dentist, the human potential for happiness and success will be considerably increased.

13 sublimation

It is not really fair to blame psychoanalysts and other psychologists for being more concerned with abnormal and lower psychic activities — neuroses, dreams, careless behavior — than normal and higher actions. There is sufficient explanation and justification for all this in the pragmatic and essentially therapeutic origins of modern psychology. What is more, dreams belong to the lower psychic activity only in the Freudian perspective. Despite the excessive importance Freud attaches to the unconscious, he has never managed to completely free his thinking from the rationalistic prejudices of his times and thus always speaks of the unconscious with a more or less pejorative nuance. We have already sufficiently stressed our unwillingness to see things in this same light. We believe that the dream can just as well give access to the deepest and most mysterious part of the soul, the part that is rooted in the common psychic fund of mankind. It is only with a good deal of respect that we thus make an effort to decipher its language.

I. Higher Psychic Activities

It is an obvious fact, verifiable by even the most superficial observation, that psychic energy, the libido, is not restricted to dreams, conflicts, and neuroses. The architect who plans and builds; the painter, the musician, the poet who express themselves in color, sound, and verse; the believer as he prays, the mystic as he contemplates — these are all mobilizing an enormous quantity of their libido in the service of psychic activities which must be called higher. Sentiments and acts of friendship, father and mother love, love of children and fraternal love; brotherhood in combat, camaraderie in work or play; the heroism of the pioneer, the explorer, the warrior; the devotion of the doctor, the inventor, the social worker, the priest — none of this is possible without an intense consumption of affective energy. The richer a person is in his supply of libido, the more he can give of himself and realize grand and beautiful things in his life.

Freudian-inspired psychology almost completely misunderstands the profound originality of these higher psychic activities. As we have seen above, in Freudian thinking the affective energy is not a force in itself, neutral and undifferentiated; it is supposed to proceed from the sex instinct. It is only because the libido is unable, due to the intervention of the superego, to fully realize these sexual purposes in certain cases that it deviates towards other functions. The only "real nature" of man is animal, in Freudian thinking, and thus everything that tends to distinguish him from the beast must necessarily appear to be more or less abnormal.

II. *Freudian Sublimation*

The psychic function which turns the libido towards these higher psychic activities Freud calls *sublimation*. It is defined as an aptitude to replace the primitive sexual goals of the libido with other goals, for example, art, religion, friendship, military heroism. Obviously there is nothing sexual in these various psychic activities. Still, as Freudian theory would have it, the appearances are very deceiving. We need only push the analysis of any spiritual or esthetic sentiment to its ultimate depths, he assures us, and we will discover that its roots are always plunged deep into the biological sex instincts.

The only difference between neuroses and inattentive acts, on the one hand, and what we have called the higher psychic activities, on the other hand, would thus consist in the fact that the former are lower and closer to their immediate cause (the sexual libido), whereas the latter are higher. But if the Freudians decided to be logical in following out these first principles, there would be nothing to make us consider the devotion of the surgeon, for example, as higher than the mental anxiety of the neurotic. In both of these two cases there is a deviation of the libido from its normal object. The whole possibility of a value judgment is alien to the very concept of Freudian thinking, or any other materialistic or naturalistic philosophy.

* * * *

Here is a very simple case history to illustrate the Freudian theory of sublimation:

From the age of five, Peter had felt intense sexual excitation whenever he heard people talking of correction and corporal punishment. Towards the age of nine, he began playing soldiers with a friend of his. When he was separated from his companion, he began to play soldiers all by himself. His favorite adolescent reading was military or combat reports; he loved to dream about divisions, regiments, attack, offensive and defensive. When, about the age of eleven, he began to enjoy drawing things, it was always pictures of military outposts and fortified frontiers, in a word, anything that had any connection with soldiers and war.

Psychoanalysis attributes his inclination towards this type of game and reading and drawing to the repression of his sadistic sexual tendency. If morality and education had not kept him from delighting in inflicting torture on other people, he would not be playing war games and would never have been interested in military strategy or designed military installations. Perhaps even, we are informed by psychoanalysis, he would never have shown any interest in any kind of reading, nor ever learned much about drawing.

In later life, Peter became a history professor. Why? Quite simply because the story of war and combat occupies a large place in history. Once again, it was the satisfaction of his sadistic sexual tendencies that he was pursuing, this time through the medium of his teaching profession.

It is important to know, in order to understand Freudian sublimation, that Peter never experienced any pleasure of a sexual nature in reading war stories or in drawing pictures of military installations. He himself was completely ignorant of the motivation behind his tastes. The mechanism of sublimation is always unconscious.

*   *   *   *

We have already said that Freud, in his various writings, is not too embarrassed at the prospect of self-contradiction. Who can blame him for that? His was a pioneer's work, and he was necessarily led to propose many hypotheses that were not always in perfect harmony with each other, gradually, as his work progressed and his thinking developed. Systematic and dogmatic in his leanings, he cast these hypotheses in the form of categorical affirmations, without taking pains to advise his readers that they were only hypotheses.

In many texts, the founder of psychoanalysis, while still considering the effects of sublimation as the result of sexuality, seems to have recognized their specific character; he would have found it very difficult, actually, to speak of Peter's repressed sadistic tendencies (in the case cited above) as the real *cause* behind his historical work.

But we have also pointed out that too many of his disciples honored none of the scruples that their master so faithfully observed. They did not hesitate to proclaim that the sex instinct is the sole and sufficient cause of the higher psychic activities. For some of them, there is no question of even sublimating the sex instinct; there is little more than a thin disguise for the instinct. There is thus no fundamental *specific difference* between art, science, morality, and religion on the one hand, and the various neuroses on the other hand. As a result, the attitude of these Freudian "psychologists" is, according to the individual case, either scornful or condescending with regard to anyone who continues to live for those realities which we shall continue to regard as higher.

III. *True Sublimation*

The concept of sublimation seems to have great value in psychology. But it must be understood in a more subtle sense, less allied with the pansexualistic philosophies of some of its chief proponents.

Sublimation appears to be not a deviation of sexual libido "towards something higher," but rather the application of the basically undifferentiated affective energies towards the higher functions of the soul. If this energy had been consumed in sexual abandon, or in a neurosis, Peter (to continue the case cited above) would certainly never have become an historian of any merit. On the other hand, the same psychic tendency can find any of several outlets and directions, according to the orientation taken by the affective energy of a person's psyche. Thus we frequently discover a strong unconscious (and sometimes even conscious) aggressiveness in the surgeon, the military man, and naturally also in the sexual sadist; still there are no grounds for considering sadistic aggressiveness as the only "normal" manifestation of this tendency, and seeing the calling of the military man or the surgeon as a mere disguise for sadism. More simply, in the former case, the aggressive tendency is fixed in neurosis, and in the other two cases it has been sublimated. Thus it would be absurd to try to destroy aggressiveness, on the pretext that it is sadistic. Sublimated, its existential value is beyond question, and it is at the sublimation of his aggressiveness that the aggressive neurotic must necessarily aim.

Too many men, unfortunately, have only a very weak capacity for sublimation. This capacity is, in the last analysis, intimately bound up with the degree of talent or genius which the individual possesses. A person who has none at all is unable to use his affective energies excepting in the lowest psychic functions. The consequences are generally not too serious, but that is because the majority of men without genius or talent are also endowed with a lesser degree of libido. Thus, though they may be dull and unimaginative, they do not present any particularly serious threat to society. It is primarily when the individuals in question are more or less highly endowed that the psychic energy, when it is not at work in sublimation, threatens to deviate towards neurosis, and thus to become dangerous for the individual and for society as well.

But it is important not to have any illusions here. Even in the most highly endowed person, even in the genius, the capability of sublimation does not extend to the whole of his affective energy. A more or less important part has to be at work in normal sex life and in the other psychic functions that might be described as "middle-level." When this is not the case, then some form of neurotic deviation is almost inevitable. This is the light in which we must understand Pascal's famous dictum: "The man who tries to be an angel will be an animal." The saints themselves, for whom grace made it possible to reach the loftiest of sublimation, did not for all that escape the common laws of our human condition. We all know of the struggles that many of them had to face in order to remain faithful to their lofty commitments. And not all of them managed to reach their goals without paying the price of neurosis.

IV. *Promoting Sublimation*

The psychologist can never be satisfied with simply noting the fact that, in the case of certain persons who are specially predisposed, the affective psychic energy can be enlisted in the service of the higher psychic functions, provided there is no obstacle in the way. His duty is to use his knowledge and technology and experience in an effort to promote this sublimation. Obviously there will be some men and women in whom sublimation takes place spontaneously, either because there are no obstacles to inhibit its development, or because their ego is strong enough to overcome the obstacles. But many, many others could realize themselves just as well on some higher human plane, if only the mistakes in their education, the prejudices and complexes, did not stand in the way of sublimation, either leading them into neurosis or restricting them to their merely biological instincts.

Parents and other educators must propose a lofty set of ideals very early in their children's life — that is the best insurance for sublimation. Important as it is, in actual fact, to pay every attention to the efficient cause of sublimation, it is just as indispensable not to lose sight of the role of the final cause. The neurotic deviations of the libido are so frequent and serious in decadent civilizations simply because no lofty ideal — religious, moral, or social — has been proposed by the collective society as a whole in an effort to lead its individual members towards a true sublimation.

It goes without saying that it is never enough to propose such an ideal on the purely rational level. There is no way to give a "course in sublimated living" in our high schools. The values that this ideal embodies must be really lived by the family and by society. Nevertheless, it is not uncommon, even in a family that is very authentically attached to an ideal, to find that the child's affective energies are not channeled towards any sublimation. The reason for this is that, without really knowing it, the family has not been able to overcome certain obstacles. Here is where the psychologist's mission begins, as a specialist in affective pedagogy.

The psychologist is an even closer ally of sublimation when he has to cure a neurosis. It is important here for the affective energy that was mobilized by the neurosis to be applied to some higher psychic activity. If this is not possible, it is better to leave the person with his neurosis. The neurosis, after all, does constitute a certain psychic scaffolding for the soul. The individual really stands to gain nothing by seeing it torn down, unless he is able to replace it with another support more solid and lofty in its ideals. To hope that, after resolving the neurosis, the subject will succeed in setting out upon some form of sublimation on his own strength is a sad delusion. Synthesis, rather than analysis, is the task of the psychologist here — the latter being only a means to make the former possible.

* * * *

In this chapter, we have deliberately kept within the general possibilities of sublimation. In the chapters that follow, we shall study some of the individual higher psychic activities that can serve as stepping stones to sublimation.

14 catharsis through art

In the artistic creation, sublimation of the unconscious affective energy plays an absolutely essential role. Poets, composers, painters, sculptors — all seem to obey the unknown forces which, more than the artist himself, appear to be the creators of artistic work. These forces are called, according to various cultures, inspiration, the Muses, demons, or angels: in any event, there is a firm conviction that something more than the conscious ego is at work in both the conception and the execution of the artistic creation.

I. *Source of Inspiration*

The project undertaken by the artist can be the work of his conscious mind. The artist can, for example, very deliberately set about glorifying mother-love, his fatherland, the conversion of the repentant sinner. But his reason will search in vain for the means to give body to his ideas. He sets out along several vague plans, makes one sketch after another. But nothing satisfies him. It is all too conventional, too learned, too cold, and it all lacks soul, life, originality. Suddenly, in the course of an afternoon walk, while he is resting, while he is busy with some other little job that does not have the least connection with his projected work of art, the artist *sees* what form his work will take and how he is to begin it. After that, he need only set to work.

Sometimes the artist will have to wait for this inspiration for many months, even many years. It might happen that he was looking for inspiration for one project, and he finds it for another.

Some artists do not need this inspiration: they can execute their artistic works "cold," because they have such a perfect mastery of their technique. But generally, they are virtuosoes rather than artists. Their works might astonish us by their sheer ingeniousness, by their formal perfection; but they cannot move or exercise any really profound influence on our living.

* * * *

Where does this inspiration come from? Where is this hidden seat of the Muses from which the artist draws his inner force?

On all the evidence, it is not possible to attribute this inspiration to the conscious psyche. It obviously does not come from any outside stimulus either. Everything leads us to conclude that it has its source in the unconscious psyche, where dreams are made up, as well as the phantasies and obsessions and anxieties that breed neurosis. Psychology, in practical experience, reveals that this is indeed the case.

While he is waiting for this inspiration, the artist, even the least nervous artist, always experiences an indefinable anxiety, sometimes just as painful as the anxiety of neurosis. This is a sign of the fact that his psychic energy, the libido, is searhcing for some way to express itself. From the moment he first has the vision of what he is to do, the anxiety ceases, giving way to a fever of creative activity. It is probable that, if the anxiety had not been transferred into a work of art, the accumulated libido would have given rise to neurosis.

The work of the surrealist artists translates these fantasies of the unconscious in what we might call their pure state. Their work possesses all the apparent incoherence and incomprehensibility of a dream. Here, obviously, I am alluding only to those surrealists who are really artists. There are very many who have looked to Picasso or his followers only for certain technical procedures. Their "surrealism" is purely a product of the brain: it does not come from any inspiration.

But even the most "realistic" art is more like a dream than we might readily care to believe. There are dreams that seem so "clear" that the dreamer asks himself whether it is a dream or something that he is "really" seeing. The unconscious mind expresses itself in very different forms and symbols. The "clear dream" is just as mysterious as the "obscure dream"; realist art, if it is truly art, has a "hidden meaning" of its own, just like surrealist art.

II. *Understanding Art*

The psychology of the unconscious makes it possible for us to have a better and more profound understanding of the work of art. Why does a certain painter or sculptor delight in representing Christ as humiliated and tortured? Why does another artist like to represent the Blessed Virgin as mature and tender, whereas a third conceives of her only in the lines of a young girl who is barely beginning to develop? Why is the music of a Beethoven majestic, that of a Wagner tormented? Why is the poetry of a Claudel, in form and in content, so different from the poetry of a Valery? Why does an author like Kafka write one book and an author like Camus write a different one? To say that it was their way of looking at things or their personal preference has no meaning to the psychologist. There is no really free and fully voluntary act that does not have its underlying motivations. Still, this does not imply a denial of human freedom in general and of the freedom of the artist in particular; the truly free act is always an act that is consciously or unconsciously motivated.

If the artist submits to psychoanalysis, this deep-seated relationship between his unconscious tendencies and the content and form of his artistic output will certainly come to light. In practice, it is impossible to psychoanalyze all the artists whose work we should like to understand in greater depth, even if only because most of them are dead. The psychologist, since he is thus deprived of the opportunity to know the unconscious of the author or artist, firsthand, finds that he has to proceed in the inverse order: he must look to the work or art itself in an effort to discover the hidden and unconscious motives and motivation that set the artist to work in such a manner. This is not an arbitrary method at all; it is very like the methodology necessarily followed by the professional historian, who also has only the footprints of the past as a basis upon which to reconstruct his history. Thanks to depth psychology, we are in a position, today, to have an infinitely better understanding of the great departed masters than their own contemporaries enjoyed. Freud himself made a thorough study of Leonardo da Vinci; Baudouin has studied Victor Hugo and Laforgue has studied Baudelaire, etc.

The one serious disadvantage to the application of such a method comes from the *a priori* prejudices and theses of too many psychologists. Convinced, for example, that sublimation can be effected only on the basis of sexual conflict, some psychoanalysts, particularly the popularizers of Freudian psychoanalysis, explain in a very facile and thus also very superficial way, that all artistic masterpieces are the result of sexual conflict in their authors. And still, the laws of psychology never have the same universality as the laws of physics. In explaining the author by his work, the strictly individual factors necessarily escape our scientific eye. But still, if it is applied with prudence and careful in its expression, depth psychology can be of immense service in this domain.

* * * *

To illustrate the preceding remarks, let us take the famous novel of Pierre Loti, *Pecheurs d'Islande*. His heroine, Gaud, a pretty young Breton, marries an "Islandais," that is, one of those fishermen who go out after their catch in the far-off reaches of the Nordic seas. Eight days after their marriage, the fisherman leaves for his work and perishes in a severe storm.

Loti's choice of subject matter can be explained without having recourse to any analysis of his unconscious mind. So many Bretons are sailors and fishermen that an elementary familiarity with the country would be enough to suggest them as the heroes of his work. What strikes the attention of the psychologist in the novel is its tragic outcome. Why does Gaud's husband die so suddenly? The fisherman could just as well have returned after he was believed lost, found Gaud alive and waiting for him, lived happily with her, and raised a big family.

Orthodox Freudian psychoanalysis thus logically concludes that the death of Gaud's husband is the result of feelings of hostility in the author's unconscious mind. The fatal destiny of the fisherman appears to be a catharsis, that is, a literary resolution of the desires of vengeance nourished in Loti's unconscious mind.

According to what we know about Loti's life from other sources, Freudian interpretation seems probable enough. The writer was himself in love with a Breton girl who abandoned him in preference to a man from her own country. Still, it is impossible, a priori, to claim that the theoretical deductions that result from such an analysis of a work of art are really in conformity with reality. As in Loti's case, it is necessary to verify them by further information about the life and personality of the artist. What is more, just as in the case of dream interpretation and neurosis, the psychologist, before attributing any of these phenomena to the unconscious, must first exhaust all possible explanations that involve the conscious mind.

III. *Artistic Schools and Current Trends*

The psychologist must not be content with explaining isolated artistic works. These works generally belong to schools, to trends and tendencies that are particular to each era. Collective psychology, analytic in slant, thus appears to be most useful in understanding the work of art.

The extraordinary favor enjoyed by surrealism after the first world war seems to be explainable in terms of the explosion of the same irrational forces which, after the years of military discipline, suffering, and anxiety, gave rise to the Russian revolution, the German putsch, and the revolts in Italy and Hungary. It is also significant that one of the principal representatives of surrealism, Andre Breton, was conversant with Freud's work and greatly admired it. The surrealists made a voluntary and fully conscious effort to make art a medium of expressing the unconscious mind. But this same preoccupation made it possible for art to fulfill its real cathartic mission. It is certainly not pure chance that many of the principal representatives of the school (Aragon and Picasso among them) also turned Communist, becoming members of one of the most disciplined of all parties.

The existential vogue of the years 1945 to 1950 must be understood in the perspectives of human anxiety on the completion of the second world war. The failure of rationalism, the invention of the atomic bomb, and the apocalyptic threats which menaced humanity could give rise to nothing but panic, particularly in the case of men and women who had no religious faith to help them transcend the absurdity of immanence.

Still, existentialism was in no better position to effect a real catharsis than was the surrealism that followed the first world war. Sartre himself was unable to finally resign himself to "existence" such as it was in the caves of Saint-Germain-des-Pres. He was active in the struggles which tended, more or less consciously, towards the creation of a perfectly rational world, a world in which freedom such as his philosophy understands the term, would have no right to exist.

IV. *Creation and Conflict*

The psychic state of conflict is obviously an indispensable prerequisite for any artistic creation. Those who do not make a neat distinction between this conflict and neurosis as such, have maintained that it is really the latter which plays the essential role in the artist's activity. If such thinkers also happen to profess a rigorous, psychological determinism, they see this determinism as a real cause of the artistic output as well. It is on the basis of these postulates that they speak so highly of what they claim to be the positive effects of neurosis. In all logic, artists must therefore fear the loss of their creative capacity whenever they undertake psychoanalysis in an attempt to resolve their neuroses.

There is no denying the fact that many artists are neurotic. This can, no doubt, be explained by the fact that their greater sensitivity is generally correlated to a certain psychic fragility. But it is still true, as we have said above, that it is not because of neurosis, but rather despite their neurosis that they are artists. Thanks to their genius, or at least to their talent, they have managed to overcome a part of the obstacles that are the result of their neurosis. Some of them have done even better: they have even managed to put their neurosis to the service of their art, reproducing their obsessions and anxieties. Salvador Dali, Toulouse-Lautrec, Rimbaud, and even Nietzsche belong to this number. Still, I find it impossible to subscribe to the theories of Dracoulides, who devoted a remarkable piece of work to the pyschology of the artist, when he claims that it is impossible to conceive of a real artist who is completely sane and healthy from a psychic point of view.[1] Otherwise we would have to regard normality as such an abstract ideal that it would never be realized fully in any individual person. Besides, in reading through the examples that Dracoulides cites in substantiation of his thesis, we note that he regularly confuses psychic ailment with the psyche in a state of positive conflict.

Suffering, not only the suffering that gives rise to psychic conflict as such, but also any suffering that is psychic in origin, frequently plays the role of stimulus in the work of the artist.

---

1. *Psychanalyse de l'artiste et de son oeuvre*, p. 103

The famous painter Millet was right when he maintained that, even if he had the power to suppress all suffering in his life, he would not dream of doing it, because it is suffering that forces the artist to work. Dostoevsky would not have become one of the greatest novelists of all times, if he had not had to spend four years in Siberia, and if he had never suffered from epilepsy. Toulouse-Lautrec loved to paint monsters, clowns, prostitutes, hideous and deformed people. It does not take a psychoanalyst to notice the relationship between his own artistic output and the physical deformity he suffered from and which humiliated him from his early childhood. What is more, the artist was perfectly well aware of this himself, and he once wrote that if his legs had been a little longer, he never would have taken up painting seriously. He loved to do his own self-portrait, making it as ugly and humiliating as possible.

Proust, from his adolescence on, experienced a veritable passion for the life of the world. His long sickness never gave him a chance to enjoy this life. It is apparently in an effort to compensate for this frustration that he depicts the social life of the salon with such exact detail, in his famous *A la recherche du temps perdu*.

Still, neither Proust's sickness, nor Toulouse-Lautrec's physical deformity, nor Dostoevsky's suffering in Siberia are the complete explanation behind their literary and artistic work.

V. Neurosis is not the Cause of Genius

Psychology can, in a certain measure, cast light on the artistic creation; but it is not within its power to render an adequate explanation. It is certainly far from our intention to underestimate the importance of sublimation, since it is sublimation that gives artistic activity the affective energy that is indispensable for it, and which would otherwise be expended in other psychic functions. Still, in no case can sublimation be considered as the real source of the work of art. It could accomplish nothing, unless it recognized a real artistic talent in the subject. As for the origin of this talent, psychology has nothing to teach us. We are dealing here with a free gift of God (or if the metaphysical terminology implied in this wording is a source of embarrassment, a free gift of nature), a gift that is given only to very few people.

But without sublimation, such talent will never show, because it will have no energy to give it impetus. Since the psychic energy is being intensely absorbed in other activities, no matter how richly endowed with artistic talent we might suppose a given individual to be, he still could not ever really create anything worthwhile. It is thus very probable that, as the result of a poor psychological education, or a complete lack of such education, some very great artistic talents are never discovered.

Sex inhibits artistic talent more than any other psychic activity. A man who has discovered intense sexual satisfaction very early in life will generally be unwilling to attempt any sublimation. Contrary to a very widespread prejudice, great artists are only rarely endowed with strong sexual urges. Sex urgency, in the artist, is weak, and that is very likely the reason why there are so many sexual inverts among artists. We have noted above, that on the basis of the numerous observations recorded by practical psychology, perverts are almost never strongly hypersexual. The instinctual impulse in hypersexual people is strong enough to tend immediately towards its proper and primary object. It is when this instinct is very weak that it can be inhibited and easily led astray.

If the opposite thesis has been so stoutly maintained, the reason no doubt lies in the fact that sexuality has been unduly identified with affectivity. True artists are, of course, all endowed with a particularly high degree of affectivity. And it is from the ranks of the affectively rich that the great majority of artists arises.

What is more, it seems that artistic talent can develop, that is, that the affective energy is sublimated, primarily in people and in milieux where a more or less authentic morality has imposed severe restraints on sexual freedom. It is certainly not mere chance that makes the Catholic countries — Italy, Spain, and France as well — produce more artists (and more mystics too) than other countries. This has nothing to do with climate. The Greeks, the Yugoslavs, and the Arabs of North Africa live in almost the same climatic conditions as the people just mentioned. Their affectivity is obviously also intense. But it does not meet with as many obstacles to expression in sexual activity as it does in the Catholic countries, and once the stimulus to sublimation is thus removed, the artistic talent remains unexplored.

* * * *

Art, says Dracoulides, appears as a need and satisfaction of unsatisfied desires which vitally interest and torment individuals.[2] This is true enough, provided always that it is not understood as according a priority of nature to satisfactions of the biological order. The expenditure of affective energy, by way of sublimation, in the higher creations of the mind, is every bit as normal and natural. Stephan Zweig, speaking of Holderin, says that the torments of his last years produced the realization of an immense literary output in his case. Thanks to these torments he was able to find the fullest expression of his poetry and create the heroic rhythm of his greatest poems.[3] This explanation is justified only within a perspective of the sublimation process that is infinitely more subtle and nuanced than that currently professed by the disciples of Dr. Freud.

On the other hand, I must take a firm stand against the theory that Dracoulides seems to be substantiating when he writes that if Ibsen had lived in our century and gotten rid of his psychic conflicts by means of psychoanalytic cure, his whole dramatic output would have been nonexistent and he himself would have

---

2. *Psychanalyse* . . . , p. 98
3. Quoted in Dracoulides, *ibid.*, p. 101

been a country druggist.[4] In the eyes of the author we are quoting, psychic conflicts are the same thing as neurosis and it is these conflicts that are the cause of Ibsen's dramatic output. If the resolution of his neuroses had resulted in killing off the artist's creative capacity, then psychoanalysis should be condemned without appeal, notwithstanding the services which it renders to the diseased psyche. The healthy normal man, as he is conceived to be by certain psychoanalysts, is a monster of mediocrity, and thus in no way can he serve as an ideal towards which we must consciously tend.

If Toulouse-Lautrec had been cured of his neurosis, or of his inferiority complex which turned into a sado-masochistic state, he would probably not have painted any more drunks or prostitutes. His artistic genius, however, would have been the same as before, and, far from being deprived of psychic energy, it would have given birth to pictures that had a different inspiration, but were every bit as artistically worthwhile.

Ibsen, had he undergone psychoanalysis, would have created dramas at least as excellent as those we are familiar with, but they probably would not have been so pregnant with mental anguish. He never would have been a "country druggist," unless he had had the misfortune of falling into the hands of an orthodox Freudian psychoanalyst. Such a psychoanalyst, essentially, would not have been satisfied with setting free the affective energy that was tied up in the neurosis; he would have been obliged to make the writer better "adapted" as well, resolving, if possible, every element of psychic conflict within him.

A psyche that is free of every conflict and contradiction, and obeys only the impulses of natural instinct, is never our ideal. Sublimation never appears to us to be a second-best path, but rather one of the most positive faculties of our psyche. Esthetic pleasure does not appear to us to be a substitute, more or less "good," for sex pleasure. It has its own specific character; it is

---

4. *Ibid.*, p. 103

irreducible. In maintaining — and we have no intention of doing so — that the normal function of the libido is artistic creation and that its preoccupation with sexuality is nothing but a deviation, the paradox would be no more intolerable than that which is currently professed by many Freudian thinkers. In reality, it is the same affective energy, undifferentiated in itself, which is at work in sex, artistic creation, and all the other higher and lower psychic activities.

When Freud claims that "beauty" and "charm" are primarily only attributes of the sex object, or that esthetic emotion derives from the sphere of sexual sensation,[5] he is speaking, not as an educated scientific mind, but rather as the worst kind of a priori metaphysician. Neither the sex organs nor the sex act appear beautiful to those who observe them. It really seems that the feeling of shame, before integrating within moral concepts, was, primarily, and still is to a great extent, of the esthetic order.

In a certain measure, the psychology of the creator explains his work. But still there is always something in the artistic work that transcends the person of the artist. It is this, perhaps, that makes us the "co-creators with God" that Bergson speaks of.

VI. Art as Therapy

Thanks to the techniques which are at the disposal of modern-day depth psychology, artistic sublimation can act as a very effective medium in the prevention and resolution of neuroses. The important element in the resolution of the neurosis is for the art which was bound up in the neurosis not to remain without positive outlet, but to be employed in some other psychic activity. Without such sublimation, there is a danger that a new neurosis will quickly replace the one that has been resolved. We

---

5. Passim, in Malaise dans la civilisation

are indebted to Charles Baudouin for an example that seems to offer a particularly apt illustration of this cathartic role of art.

A young girl of sixteen went to the psychologist. She was a very pretty girl, but seemed to have a horror of every form of coquetry: she dressed with extreme carelessness, never took care of her hair, etc. Still, on the other hand she spent a good deal of time dressing and caring for her collection of dolls. She also spent a lot of time taking care of the flowers in the family garden. With the plants and with the dolls, she gave every evidence of real taste: obviously it was no lack of *savoir-faire* that made her so negligent about her own person.

Every month, during her period, this young lady gave evidence of serious psychic problems, and that is why she went to see the psychologist. There was no visible connection between these troubles and her refusal to be a woman. But, it came out in the course of the analysis that her delirium and the ideas of persecution which beset her every month all began on one very definite date which she remembered very well. At the age of twelve, on the very day of her first menstrual period, another person made some impure gestures in her presence that greatly shocked her. Unconsciously, she connected these disgusting gestures with her own budding femininity, which she regarded somehow as soiled and dirtied by them. Thus there was always a close relationship between her refusal of the most elementary feminine conduct and the ideas of persecution and delirium that beset her every month.

Is it enough to have uncovered the origin of a neurosis in order for the young lady to consider herself as cured? Certainly not.

She had, all by herself, discovered a certain sublimation of her repressed femininity in her exaggerated care of the dolls and the flowers. This sublimation probably succeeded in keeping her neurotic symptoms from habitually manifesting their presence and restricted them to certain fixed times and periods. The psychologist took all this into account and thus tried to complete this process of sublimation. He encouraged the young lady to get very interested in art, since he quickly discovered that she had a real gift for artistic expression. Six months later, all the neurotic symptoms had completely disappeared. Her interest in art gradually developed her esthetic sense, and she naturally began to take more interest in herself as well, and show her natural beauty by careful attention to her person.

Still we must insist once again on the fact that artistic sublimation is possible only for those who have real artistic talent. It is the task of the psychologist to discover the gifts of his patient, either for music, or for poetry, or for painting, or for the dance. When this talent is lacking, the efforts at sublimation must bear upon some other area of human experience. It might be possible to find an outlet in social dedication, sports, even politics. The psychologist has a real problem when he is dealing with a person who is not well suited for any form of sublimation. Fortunately, these minus quantities among people are much less numerous than we generally like to believe, particularly in the case of neurotics.

15 psychology and morality

It is not within the province of psychology to establish a new system of morality. Even if psychology were to attempt such an enterprise, the results, would hardly be any more successful than those of the "rational morality" which marked the end of the last century. This is not the place to reopen the age-old controversy as to the existence or non-existence of an eternal and universal morality, obligatory for every human being, or to decide whether there are, instead, systems of morality that are proper to a given civilization or social class. The psychologist, no matter what his own personal religious or philosophical convictions might be, always looks at the problem of morality under a markedly different point of view from that adopted by theologians and moralists.

The moralist always centers his attention primarily on the objective foundations of morality, either metaphysical or sociological. Whether the moral law has been promulgated by a God who revealed it to mankind, or decreed it by "universal reason," or merely imposed by the instinct to preserve society's self-conserving instincts, it is always a principle external to the person himself. The individual is obliged to obey it, voluntarily by preference, but, if need be, despite himself. The worth and importance of such a law, both social and individual, seem to be incontestable.

The psychologist, on the other hand, is interested in *subjective morality*. His work is to untangle the personal motivations that incline each individual to one or another kind of moral conduct. Subjective morality is not necessarily opposed to objective morality; it can even be the interiorization of external morality. Here is a good example of the distinctions to be made.

Catholic morality forbids divorce. All Catholics are bound to conform to this law which takes no considerations of the personal order into account. The psychologist, on the other hand, observes that Catholics, unhappy in their marriage but unable to get a divorce, are frequently guided by subjective imperatives that are extremely varied. One person might observe the law out of loving obedience to the will of God as expressed by the Church. Another might obey because divorce is looked down upon in the social environment in which he happens to live. A third might obey because he is afraid of the problems that his new found freedom would pose for him. Whereas the first, no matter how serious his conjugal difficulties might prove to be, always discovers a certain sense of peace and profound joy in his obedience to the law, the other two are not so fortunate. The moralist, in strict logic, can always ignore these subjective differences; but in the eyes of the psychologist they are essential. His task is not so much to suggest divorce for those who are unwilling to attempt divorce for reasons that they do not deem solidly worthwhile, but rather to help them find new and more authentic motivation for conjugal fidelity.

I. *Psychological Determinism and Moral Conscience*

It is no surprise to discover that Dr. Freud and his disciples were interested almost exclusively in the unconscious motivation of moral behavior. They have a tendency to see man merely as an irrational being, determined by implacable biological laws, evolving as a function of his instinctual conflicts. Psychological freedom is only an illusion, in their eyes, and thus a man never behaves freely in any particular choice of activities he makes. Psychological determinism is absolute in their eyes, and a man has to obey its mechanisms. Breaking with this universal determinism, according to Freud, even on one single point, would upset the whole scientific conception of the world. His hostility towards all objective morality is thus a perfectly logical conclusion. Morality, with its obligations, sanctions, and eventual recompenses, could have meaning only in the case of free persons. Since man is not free, he must not ever be considered as subject to any kind of morality.

In this perspective, it is impossible to explain moral conscience, and yet no psychologist could ever doubt that it really exists. Freud attributes it to events that took place in the far distant past of collective humanity. Together with certain sociologists who were popular in his day, he presumes that our earliest ancestors lived in hordes. No one in this vast horde had any particular awareness of his own individuality, and thus there could be no question of any moral law. The only law that the horde obeyed was the law dictated by instinct, especially by the instinct of self-preservation. Here too, it was not a question of the individual's self-preservation, but that of the group. But one day — by some fatal chance — disorder and discord entered into the peaceful existence of the horde. A young member of the group killed his aged father in order to steal his woman. The collectivity immediately decreed severe sanctions for this parricide. Thus it was the famous Oedipus complex that gave birth to moral conscience.

Obviously, Freud continues, no one of us has any present-day recollection of this ancestral crime. Still, the interdicts promulgated on that occasion have been sharply registered deep in our collective unconscious. As a result, whenever a man acts with a feeling that he is doing good or evil, that is, behaves in a morally conscious manner, he refers unconsciously, in the last analysis, to these repressed feelings of incestuous sexuality. The famous "path of conscience" does not thus come from God; it is not a dictate of principles that are ingrafted into the spiritual nature of man. It is only the expression of age-old prohibitions, whose origins are long forgotten but always at work within the unconscious mind.

Obviously, Freud judges all moral prohibitions with extreme severity, particularly in the area of sexual morality. Since the moral conscience is the consequence of sexual crime in the beginning, in his theories, all other moral precepts can only be unconscious disguises or prolongations of the primitive sexual prohibition. This prohibition against incest goes counter to instinct, and thus, in his eyes, it is "the most frightful mutilation ever imposed, in the whole course of history, upon the love life of the human person."[1]

Hedonism alone is supposed to determine the goodness of human behavior. It is simply the pleasure principle that determines the goal of life, writes Freud, and governs all the operations of the psychic functions from the very first.[2] Freud is not embarrassed at the fact that, for current morality, evil frequently does not consist in what is harmful and dangerous for the ego, but rather in what is desirable and what procures pleasure. Thus an outside influence is decreeing what must be called good and evil.[3]

The principal shortcoming in this Freudian theory of the origin of the moral conscience is that it is not based on any demonstrable fact. No serious ethnologist could any longer maintain that primitive man lived in a horde. Even if this were the case, it is hard to see how sexual rivalry between father and son could have led to such evil consequences, since, by definition, no one had an awareness of his own individuality. Freud invented a fable, which some thinkers might find beautiful, but it could never hope to serve as the basis for theories that claim to be scientific in any sense of the word. If we were to follow him to his logical conclusions, then the psychologist's mission is merely to set man free from all his moral obligations, to take away every restraint

1. *Malaise dans la civilisation,* p. 730
2. *Ibid.,* p. 703
3. *Ibid.,* p .740

from the free play of his natural instincts. In the perspectives of a dogmatic biologism, how can we be expected to believe that the role of instinct in man is not identical to the role of instinct in the animal? In the animal, instinct is the only force that regulates behavior, whereas in man, a being endowed with the use of reason, instinct never has the same scope or precision. What is more, it must necessarily be this way; otherwise the mind would have no way to develop.

No matter how hazardous certain of Freud's philosophical speculations might have been, he was too scrupulously honest a practitioner to let himself be sidetracked by his own theories, in the actual exercise of his profession as psychotherapist. Here once again, those who take their inspiration from Freud have frequently gone far beyond the limits observed by their master. They actually treat morality as if it were the worst enemy of psychic health, and they disapprove of every form of discipline that it tries to impose on human instinct. There is no need to insist on the lamentable results of such an attitude in the practice of psychology. We find here a further confirmation of the truth that the elucubrations of the theorists are not always so harmless as certain people claim and that, as a result, their intellectual responsibility is always very serious.

Doctor Charles Odier,[4] though he is still faithful to the broader theses of Freudian thinking, has produced an infinitely clearer, more profound, and more detailed explanation of the psychological content of morality. Though we cannot follow Odier on every point, it does seem that psychologists as well as moralists would do well to ponder his reflections.

We think, together with Jung, that the moral attitude is a real factor which the psychologist must take into account if he does not mean to risk the most classical blunders.[5]

---

4. *Les deux sources, consciente et inconsciente, de la morale.*
5. *L'homme. . . . ,* p. 29

II. *Morality and Unconscious Motivation*

Morality does not come from outside, nor is it imposed by any human power. It constitutes a "function of the human soul, as old as humanity itself."[6] Without morality, there would be no way for men to live in society and thus satisfy one of the greatest exigencies of their human nature.

The psychologist as such does not need to be preoccupied with "norms" that are to guide the behavior of man: that is the domain of the moralist. Our professional attention is directed to the fact that men react with extreme diversity in response to the demands of moral law. Thus we observe that the prohibition of extra-marital sexual relations in Christian morality sometimes promotes the highest spiritual or artistic activity, sometimes gives way to the most painful neuroses, or even leads to open crime. For the majority of mankind, it serves as an incentive to proper marriage and the establishment of a normal family life. It is the psychologist's job to untangle the reasons behind such radically different forms of behavior and, as the case demands, help the moral law to produce better and more consistent results.

As long as it is merely a question of instincts, rigorously biological needs and drives, there is not yet a question of morality. Morality comes into the picture only when the conscious and free ego enters into play. On the other hand, because of the close solidarity between mind and body, even in our freest acts, those that are most specifically spiritual in nature, there is always an element of determinism. Often, the simple study of the conscious elements in a situation will permit the trained moralist to arrive at more or less accurate approximation of what is the work of freedom in the human act involved and what is the work of determinism. "Attenuating circumstances" as they are admitted

---

6. Jung: *Psychologie de l'inconscient,* p. 62

by judges in deliberating the gravity of an offense — when the criminal has acted under the influence of violent passion, or because he was psychically damaged by an unhappy childhood, or because his parents were alcoholics — are based precisely upon the possibility of establishing such a distinction. The confessor, in his turn, is always ready to admit that what might be *objectively* a "mortal sin" is often not mortal sin *subjectively*, because the act in question can be explained more by determinism than by psychological freedom.

Frequently, however, a serious discord exists between the conscious and the unconscious motivation of a moral act. Anne, married for ten years, decided to observe chastity throughout the season of Lent. In her conscious mind, she was convinced that she was acting solely out of love of God. When various psychic troubles made their appearance, she went to see a psychologist. He quickly discovered that in Anne's unconscious mind, her decision to observe chastity during Lent had been motivated by a violent resentment towards her husband, by the desire to avenge herself on him for not having been tender and affectionate enough towards her.

Even from the point of view of positive Christian morality, the knowledge of unconscious motivations always has a great practical utility. Thus, Anne's confessor, who was familiar only with the conscious motivation behind her decision, could only praise her for her "piety." If he had the necessary insight into her unconscious motivations, he would soon enough understand that it was his duty to advise her immediately to give up her Lenten resolution.

Even a well-informed confessor, however, can do nothing to resolve the unconscious hostility Anne feels for her husband. It is the psychologist's task to complement the activity of the confessor in this respect. Most of the time, in such cases, the confessor's exhortations to his penitent will be effective only after the psychologist has been called in as well.

248 / THE DEPTHS OF THE SOUL

III. *Morality and Instinctive Act*

As we have just seen, the same objective behavior can be at once moral and immoral, according as it is seen from the point of view of the conscious or the unconscious. Or, more exactly, since only the conscious mind is the seat of morality, moral behavior can be heathy at one time and diseased at another.

Still, the instinctive act must not be indiscriminately regarded as the opposite of morality. In certain Christian circles, there is still a strong inclination to measure the moral value of an act in terms of the gradually diminishing degrees of pleasure associated with it. I have often heard fervent believers say, with a strong feeling of guilt and regret: "I'm not getting any merit for acting this way; I enjoy it so much." Here once again we run headlong into inadmissible prejudices against the flesh. The fact that a mother's love for her children has strong roots deep in the flesh does not for that matter make it any less beautiful or noble. Thanks to the progress of psychology, we are beginning to admit that even the pleasure experienced in the sex act, far from constituting an immoral imperfection for the Christian husband or wife, is in itself something good and even morally praiseworthy.

A young man has chosen a military career. Consciously, he has made his choice because he is convinced that in this field he can give the most concrete expression to his burning love for his fatherland. But unconsciously, the career of officer offers him a means to satisfy his strong aggressive tendencies, and his instinctive need for an exciting and adventurous life. Here once again, the unconscious motivation does nothing to diminish the moral value of the conscious choice. Aggressiveness, far from being a naturally evil thing, is really an evidence of normal vitality. When, in virtue of conscious choice, it is enlisted in the service of an objectively good cause, it must be considered as morally good. The situation changes when, as in the case of Anne, the conscious behavior is only a pretext for unconscious feelings that are bad in themselves.

A certain person is prodigal in his little attentions and the little gifts he gives. Is that generosity? Perhaps, but not necessarily. The unconscious can also be at work here, trying to find a solution to a loneliness that has become insupportable. In this hypothesis, the generosity is no more than apparent, and still the prodigality is not morally reproachable. Things would be much different if a person were to make such presents only in an effort unconsciously, to oblige other people to give something more in return.

Durand is vehement in criticizing corruption in public officials, the immorality of youth, the dishonesty of businessmen, etc. Looking at things only superficially, we might be inclined to think that he is a man with a particularly lofty moral sense. But the psychologist knows that the conduct and activity of such do-gooders is generally based on their own unconscious desires to accomplish the very things that they so violently criticize in others. If you find a woman who is particularly harsh on the disloyalty of other women, particularly her close friends, you must not be too surprised to learn that she is "cheating" her husband.

IV. *Morality and Psychosynthesis*

The Freudian doctrine of repression, according to Jung,[7] acts as if there were only "overly moral" people in the world, people who are suppressing their immoral instincts and nature. If his point of view were true, the immoral person, who lives his instinctive impulses without any check or rein, would necessarily be completely immune from the danger of neurosis. Naturally, as experience has proven, this is not the case. If we analyze the problem, we discover that in the case of the immoral man it is merely his moral sense that has been repressed.

---

7. *Psyhcologie de l'inconscient*, p. 61

Stripping away the pretext of false morality does nothing to prejudice the existence of true morality. If it is true that, often bad faith is lurking behind the appearances of good faith, and that love frequently serves as a mask for hate, and that devotion is often no more than a tool towards self-seeking, the psychologist is still not authorized to conclude, with Sartre, that neither faith nor love nor devotion exist in any pure form. We denounce pseudo-morality only to insure that moral consciousness establishes its proper autonomy over unconscious determinism.

The psychologist's mission as such is not the promotion of moral perfection. Even if psychology claimed such a lofty goal, its techniques are incapable of reaching it. In making an effort to reduce unconscious motivations, it is the acquisition of *moral wholeness* that it is promoting. In certain specific cases, moral perfection can coexist with unconscious feelings that have nothing particularly moral about them; the unconscious sentiments can even serve as a stimulus for the morality. This was probably the case with those saints who kept accusing themselves of being "great sinners," without ever being able to say precisely in what their sin consisted. St. Anthony and other ascetics, in their Homeric combats with the Tempter, were probably caught up in a violent unconscious conflict. Would it have been the best course to reduce these psychic conflicts and reestablish their full moral health? The answer is by no means obvious, particularly when dealing with men of this stamp, in whom unconscious motivations have no chance to prevail.[8] As for the common run of men, moral health could only promote their progress towards moral perfection.

* * * *

Under the pretext that unconscious motivation is less pure than conscious reasons, the psychologist must obviously not try

---

8. Obviously it is not our intention here to deny, *a priori*, the intervention of the devil in the temptations of the saints under discussion. But it is precisely on their unconscious mind that the devil always acts.

to dissuade his patients from being chaste, loyal, and honest, or from showing love. A psychoanalyst whom I knew very well had just observed that one of his patients had transfered to his wife the feelings of affection which, in his childhood, he had felt for his twin brother. Now obviously it is not "healthy" to love your wife the way you love your brother, no matter how pure and noble we suppose this fraternal love to be. In order to reduce the fixation on the twin brother, the psychoanalyst, unable to see beyond his ingrained principles, thought he also had to destroy the patient's love for his wife. As we might well imagine, the result of such a therapy could only be disastrous. In the abstract, it is possible for the man in question to still arrive at a fuller degree of moral health. But it is existentially certain that he will draw much father away from moral perfection. The psycho-analyst, in order not to damage this morality, should have made every effort to guarantee that only those elements in his client's love for his wife that could really prove harmful to authentic conjugal love would be liquidated — the promotion of this love always remaining the primary objective of his activity.

John had an unhealthy fear of women. He felt that his religion obliged him to avoid women as a permanent occasion of tempta-tion and sin. He was also afraid that by having too much to do with women he would contract a venereal disease and waste all his money. He masturbated with a frequency that was excessive even from the point of view of his health alone. The psychologist gradually succeeded in freeing him from his obsessional fear of women, and convincing him that his attitude towards women had nothing to do with either religion or morality. His habit of masturbation stopped after he became aware of these facts. Obviously there is no question of advising John to take advantage of his newly recovered moral health and give up his chastity with the first woman that comes along. John's moral conscience would not approve of extra-marital sexual relations, and thus the psychologist does not have the right, under the pretext of safe-guarding John's mental health, to advise anything counter to his moral conscience, even if his own convictions in this area are not identical with those of his patient. While waiting for John to get married, it would be very important to help him maintain his chastity, not out of fear of committing sin or contracting a disease, but simply as a means to safeguard the moral perfection towards which John is striving.

* * * *

Psychological morality must not ever attempt to replace religious or social morality. It might perhaps be possible for a "superman" to live a purely subjective morality, without any reference to external or transcendent principles. But even that is not probable; witness the personal tragedy of Nietzsche.

Making no fundamental distinction between false and true values, and refusing, on principle, to see religious or social morality as anything other than the irrational constraints imposed by the superego, certain psychologists attempt to free their clients from every "moral complex." They advise their patients to impose only those limits upon the impulses of their instincts that are dictated by their own individual reason. The conception that such psychotherapists, at least implicitly, have of human freedom is very close to the philosophy of Sartre. Our own personal observation has been that, based on practical results, those patients who have been emancipated from all objective morality are not supermen but slaves. On the basis of all the available evidence, subjective psychological morality has meaning and justification only when it is applied to promoting objective morality, moral perfection.

Taking things as a whole, both for society and for the individual himself, it is preferable for the individual to act on the basis of an inauthentic and unconscious morality, than without any morality whatsoever. It would indeed be desirable for husband and wife to be faithful to each other out of mutual love or because they believe in the sacred character of marriage. But rather than infidelity and adultery, even a fidelity that is based, for example, on the fear of scandal, is morally justifiable. The psychologist must not work towards the liquidation of this false fidelity unless his efforts will also give rise to a true basis for fidelity. Supposing that this true fidelity appears to be impossible, in a given case, then it is always preferable to leave the inauthentic morality undisturbed.

V. Promotion of True Morality

From the psychological point of view, behavior is really moral when it is in conformity with the inner truth of the subject, with his honesty towards himself and others, when it makes him assume the responsibility of his own destiny and the destiny of others who are in his charge. The Christian finds nothing in this that is not perfectly in accord with the religious morality he professes. It can only be great ignorance that prompts certain people to believe that religious morality is a form of blind obedience to commandments that are foreign to the inner exigencies of the human soul. Still there is always an important difference between Christian morality and psychological morality: the former is interested only in the harmony that exists between behavior and conscience, whereas the latter stresses primarily the unconscious motivations of behavior.

We can only rejoice to note that psychology has unmasked certain serious deformations of Christian morality. We know that the deep-lying motivation behind the sufferings that certain people impose upon themselves, claiming that they are a form of Christian virtue, is not always really pure. Maurice, although he is a very lukewarm Christian in his everyday life, takes the discipline (scourges himself) every day and periodically imposes painful privations upon himself in fasting and abstinence. The psychologist he went to consult on the subject of certain psychic troubles, had no difficulty in dicovering that the love of God and the desire for Christian perfection had no real place in his austerities. It was not yet a question of masochism properly so called, because his sexuality appeared to be quite normal. It turned out that Maurice used to take great delight in criticizing the mediocrity of Christians whom he knew and that he made his censorship of their living a sort of specialty. In order for him to feel authorized to assume such a role, his own Christianity had to be perfectly pure. As it was, however, Maurice felt no particular call either to mysticism or to morality, or above all else even to charity. His unconscious mind thus invented a variety of masochistic practices that served as his credentials for criticizing other people's conduct.

The sufferings a person inflicts on himself are often tainted with more or less neurotic elements. Realizing this, spiritual directors who have some grounding in depth psychology hardly ever recommend such behavior. It is far better to have a Christian acceptance of the sufferings and adversities that come our way in the normal course of living.

The psychologist is never an enemy of positive morality. Unless he is a super-orthodox Freudian, he never considers the precepts and practices of current morality as something superfluous or harmful to psychic health. But, thanks to his professional aptitude for seeing things in real depth, he can also observe that far too often the forms have become void of all content. Still, instead of shattering these empty forms, he must make an effort to fill them once again, helping the subject to rediscover the basic demands of fundamental morality. He knows, contrary to what many people believe, that these demands, instead of constituting an obstacle to the free development of the human psyche, are a powerful aid and even an indispensable condition for psychic development.

Thus, it is not their ingrained hostility towards morality that makes psycholanalysts and some other modern psychologists take a rather severe attitude towards current sex morality. They have observed that this morality is at the root of many crimes and numerous neuroses. The reason for this is not the fact that this morality imposes constraints on the sex instinct, but rather because these restraints have become *taboos,* too often, in our modern civilization, they no longer have any real point of reference to conscious morality, freely accepted; since they have been reduced to the level of an irrational constraint, they have nothing to contribute to the advancement of mankind. Psychosynthesis, here once again, does not contemplate the destruction of morality, but rather its revitalization.

VI. *Sin and Unconscious Guilt*

The idea of morality, at least in the mind of the Christian, is intimately bound up with the idea of sin. Whatever is not sinful is moral, and vice versa. This conception of things is obviously in contradiction with the spirit of the Gospels. The Old Law was a law of constraint, whereas the obedience demanded by the New Law, the Law promulgated by Christ, is supposed to proceed from the love of God.

Any least acquaintance with the Christian world is enough to demonstrate the fact that very many people experience genuine scruples and anxieties, and act as if they were always under accusation, and always needed to prove themselves not guilty. In a word, we get the impression that many Christians are not really living the Law of Love. What is more, a philosopher who was so deeply rooted in faith as Soren Kierkegaard has noted that man cannot come into the presence of God without feeling guilty and sinful.

On the basis of their natural opposition to such exaggerated attitudes, many psychologists severely condemn Christian morality. Since the guilt feeling always plays a disastrous role in the majority of neurotics, it is easy to blame Christianity as the force that is responsible for their sufferings. This is, fundamentally, the opinion of Freud and many other psychologists. In their eyes, there is no essential difference between the Christian doctrine of sin and primitive taboos. Dr. Hesnard, in the name of psychic health, has attempted to establish a system of "morality without sin." We are here involved with a misunderstanding that it is most urgent to correct, for the good of both religion and psychology.

* * * *

What characterizes almost all neurotics is their unconscious feelings of guilt. Without knowing either why or how, they feel that they have committed sin. The absurd rites to which they feel obligated to turn, are aimed primarily at redeeming themselves from this sin, but even more frequently they are an effort to escape its disastrous consequences. If the neurotic, in general, is afraid to live a happy life, and if his unconscious mind normally leads him to destroy his own happiness, if in everything he undertakes, he necessarily acts in such a way as to insure its ultimate failure, that is all an indication of his fundamental guilt complex: he feels that he has no right to happiness or success. He is afraid, that, if he is successful or happy in any respect, he will have to pay dearly for it later on.

This unconscious feeling of guilt works not only against the neurotic himself. The neurotic also presumes, without any valid reason, that other people are equally guilty, and he cannot keep from playing the role of avenger. This he does particularly in the case of those who are most dear to him. It is almost as if, in accusing and punishing them, he hoped to keep them from other more terrible punishments. It is largely owing to this tendency that the presence of a neurotic person is such a source of pain to everyone around him. And at the same time he is unwilling to accept the least criticism, the least disapproval on the part of others, because this only reinforces his own feelings of guilt.

In the eyes of the Freudian school, the guilt feeling is obviously sexual in origin, the result of the Oedipus complex. Moral education, since it lays particular stress on the prohibition of sexual pleasure, only aggravates this complex. Christian morality, in particular, appears dangerous, and thus its ultimate destruction appears to be a prerequisite condition for any effective combat against neurosis. Let a man no longer see himself as a sinner, and all will be well!

We must note that, for these psychologists, there is no opposition to the concept of culpable act, but merely the feeling of guilt. Objectively speaking, says Dr. Hesnard, human acts must be evaluated only on the basis of their social usefulness, in reference to other people. What makes the guilt feeling so harmful is the fact that it undermines the soul. The importance that Christianity and every other religion always placed on the interior life is to be condemned out of hand, he claims. Thus Hesnard's psychology comes very close to the Marxist conception of moral values.

This whole psychology of sin and guilt shows a complete misunderstanding of the Christian doctrine. It is not the *feeling* of guilt which characterizes the Christian, but rather the fact that he is *conscious* of his sin and knows *why* he is guilty. He also knows that God can deliver him from this sin. His consciousness of sin cannot therefore give rise to neurosis, but rather to repentance, which is the condition for divine forgiveness. Neurotic guilt, on the other hand, is imprecise and vague, because it is unconscious in origin. On the religious plane, it is encountered primarily in the phenomenon of scrupulosity.

The scrupulous person, in confession, never accuses himself of precise sins, really committed, as Catholic morality requires. He feels unhappy; and he knows, in a vague and diffuse manner, that he is guilty. He does not confess so much in order to be forgiven as in the magic hope that he will thereby escape the dangers that threaten him. Basically, he does not really believe in forgiveness, because he keeps coming back to the same sins, real or imaginary, sins for which he has already received forgiveness several times over. He has an obsession with unreal sins. Claire, a young medical student, brought up in an excellent Christian education, regularly accused herself in each one of her many confessions —

and to the great scandal of her confessors — that she wanted to make love to Christ, or to the saint whose feast it happened to be, or with a highly placed religious personality. Was she a sinner? Certainly not, in the Christian sense of the concept. But she did have a strong unconscious guilt feeling, which expressed itself in the most absurd manner, in radical opposition to her conscious personality.

Only the grossest ignorance can excuse the confusion, so frequent in the case of psychoanalysts, between the Christian dogma of original sin and the unconscious guilt complex. The dogma has no real relation to any more or less diffuse "feeling of guilt." What is more, how can we forget that theology is so intimately bound up with the realities of a loving Redemption that it could not possibly give rise to any feelings of anxiety?

VII. Psychological Necessity of Morality

Unconscious guilt feeling is, beyond the slightest doubt, harmful to any human being, even if it does not always result in neurosis. Still it is not morality, but rather the lack or distortion of morality that is responsible for neurosis. A person who claims that he behaves as if there were neither good nor evil, still cannot very well manage to eradicate his inner feelings of both good and evil. Obviously, each civilization has a more or less original idea of what is good or evil. Thus we might well say that there are several moralities, even if we believe that one of them is more excellent than others, or even the only morality that is really in conformity with "human nature." We simply observe that human nature is *actualized* in different manners according to the various classes of individuals and civilizations. In any hypothesis, morality is a function of the ego and its degree of perfection is always in proportion to the solidity of the ego.

When this ego, for lack of innate strength or by reason of

intellectual error, refuses to accept any concept of morality, then it is the unconscious, that, in its own anarchical way, develops its own distinctions of good and evil. But the unconscious might very well consider something evil that, objectively speaking, is actually good, and vice versa; above all, it never has a really clear concept of what is good or evil for "unconscious morality." Hence the diffuse and anxiety-ridden character of unconscious guilt.

This more or less neurotic sense of guilt is frequently the result of poor education. Morality is, after all, a factor in promoting human progress only if it springs from a mystique, from a transcendent love. All too frequently children and adolescents are trained in the pursuit of a morality that is purely formalistic. Instead of freeing and elevating the soul, it imprisons the spirit. And then the unconscious mind might well refuse to submit to it.

* * * *

The idea of sin in itself is not at all morbid even though, like so many other basically good things, it can very well become morbid. From the mere psychological point of view, the concept of sin is frequently a very effective stimulus towards spiritual progress.

Some psychologists consider the guilt feeling as the only source of evil in man. Psychoanalysis, in resolving or liquidating this disastrous feeling of guilt, could thus, allegedly, make everyone good. But we need only express this extremist thesis in order to realize how fragile a morality would have to be if it were only psychological in its basis. It is infinitely more true to say that it is really the recognition of their sins, not a mere theoretical admission but a knowledge accompanied by repentance and a purpose of amendment, that can make men absolutely good, or at least make them much better.

Knowledge and admission of sins give rise to no guilt complexes. Quite the contrary, many psychologists have observed that an awareness of sin is frequently the very best remedy against neurosis. In this repect we have already mentioned the opinion of C. G. Jung, according to whom neurosis is relatively less frequent in fervent Catholics than in any other sociological category. If, in certain countries, particularly the U.S.A., so many persons make a habit of retaining and regularly visiting a psychologist, might not the underlying reason for the popularity of psychologists be the fact that they are really replacing the confessor in people's lives? Unfortunately, this "confessor" does not have the power to absolve and pardon, and thus there is not very much he can do to counteract the conscious feeling of guilt.

Still in no case could psychoanalysis ever be a substitute for examination of conscience. This process, as its name indicates, is never concerned with unconscious complexes, but exclusively with that part of human behavior which relates to human freedom and thus personal responsibility. On the other hand, contrary to what certain spiritual directors seem to think, the examination of conscience is not in a position to replace analytic catharsis, which is concerned exclusively with unconscious conflicts. Still it is always true that the examination of conscience and confession and sacramental absolution can, in many cases, keep moral conflicts from being repressed into the unconscious mind.

The psychologist's task, with respect to persons who are suffering anxiety and guilt feelings, is not to persuade them that they are not guilty. He must help them to distinguish between real guilt and neurotic guilt. A person who is aware of the moral faults that he has really and truly committed is not likely to seek refuge in a barren sense of fear; he will assume full and courageous responsibility for all his acts, including the sinful ones. Flight from responsibility is, actually, one of the primary characteristics of neurotic guilt feelings. On the other hand, the man who admits that he is wholly responsible for his own behavior can always rise to a higher level of existence, and repair the faults he has committed, and master his instinctive impulses without doing any harm to his psychic health.

16   psychology and religion

In the nineteenth century, Science (with a capital S) claimed to be a substitute for religion, claimed that it could furnish not only an explanation for everything in the world, but also give reasons for living. Today, in recalling these vain ambitions, we can only smile. Still, there are many scientists of this stamp, among psychoanalysts more than anywhere else. Without being able to defend their thesis on a theoretical basis, they believe more and more strongly that psychology can assume a larger proportion of this role than is traditionally attributed to religion, in the lives of individuals and society as a whole. The naturalists of the last century conceived of religion as something that responded to the human appetite for knowledge — by means of its myths and supposedly revealed dogmas. The spiritual heirs of Freud think that religion is born of anxiety, irrational fears and uncertainty, all provoked by a conflict between the unconscious libido and the conscious ego. The gods and demons are supposed to be nothing more than complexes. Psychoanalysis, after liquidating them, is supposed to take over the existential functions they have been performing so poorly up to the present time.

I. Freud and Religion

Freud's personal attitude towards religion was one of open hostility. The mask has fallen, he writes and psychoanalysis is finally leading to the denial of God's existence. Far from adapting or toning down this attitude as his studies progressed, Freud's hostility towards all religion kept growing — evidence is to be found in the two books he devoted particularly to this subject: *Totem and Taboo* and *The Future of an Illusion*. He equates religious feeling to obsessional neurosis, as produced by the Oedipus complex. When the child, in growing up, sees that he will always have to remain a child in some respect, that he will never outlive his need for protection against sovereign and unknown powers, then, according to Freud, he endows these powers with the characteristic traits of a father image, creating gods for himself, gods whom he fears and tries to make propitious, gods to whom he assigns the task of watching over him on earth.[1] Once again: he says that all the religions of humanity must be considered as collective delirium.[2]

There is thus supposed to be no fundamental difference between magic, superstition, and religion. All faiths, even those of the most spiritualized religions, are only superstition; all rites are only magic. Primitive man, according to Freud, had an obscure sense of fear in the face of the instinctual impulses that he experienced within himself. He could only attribute them to an outside cause, to a spirit, a demon. In large measure, says Freud, the mythological conception of the world which is in evidence in even the most modern religions, is nothing more than human psychology projected onto the outside world. . . . It would be a worthwhile service to humanity if psychoanalysis were able to "decompose" these myths of paradise and original sin, God, good and evil, immortality, etc., by taking its stand at the original point of departure for the myth.[3] What is more, "repression, the renunciation of certain instinctive impulses, also seems to play a large role in the formation of religion."[4]

1. *L'avenir d'une illusion*, p. 64
2. *Malaise dans La Civilisation*, p. 709
3. *La psychopathologie* . . . , pp. 298-299
4. *L'avenir*. . . . , p. 178

What we traditionally call *metaphysics* is in reality only a *metapsychics*. Since the unconscious mind, by reason of the original Oedipus-complex crime, has been contaminated by guilt feelings towards the father image, it is supposed to have invented the image of a Father-God, all-powerful, and capable of taking vengeance. Since they are more or less directly the result of the Oedipus complex, all religious emotions and feelings could only be fundamentally sexual in origin.

Freud sees art as a noble sublimation of repressed sexuality, and thus considers it to be legitimate. On the other hand, he has only contempt for religious sublimation. It has nothing valid or valuable to offer humanity. It is an obsession in itself, and thus religion is only qualitatively superior to the other neuroses. Freudian psychoanalists, in later years, could consider a psychoanalysis as truly successful only when the religious neurosis was also liquidated. Moreover, the master himself firmly believed that every religious need would disappear with full psychological maturity.

II. Religion Transcends Psychology

There is no real scientific basis behind Freud's contempt for religion. It is based only on postulates and hypotheses, all of which are narrowly bound up with Dr. Freud's own personal complexes. In his considerations on the subject of religion, we can see a quarrelsome attitude at work which no really scientific mind could ever approve on the basis of any scientific observation. The fact that he was a Jew, in the diaspora, and in a traditionally Catholic country,certainly explains most of his reactions in this area. My own experience as a psychologist has enabled me to observe that almost all Jews who call themselves atheists are much more vehement about their atheism than any other group of people. It is easy to realize that this revolt is not addressed so much against God as it is against their own Jewish stock which sets them apart and frequently makes life very difficult for them. In their atheism we can also see an attempt to take revenge on the Christians (or Moslems) among whom they live and face constant humiliation.

We should have to be very naive indeed to look for any solid arguments against religion in the area of psychology. At the most, some of Freud's habitual accusations and complaints might very well be strictly applied to some of the inferior and deviated forms of religion.

It is just as pointless to look to psychology for proofs in favor of religious truth, particularly in favor of any one given religion. The task of religious psychology is a more humble one. It can only give us a good insight into the role played by religious faith in the maturity and accomplishments of a human person. It can also help us distinguish between authentic spirituality and its counterparts; it furnishes us with a means to get beyond religious pseudo-values, and let real values exert a freer activity. Obviously, such services are not to be disdained.

Psychology is not in a position to say who or what has stamped the idea of God on the human soul. But it can observe that this idea exists almost everywhere and among all peoples, no matter how great the deformities and falsifications that might vitiate it in one or another given instance. Jung observes that the idea of God strikes the psychologist as the most fundamental and basic of all the archetypes.

The most primitive idea of God appears as that of a power, a mysterious and unexplainable energy. Gradually it personifies, expressed under symbols such as the sun, a certain animal, a spring, etc. Did mankind really need a revelation in order to arrive at the conception of one sole God, sovereignly personal and spiritual, as he is conceived of in all the great monotheistic religions? The psychologist, as such, has no information on this subject. Still there is nothing in what he is able to observe that is opposed to the concept of a direct intervention on the part of God. Dr. Odier is not completely wrong when he says that the psychologist must hold to the methodological principle of excluding all transcendence, but not of denying it.[5] Thus he is not, *a priori*, either for or against Revelation.

Drawing on his immense personal experience, Jung is able to write that, "of all the neurotic patients who have reached middle age, that is, more than 35 years old, there is not a single one whose most fundamental problem was not posed by his religious attitude. Every single one of these patients was sick, in the last analysis, because he had lost the things that a living religious faith has always given to its followers, and no single one of them was ever really cured unless he was able to recover, at the same time, a religious attitude in keeping with what he had lost."[6]

The psychologist who is free from all rationalistic prejudices hardly ever needs to explain why a given person believes, but rather why it is that certain people do not believe. Everything inclines us to think that a man is religious on the same grounds that he is a thinking being, and free, and sexed — that is, that religion is not a question of something imposed from without, but one of the basic structures of his innermost being. Neither the moral law, says Jung, nor the idea of God, nor any religion has ever taken hold of man from without, as if it had somehow fallen down from heaven; on the contrary, from the very beginning, man was born with all this within himself, and that is why, every time he manages to put religion aside, he always has to create it for himself all over again. The idea of morality and the idea of God are part of the primitive and ineradicable substance of the human soul. In psychology, the notion of divinity is an unalterable magnitude with which we must always reckon.[7]

Psychological analysis is witness to the fact that, often, those people who are most "worked up" over the problem of God are precisely those who call themselves atheists. It even seems, in the

---

5. *Les deux sources . . .* , p.; p. 241
6. *La guerison psychologique*, p. 282 (French edition)
7. *L'homme a la découverte de son âme*, pp. 276-277

light of experience, that the repression of the psyche's religious function is the most disastrous of all the many possible repressions and the cause of most neuroses and of the most distressing ones. It is moreover an undeniable fact that the number of neurotics grows in strict proportion to the degree of decadence in the religious life of a civilization. The philosophical materialism of the Russians and the pragmatic materialism of the Americans are two equally serious threats to human progress. At the moment, neurosis and mental disorder are much more widespread in the U.S.A. than they are in the U.S.S.R. — but this is no grounds for concluding that Communist materialism is less dangerous than capitalist materialism. To put it more simply, the psychologist must admit that the Russian's greater resistance to mental disease is the product of his long and profoundly religious past. At the very most, up to the present time, Communist propaganda has managed to give idolatry the upper hand over real religion.

III. *Religion and Civilization*

Jung and his disciples have been reproached for their religious eclecticism and for their antidogmatism. This is a serious misunderstanding of the role of the psychologist. The psychologist is not to take the place of the theologian. His own faith, in keeping with the teachings of a given religion, is never upset or disturbed by observing the fact that, psychologically, other religions can accomplish the same functions in other men.

In people of our Western civilization, the psychologist observes that the Christian religion is undeniably the best equipped to satisfy the higher aspirations of the psyche, and thus promote psychic equilibrium. But is Christianity equally well adapted to the Asiatic and the African? Jung denies that it is, and takes a very strong stand against the concept of Christian missionary activities. As a result, many Christians have taken offense at Jung's positions and have accused him of a very dangerous moral and religious relativism. But perhaps these people have not reflected sufficiently on the real evidence behind the problem which the missions pose for the psychologist.

It is difficult, if not impossible, to present the Christian message to the peoples of Africa or Asia, in anything like its pure state. For two thousand years, it has been the ferment and cement of European civilization. Inevitably it takes on a certain stamp from these civilizations in its turn. I have always felt a certain sense of fraternal pity whenever I saw black-skinned priests, dressed in a Roman cassock, celebrating Mass and reciting the breviary in Latin. An educated twentieth-century Frenchman, whose culture is Greco-Latin in inspiration, already has some difficulty in understanding the catechism because its concepts no longer tie in with the mental structures of our own times. What can be expected of Chinese or the dwellers of the Gold Coast, when they have to learn the same catechism and the same theology? It is no wonder, under such conditions, that the Christian faith seems to work its miracles of renewal and cure much less readily in their psyche than in the Western soul.

These considerations are further aggravated by the great differences between the level of mental development and material civilization. The Church is always the first to recognize the fact that a certain elementary level of civilization is an indispensable prerequisite for the preaching of the Gospel. That is why missioners establish schools and teach hygiene, and do everything they can to improve agriculture and technology in the countries in which they preach — their activity is not dictated by mere pity.

Slightly qualifying what might be too absolute in Jung's position with respect to Christian missions, it seems we have an obligation to point out that Christianity, for peoples other than those of the Mediterranean civilization, could be a factor in psychological health and progress only on two conditions: 1. if the missioners make every effort to raise the standards of the material and cultural civilization of these peoples and, 2. if the Gospel message is transmitted in as pure a form as possible, so that it will not look like something foreign, something that came from outside. What is more, we must recall the words of Emmanuel Mounier, "that a non-missionary faith is a dead faith."[8]

IV. *Rites and Symbols*

When a sociologist or ethnologist undertakes the study of a given religion, what he most easily observes are its cultual rites and ceremonies. Unless he is completely closed to spiritual realities, he will soon observe that these rites and ceremonies, far from being simple "affectations," have a profound meaning. The important thing (in an effort to really know a religion objectively) is to discover what is being expressed by a given rite in a given religious setting. It is not uncommon for the same ceremonial gestures to be repeated in very different religions. Whereas the superficial observer might conclude, on this basis, that two given religions are fundamentally identical, the observer who looks more closely will soon see that the same forms do not always have the same content.

One of the primary causes of the psychic disorder of our age certainly consists in the fact that men, under the malevolent influence of rationalism or materialism, have lost their whole understanding of symbols. Ritual gesture, liturgical ceremony, biblical parable, etc., no longer seem to be anything but magic in their eyes. Even if we had no other reasons for wanting to see Jung's psychology spread over a larger domain of professional influence, the fact that it can reeducate us in the language of symbolism is reason enough in itself.

One of the main differences between the psychology of Freud and Jung consists precisely in the fact that the former aims at curing man of religion (religion being considered as a neurosis in Freud's eyes), whereas the second proposes to cure the sick soul

---

8. *Traité du caractère*, p. 685

by religion. It is hard not to prefer this second perspective to the first. The psyche, as experience has shown, is fundamentally religious, or, as Jaspers puts it, there cannot ever be any real existence without intrinsic reference to transcendence.

V. Religion and Libido

When we get beyond the superficial appearances of things, it becomes evident that religion could not possibly be considered as the simple reorientation of the sexual libido. Still, it is equally impossible not to recognize a certain relationship between the two.

It is most difficult to believe that it is only by pure chance that some of the most famous mystics — St. John of the Cross, St. Therese, St. Catherine of Siena, etc. — in their descriptions of the communion between the soul and God, regularly fall back on images and expressions whose sexual overtones are incontestable: espousals, exchange of love, etc. In the Old Testament, the Canticle of Canticles could just as easily pass for a profane love song as a hymn of divine love. The prophets of Israel, in their turn, make important use of the sex symbol.

Those who refuse to admit any distinction between true and false mystics, claim to see a perfect identity between the facts we have just mentioned and lyrical or hysterical outbursts. In the case of hysterics, the claim to divine revelations and divine communications is really only a poor disguise for very specifically sexual desires.

A psychologist who has some grounding in religion has no trouble in distinguishing between true and false mystics. The fact that the outbursts of some particular hysterical person proceed from his repressed sexual libido does not ever authorize us to conclude that Theresa and Catherine, John of the Cross and Henry Suso, were merely projecting their unsatisfied sex urges on God or the Blessed Virgin. But it sometimes takes more than a psychologist to realize this.

In order to understand the use that the most authentic mystics make of sexual symbolism, we must recall what has been said about the libido as affective energy. It is indeterminate in itself and it can be utilized by any psychic function. Love activity is, obviously, a great consumer of this energy, if not the greatest. This explains Dr. Freud's error, when he makes sexuality the very source of all psychic activity. But it also explains the mystics. The direct experience they have of the divinity is, on their own admission, absolutely ineffable. In order to give even an approximate idea of what they have experienced, they naturally turn to ideas and images that belong to the most intensively affective of psychic functions.

VI. *Interior Religion*

Some people think — and there are authentic believers among their number — that dogmas, rites and religious symbols are outmoded, since they no longer respond to the spiritual needs of modern men. They do everything they can to make active charity the one and sole foundation of religion. Such a spirit is expressed particularly in the Anglican Broad Church, in liberal Protestantism, and even in some Catholic circles.

The experience of psychology is a direct denial of this illusion and these reformers. It is impossible not to realize that the desertion of the masses but above all of the elite is infinitely greater in purely philanthropic religions than in those which have a solid dogmatic and liturgical foundation. Modern social organization tends towards a progressively broader degree of State control over the sick, the poor, the aged, the retired, etc. What men are looking for in religion is the inner certitude, the deep-seated reasons behind life. Religious liberalism is not able to give any of these certitudes or reasons.

The psychologist's task is not to recommend dogmas and rituals for disturbed psyches. Quite the contrary: whenever he is dealing with Christians, or with persons who want to be Christians, he must, in the name of the psychic health that he is sworn to promote, make such people understand that Christian authenticity consists in the imitation of Jesus Christ. Neurotics have a marked tendency to rely primarily on practices and rites whose meaning they do not generally understand and which are, in their eyes, something magic. Such Christians must be made aware of the fact that the imitation of Christ does not consist in purely external attitudes. They are not supposed to dress, for instance, the way Jesus dressed, eat what he ate, work the miracles he worked. It is along his own individual path that each disciple of Christ must walk with the same authenticity that the Master himself brought to the full accomplishment of *his vocation*.

The essence of Christianity is love. Now the neurotic is a person without love. He does not love others and, above all, he does not love himself. It is because he does not love himself that he behaves, unconsciously, in such a way that others will not love him either. By attaching firmly to what is the alpha and omega of his religion, he will be capable, according to the individual case, of forgiving others and especially himself. The result will be a sense of reconciliation with himself, with the world, and with God, and thus a greater joy in the prospect of living.

* * * *

Depth psychology gives us a better yardstick to measure the extremely harmful results of rationalism on the religious plane. Only what is rational passes for reality, and thus the theologians of the last centuries have tried to make religion come into perfect conformity with reason. The religion of pure reason, such as propounded by Immanuel Kant, is, basically, only the logical excess of the general trend of his times. Now, reason embraces only a slight portion of the psychic totality. Proofs and arguments of the rational order can touch the soul only superficially. The soul, deprived of religion, is abandoned to the anarchy of its instincts, the modern superstitions which are Science, Progress, Revolution. The result is almost certain to be the utter impoverishment of affective life which today characterizes western civilization.

Because of prejudices and distortions in religion, many modern men, who are more or less conscious of their religious needs, are not able to find their way, unaided, to a real life of faith. The psychologist's help is frequently necessary. Obviously this is not a question of submitting all catechumens to psychosynthesis, children and adults alike. It is enough that those who teach religion or are involved in religious education, have as profound and extensive a psychological grounding as possible. Then they will be in a position to evangelize, not only the reason, but the entire soul.

VII. *Psychological Function of Religion*

We have seen, in the chapter devoted to the sick soul, that neurosis is characterized, among other things, by a fixation on an infantile stage of affective development. The neurotic lives in the past, refuses to face the present, and is afraid of the future.

From the psychological point of view, the great merit of Christianity is that it has located the ideal towards which all mankind must strive, in the future. The earthly paradise is a state that has definitively passed away, and there is no returning to it. But there is another paradise, incomparably superior to the earthly one, waiting in the future; it is this paradise towards which we are to tend. Obviously the influence of this Christian eschatology has been immense, particularly in so far as Christian peoples, more than any others, have been active in all fields of progress. The Christian religion is not a religion of nostalgia, but of hope.

Rationalistic theologians have frequently reproached mystics for the fundamental immanence of their faith. Concentrating on certain expressions of Meister Eckhart, for example, we might get the impression that, for him, God is not fundamentally distinct from the soul, or at least that the two are intimately interdependent. "God is born in the soul"—"The soul is born in God" — "I am a cause of God's existence"—"God draws his being from the soul"—"God comes into being and passes on," etc. On the basis of such expressions, and many others as well, we might be tempted to establish a rigid parallelism between the God of this great Rhenish mystic and that of Angelus Silesius, a genuine pantheist, who expresses his philosophy thus in his famous poem: "I know that without me — God could not live for a single instant; — If I ever happen to disappear, he will — necessarily have to give up the ghost." Similar "immanentist" expressions can be found even in the writings of St. John of the Cross.

Still, Jung is absolutely incorrect in concluding that, for Meister Eckhart and the other mystics, God is basically only a "psychodynamic state," a function of the unconscious mind.[9]

What the mystics are simply trying to do is to use the language of poetry in an effort to express something of the intimacy that exists between God and man. From the point of view of rational theology, they might not appear to be entirely orthodox. But still, reflecting on the subject without *a priori* prejudices, and consulting the revelation of Scripture, we cannot help being struck by the fact that the poetry of the mystics is infinitely closer to the truth than an extrinsicist theology which considers the relationship between God and man in the same light as those that exist between a watchmaker and a watch.

For us to be in a position to live a Christian life, and for our faith to really promote the spiritual progress of our soul, it is not enough to know that God exists, that he has created us, and that he will one day be our judge. If this were all there was to religion,

9. *Types* . . . , p. 250

many people could probably subscribe to Lenin's famous quip, that if God existed, that would be an added motive for combatting him.

What we have to realize is that God is present in the most profound depths of our soul — *intimior intimo meo* as St. Augustine puts it — and then God will appear existentially indispensable. Once the watch is completed, it can get along without the watchmaker, but man would fall into nothingness if the hand of God, even if only for the slightest moment, ceased to support him in existence.

Immanence, however, far from being opposed to the trascendence of God, or even denying it, presupposes and demands it. In saying, with Jung and the mystics, that the notion of God responds to an absolutely necessary psychic function,[10] we are not claiming that the notion of God is nothing more than this psychic function. Quite the contrary, it answers these needs so excellently only because it infinitely transcends the soul and all its functions. God is, to take up the famous quote from Augustine once again, *intimior intimo meo,* only because he is at the same time *superior summo meo* — higher than the highest principle within me.

From the mere psychological point of view, once again, the depreciation and repression of a function as important as the place religion fills in the human soul can never be free of disastrous consequences, both for the individual and for the social collectivity. We cannot ever forget that the atheism propagated by the "age of light" led directly to the Terror, and then the French Revolution. Nor is it any mere chance that the triumph of rationalism, thoughout the whole of the nineteenth century, was directly followed by the horrors of the Nazi extermination camps, Communist dictatorship, and the invention of the atomic bomb.

---

10. *Psychologie . . . ,* p. 140

VIII. *Religious and Psychological Maturity*

The function of authentic religion in the soul is a healthy and positive one, and any deviation in true religion is always disastrous for the psyche. When religion ceases to be an active and creative force in promoting human welfare and freedom of the human spirit, and turns into a mere instrument of spiritual and temporal domination, we are then faced with clericalism, the spirit of the inquisition, intolerant sectarianism, and, as a result, the worst forms of atheistic materialism.

Contrary to what the Freudians may say, it is not religion, but rather the lack of religion, which dates back to magic and superstition and conjures up all the fears that plagued the souls of primitive men. We must recall here that, historically, the first doctrinal atheism, that of Epicurus, was invented precisely in an effort to combat the fear of death. But as it works out, the denial of heaven and hell, far from doing away with the fear of death, only increases it. Every psychologist can observe that fear and anxiety disappear when a man has discovered a transcendent God in the depths of his own soul.

For religious feeling to accomplish its primary role in the promotion of human existence, it is indispensable for it to be gradually metamorphosed, in keeping with the general maturity of the person. Nothing is more "normal" than the religion of the "Child Jesus" in the child, popular devotions to the Blessed Virgin and "special" saints in poorly developed minds. The religion of the coalman is a perfectly satisfying and admirable thing — for the coalman. The study of the Old Testament is very instructive on this plane. The different *books* which make it up have been revealed over a spread of time that covered roughly fifteen centuries. Think of the mighty difference between the very anthropomorphic conception of God as presented in the first chapters of Genesis, and the highly spiritual conceptions encountered in the latter prophets. Still, it would be absurd to see this as an indication of any internal contradictions in the revealed text. How could the simple nomadic pastors of Abraham's day have understood the preaching of an Isaiah or Jeremiah? Only a very simple religion, in which the fundamental truths were transmitted by ancient and familiar legends, could have answered their religious needs. On the other hand, so elementary a religion could never have furnished the more educated Jews of the time of the Babylonian Captivity and the return to the Promised Land with the faith in life they needed. God took on the role of teacher.

Christianity, more than any other religion, has shown itself capable of promoting the spiritual life of educated and cultivated men of extremely diverse civilizations. But, beneath this fundamental unity, there is a great proportion of individual differences, and it could not possibly be otherwise.

The dogmas believed by the peasants of Brittany, the Negroes of the Congo, the Indians of Central America, the great thinkers, philosophers and artists of France or Italy, are obviously not the same. The psychologist as such, however, is not particularly interested in the intellectual and objective aspects of religion. His domain is the subjective content of faith. It is not hard to recognize the very great differences between the one religion and the manifold ways of believing in it. The fact that the religion of Christ is capable of metamorphosing into so many different beliefs is already a proof of its essential transcendence. It thus appears to be *the* "dynamic religion" *par excellence*, in the Bergsonian sense of the word.

* * * *

Still the spiritual beliefs of a man do not always keep pace with his growth on the intellectual and even the psychological plane. It is a mistake to be sentimentally struck by the fact that a certain outstanding intellectual, for example, still has the "simple religious faith of a child." The faith of the coalman, as we have said, is something beautiful and worthy of admiration only in the coalman. In other people, such a faith responds only to that part of their psyche which has not evolved with the rest of their spiritual growth, that part which has remained fixed on an infantile stage. Whatever is really adult in a person necessarily escapes the influence of such a faith. This explains why so many educated Christians consider it necessary to divide their lives into several small compartments, each one tightly shut off from all the others. They are Christians in church, in the parish circle, sometimes even in the family; but in their profession and in their public life, they act like unbelievers.

One of my friends, an avant-garde philosopher, used to say he was very proud that he had remained attached to the faith, just as his pious old mother had taught it to him — he had been very attached to her and had been orphaned when he was still an adolescent. It was, in fact, a very tender thing to see this intellectual burning candles before the statue of the Little Flower, receiving Communion scrupulously each First Friday, making novenas, gaining indulgences, etc. The parish priest never tired of praising him for his "childlike piety." But as for the philosophical teaching of this same pious Christian, it was completely secular. Not that he renounced his Christianity in the classroom. He always made it something of a point of honor to admit his religious affiliation to his students at the beginning of each lecture. But his faith had nothing to offer to his intelligence. Towards the age of forty, this fervent Christian was disheartened and surprised to discover that he no longer had any faith.

There was no question of any moral crisis in this philosopher. It is merely that there was a considerable lag in his affective maturity, compared with his intellectual development — a not uncommon situation in professional men of his calling. His little-boy religion corresponded perfectly with the infantile stage of his psyche. This situation might well have lasted throughout his whole life, as it sometimes does. But, towards the age of forty, he finally became an adult emotionally, and then the religion of his childhood no longer filled any real psychological function for him.

Still, we do know that, thanks to psychoanalysis, no matter

how highly civilized and adult we suppose a man to be, the primitive and child within him will never be completely dead. By that very fact, our faith itself will not ever arrive at that absolute "purity" which so many reformers have dreamed of achieving. We must not be surprised to encounter certain remnants of mythical and animistic religion even in the most authentically adult believers. What is important for the spiritual life of this category of believers is the fact that the vestiges of primitive or infantile religion do not make up the whole, nor even the principal part, of their faith.

IX. Faith-Healing

We do not need to refer to the Gospel miracles to discover that faith can exercise a therapeutic function. Christian Science and the other faith-healing sects are not pure charlatanisms.

Jung and many other psychotherapists have observed that by removing the obstacles that prevented the religious function of the psyche from exercising its normal role, it was possible to greatly advance the progress of the psychoanalytic cure. And still it would be a serious mistake, on the part of the psychologist, to consider religion primarily under its therapeutic aspects.

It is the strong, virile, creative religion of the normal man which must serve as our model here. It alone can really free and elevate a soul, whereas the neurotic always presents an inferior form of religion.

Even without adopting the absurd Oedipus mythology, it is hard to miss the fact that many persons conceive the divine fatherhood of God in terms of human fatherhood. Having generally been disappointed by their natural father, neurotics look to their Heavenly Father for everything their natural father was not able to give them. Those who, in their childhood, had to suffer from the brutality of their father, his unjust severity, or his lack of understanding, find it very difficult to believe in the goodness of God, or feel complete confidence in him.

Louise, about forty years old, cannot bring herself to believe that God loves her personally. She is not an atheist, far from it. She believes that God exists and that he exercises a sort of general providence over the universe. She is even prepared to admit that he sometimes intervenes in the lives of certain persons, but never in her own. In the course of a psychological treatment, it turns out that her parents had been very careful to observe strict justice in her regard, but never bothered to show her any particular tenderness and affection. The result was an intense feeling of inferiority which also marks her religious life. Since she was never sure that her parents loved her, how could she know that she is loved by God?

* * * *

Among the psychologists of the Freudian school, Dr. Odier was one of the first to recognize the fact that *real religious values* and morals actually do exist, along with false ones. Only pesudo-religious phenomena need to be attributed to the workings of a complex. Obviously it is not always so easy, particularly when the psychologist does not have any faith himself, to distinguish the authentically religious person from the religious masquerader, but it is still an incontrovertible fact that religious people do exist.

Here is a man, educated atheistically, who is a convert to Christianity. Is this a genuine discovery, prompted by the activity of divine grace, of the beauty and truth of the religion of Christ? Or was he more or less consciously trying to avenge himself on his tyrannical father, a fanatic atheist? This man's religion would have an entirely different essence and value, both religiously and psychologically, depending upon which of the two hypotheses is assumed to be true. Generally, when the conversion is due to a neurotic complex, there will soon be some signs of inauthenticity about his conduct. The subject will find it hard to live his Christianity with joy and dynamism; he will show himself intolerant towards anyone who does not share his convictions, etc. The psychologist who also happens to have a genuine religious life will not find it difficult to distinguish between really religious behavior and its false counterparts. Obviously, he is not to advise the inauthentically converted Christian of the necessity of renouncing his faith and returning to his former state of unbelief. It is very probable that the grace of God has had some role in this conversion, and that the subject's psychological situation has prevented it from producing fuller fruit. The psychologist must then work at clearing away the obstacles which hinder the activity of grace.

It would be a serious mistake to take intransigence or intolerance as a sign of authenticity in faith. Psychological experience has shown that "dogmatists," fanatics, witch-burners, and all other "integralists" are really the prey of doubts and hesitations in their unconscious minds. In persecuting error and denouncing weakness and luke-warmness in others, it is really themselves they are trying to convince and reassure. It is doubtless true that very many atheists are believers without realizing the fact. But it is just as true that very many believers are atheists without being aware of the fact. An atheist is never so sectarian in pursuing his beliefs as when the foundations of his atheism are about to crumble. Bigotry, on the other hand, is psychologically very close to sacrilege.

Psychology, in learning to distinguish between true and false values, to sort out the conscious and unconscious factors, is in a position not only to restore equilibrium in an unbalanced soul, but also to render some very important services to the progress of religion.